MW01503922

A Woman Whose Calling Is Men

The Memoirs of a Priestess-Identified Prostitute

Book One

Aphrodite Phoenix

ISBN 0-7414-4807-6

Cover illustration by Hannah Seaman
Cover design by Mianna L. Vaccaro

Published by:

PUBLISHING.COM

1094 New DeHaven Street, Suite 100
West Conshohocken, PA 19428-2713
Info@buybooksontheweb.com
www.buybooksontheweb.com
Toll-free (877) BUY BOOK
Local Phone (610) 941-9999
Fax (610) 941-9959

Printed in the United States of America

Printed on Recycled Paper

Published August 2008

The courage to speak your own truth
always gives someone else the courage to speak theirs.

Oprah Winfrey

I am proud to be called "whore."

When I became a whore, I declared my religious convictions.

When I became a whore, I declared my creativity to be as worthy as motherhood.

When I became a whore, I shouted my defiance of the machine that is our "male-voiced culture."

When I became a whore, I transformed tragedy into strength, loss into freedom.

Having become a whore, I have become a teacher of spiritual and psychological transformation.

Having become a whore, I have been honored as poet and performer.

Having become a whore, I have discovered my true voice. I live by the rhythms of the moon and the wisdom of my body.

Having become a whore, I have been enlightened by the tender and worshipful nature of men's desire for "the Wondrous Vulva."

Cosi Fabian

He kissed me on the cheek. "Let me have a good look at you!" The way he said it, I did not feel like a piece of meat but like a woman who was appreciated by a man.

In this one quick encounter, I was knowingly, willingly violating ten years of blind obedience to the law. Yet it didn't feel wrong.

I....had just committed my first *honest* act of prostitution....I touched the bills....two hundred and twenty dollars....

What sinful act did I commit to earn that kind of money? Nothing I hadn't already done...before--- except then I hadn't charged for it....

With a tenderness I never knew one could feel for a complete stranger, I kissed him.....

Norma Jean Almodovar

In the following account, some names have been changed, to protect individuals' privacy.

ACKNOWLEDGMENTS

This is for my children, who are the source of my will to prevail.
This is for my mother, who died, but didn't leave.
This is for my father, who saved me as only a girl's Daddy can.
This is for my aunt, who taught me that loving God is life,
and that loving life is God.
This is for my lover, just for loving me.

This is for all the activist sex workers and
all their feministic supporters.
Inexpressible, uncountable thanks to you all for speaking out,
hanging tough, and validating our work.

This is for all of my clients.
Many thanks for your patronage.
And special thanks to those of you
who contributed valuable sources.

And many thanks to each of my friends, as well as each blood
relation, who accepts me for everything I've become,
and can read this book with love.

TABLE OF CONTENTS

PART ONE

SCENES
AND
ROUTINES

To give away yourself

keeps yourself still,

and you must live

drawn by your own sweet skill.

William Shakespeare, Sonnet 16

MY SEXIEST "ESCORT" EXPERIENCE

Sluts and whores and erotic entertainers are
not the enemy of the matriarchy. [1]

I've been with so many wonderful lovers. It astounds me to think of them all. Most guys do their homework, and they do it very well. They're determined to learn how to satisfy a woman, and some of them truly succeed.

Even if I'm being true to a lover and therefore, I won't come for clients, I can see that the best of them have what it takes. They must send their women to heaven. They have the right touch, just the right presence, just the right combo of technique and tenderness.

Some of the others are all thumbs. Their natural touch is an irritating jitter. Or maybe they drink, they feel that they have to. The alcohol makes them insensible, clumsy.

Whatever. No matter how well or how badly they perform, I give most of them A's for effort. Most of them defer to the clitoris as though it were a five-carat diamond. Most of them search for the G-spot as though it were a sunken treasure.

The guy who's in bed just to get his own jollies is a relic, a throwback. He's almost extinct. Men, for the most part, have discovered something big. A way to proud manhood is to make women come. And boy, do they ever try to. Getting us off is a major-league issue. If a guy doesn't do it, he feels like a loser. And a guy will do all that's required to win.

And some of them are just being fine human beings. They understand that to make a girl come is nobler than just feeling manly. To be good to a woman is the right thing to do.

Imagine the pressure that puts on an "escort". Especially one billed as the Girl Friend Experience! Three-quarters of my clients want me to come, they shell out big bucks just to make me. Of course, there are plenty of times when I can't! But I do make sure to tell them what good lovers they are. They need to know they are, they try so hard to be, and most of them deserve a big pat on the back.

Okay, that's a fanfare, a tribute, that I'm making here and now, to men. That's my heartfelt acknowledgement, my sincere declaration, my knighting of the gallantry that men show in bed. Innumerable clients have earned it.

And now, with that said, with good mentions all made, I'll get on to the winners, the champions. For me, the winners aren't men. It's been couples. Bisexual trysts are the sexiest for me.

It's not that I'm strongly bisexual. I've never felt sad without a woman to sleep with. I've never had a girlfriend for a lover. What I need is that one special man in my bed, and without him, the blues do their number. But then, I do enjoy breasts. A lot. I love to look at them and touch them and hold them, especially the big ones, big firm ones. But if I never touch another pair of tits again, that will be fine with me. What I need all the time is a big hairy chest. And I totally worship the penis. I've got to have a meaningful cock in my life. But I don't require a pussy.

Gays have told me that means I'm straight. But open, empathetic, just a tad from dead center, able to truly enjoy my own gender, if that's what's requested of me.

Yeah, that sounds about right.

I've been with a number of couples. Each time, it's been almost ineffably sweet. I get this big sense of full-circle. And I feel a tremendous respect for the woman. She's being so strong and enlightened. She's understanding her man. She's loosening her grip, she's letting him play, there's just one big rule, they'll do it *together.* That's usually the reason they've called me. That and her "bi-curiosity."

Really good, sensual porn actresses, the ones who really get off, always arouse me like crazy. Well, just imagine where an *in-*

the-flesh woman coming takes me! And a guy's right there with us, adding maleness to the mix! I feel something perfect and whole about that, that male and female sexual passion, going on right in front of me. And once, it even got *on* me...

That brings me around to my favorite sexy story.

One day, a new guy left a message. We talked, and I found out his age, the late fifties. When he mentioned where he lived, I thought *yes!* He lives in heaven!

It would take me a while to get there, but in this case, I didn't care. He lived in a beautiful town by the sea, and I knew that his zone was the wealthiest. He was probably close to the water, probably in a magnificent house; if he passed all my tests, I'd be eager to go.

Then he mentioned his girlfriend. She was forty-five, but he said she looked younger. He described her as very pretty. She also wanted to see me. Did I like girls?

"Sure!" I responded.

"You mean that? You're not just saying that?" It was a very legitimate question. Prospective clients are rightfully afraid that sex workers just "play along" for the money.

"No, I mean it," I said. And to show my sincerity, I asked about her tits. I really wanted to know if she had big, beautiful tits.

"Oh, yes, they're very nice," he said. "All hers. Not huge, but definitely not small. All round and firm. They're perfect."

"Ummmm!"

Now he knew I was serious. "You're gonna love her," he told me. And what he said next left me spellbound. He lowered his voice, and he murmured with awe:

"She comes all over. *All over.*"

Oh my God, I thought. *She's a squirter!*

This caller and his "squirter" could not have come through at a more perfect time in my life. For the past several months I'd been educating myself about women who can do that. I'd been hearing about them from men who'd been with one, and I'd recently seen them for the first time in porn films, and they drove me out of my mind. I was jealous because I couldn't squirt. But most of all, I was extremely turned on. Every time I saw a "rain woman" splashing her stuff in a film, I'd come fast as a teen-aged boy.

And now I was going to meet one! And get paid lots of money to see what she did!

Because I was seeing two people, I quoted four hundred-fifty dollars.

He had no problem with that.

I promised him a leisurely, unhurried hour. "But I have to talk to her first," I concluded.

That's standard procedure for a couples call. To *always* make certain that the woman wants to do it. Not to take the guy's word. To hear, straight from her, that she's cool with it.

In my experience, most men are eager to jump right in, but a woman might need more time. She might need to think about it more. Maybe the fantasy's enough. And maybe her man's got it wrong. Maybe he doesn't realize she never really meant it…

So I was making sure.

He put her on the phone.

"Hi," she said, and we got to the point. Her voice was soft, her manner held-back. Somehow, I'd known it would be. She could do something wonderful—female ejaculation—-but to hear her shy sounds, I'd never know it. If I ever saw her socially, I'd never, ever guess.

Irony. It usually rules.

We talked for five minutes, and I knew she was for it. She craved a bisexual tryst. And she wanted to please her man. She completely accepted the Number One Male Fantasy: to watch two women make love, and have them all over him, too.

Good. She had the perfect female attitude for an amicable three-way encounter. We set up the time and hung up, and then I looked forward to my trek to their town.

On the way out there, my usual feeling of drag about driving never came over me. And I didn't feel any of my usual tension with regard to a new client. Part of the reason was *her*. Whenever there's also a woman, there's a sweet camaraderie feeling. But most of my balmy emotion was because of the *place* I was headed.

Our appointment was at night, so I wasn't going to see much. But when I got into the area, I couldn't mistake where I was. I had rolled down the windows—to hell with my hair—just so I could feel the sea breeze, just so I could smell it. The darkness didn't lessen my awareness of the ocean.

This wasn't just *any* environment by the sea. I was born and raised on the East Coast, so for me the Atlantic was humdrum. But this place was special. This place was mystical. This place was so full of beauty and soul that I'd actually cried here, times in the past. Why? I don't know. This place had a power. I could feel it every time.

I'd come here, and something would speak to me. It told me the whales aren't just beasts, they're my brothers. It told me the eagles are sacred. I'd take in the woods and the sea and the dunes, mostly unchanged since the pilgrims first moored here, and something would whisper what I'd known for millennia, but couldn't remember til now.

Summer tourists put themselves through hellish drives to get out here. The wealthiest of them pay insane amounts of money to build their retreats, way out on the bluffs, right in the wind, the edgier the better. They put up with clogged roads and tourist-trap prices, and come back, year after year. Nothing could keep them away.

I felt honored, privileged, special, just to be living only thirty-five miles distant.

Now I saw the landmark my hosts had described, a lone little store with two out-of-date gas pumps. It was next to the turn-off that led to their house. I left the main highway, which had dwindled to a strip, and drove on something narrow and curving. I felt my car surging on paved swells of sand. It was black here, no streetlights, but I felt safe and happy. I knew there were beautiful homes all around me, up the steep rises, obscured by the woods. And I knew I could walk to the sea in a heartbeat.

I was a little bit lost, but I felt I'd come home.

Their driveway veered off to the right, kind of sudden. Their house was high up, through a thicket of beach pines. It took me a moment to get there, to see it. It was large, as I'd figured, but humbled by nature. I got out of my car, and the stars overwhelmed me. I could hear the surf pounding in.

Outside it was windy and chilly, but the house warmly glowed from within. I saw soft yellow flickers, maybe candles. I stepped onto a deck just as big as an apartment. He was there at the entrance, with a welcoming grin.

He ushered me into a contemporary design, huge windows, slid doors, and high, skylight ceilings. Embers were burning in a raised stone enclosure, the only thing that cleaved the spacious living room from the dining. All of the areas to lounge were plush leather. The wood flooring looked to be brand-new and lustrous, and I knew that when I got barefoot, it would have a silky feel.

He lived here alone, she had yet to move in, so the decor was still very masculine. Very affluent masculine. His Mideastern carpets were wide, long and deep. His blinds, austere but top-quality, were tremendous to fit his big casements, so they must have cost him a fortune, they must have been custom-made. His paintings and sculptures were nautical, the high-priced originals of gifted, famed locals. He was obviously one of the dwellers who made all their art work worthwhile.

He was an average-looking man, relaxed, with a robe on. His eyes held a mischievous twinkle.

And here she was, well-proportioned, five-four, and she still wore all her clothes. She was demure and gently pretty. A subtle little smile graced her face.

Later on, I would realize she was like the Madonna.

He was attempting to run the show. Though his house was all spaces for lounging, he herded us into the heart of it, the kitchen. We seated ourselves on retro stools at a free-standing granite counter.

She was perched next to me. He sat across from us. He poured us all generous goblets of wine.

She remained rather quiet, but her eyes told me volumes. I needed to pick up on that; every moment, I needed to read her. I smilingly looked her way, over and over.

Whenever I'm with a couple, I completely defer to the woman. No matter what the man does, as far as I'm concerned, she's the one in charge. Usually the man understands that, too. It's a potentially dicey situation. She's letting him touch another woman. He and I watch her feelings, every step of the way.

Well, this gal was looking quite peaceful. While she sat there in passive, contented-looking repose, her man and I avidly chatted. I could tell that all this was natural. He and I were both extroverts, and she was soft-spoken by nature.

Every few minutes or so, he would shut himself up, and leer. His eyes would roll from her face to mine, and back to hers again. He was waiting for the two of us to say something, negotiate something, get this thing going, *just do it.*

He didn't seem to quite get it: she and I were all set.

He made me think of a business meeting. He was tensed up for some kind of contract. Whenever he stopped talking and bore us with his eyes, to please him we turned to each other, and smiled.

But she and I didn't discuss things. We didn't need to. We understood.

We remained there a little while longer, bestooled in his neutral kitchen, not ready to move to The Place Where It Happens, and not worried about it, either, at least not us girls, that is. He anxiously poured us more wine. He and I small-talked, she and I glowed, and we listened to the ocean make her own love, we heard her heaving and frothing with her passion for the moon.

I don't recall how we got to the bedroom. At one point, we were just there. He had a big, soft, beautiful bed. She took off her clothes, and I followed suit. Her breasts were just perfect, just as he'd said; I couldn't wait to touch them.

She wanted to touch mine, too.

He watched us for a while.

All of us knew we were waiting for her to squirt. I didn't want to talk about it. I didn't want to make her feel pressured. So I just made love to her. And then he joined in. I don't remember what he did, but it was her he did it to, and I was touching her with him, and then there it was, she gushed out all over. She came on our hands, and the sheet.

She wasn't a screamer, and she didn't take long to come. She would moan a bit and gush, moan some more and squirt, and soon the bed was sopping beneath us. She was deep in her passion, quiet but intense, and whatever came out of her was clear as a brook; it didn't smell, it wasn't yellow, there was no way that was pee; it was just this incredibly sweet thing she sprayed.

Then she needed to rest.

She and I pleased him for a while. We got down on him and sucked him together. He played with four tits and two pussies, he enjoyed himself in male heaven. But the main thing he and I wanted was her. We wanted her to *do it again*. We kept our mouths shut, however; there was no way we'd push her.

My intellectual amazement was so strong that my body had not yet succumbed. I was aroused, to be sure, but I wasn't experiencing anything like my automatic comings when I watched the girls in porn. I was just so deep in wonder!

Nevertheless, I had no doubt that I'd come pretty soon. And I knew it would be the greatest.

When she felt herself ready to respond again, we asked her to sit on my face. I licked her for only a minute, and then—oh, how can I describe this! She was like a magic fountain! She put male spurting to shame! Her sweet pretty pussy, on top of my mouth, was suddenly an overturned pitcher! My face and neck and chest got soaked, and so did my upper back!

I'll always remember that trickling, that cascade down both of the sides of my neck. She even wet my hair.

She moved herself down to squat on my middle. She remained on top of me for a minute, shoulders slumped, head bent, eyes closed, just as though she were in prayer. Clearly, her feat overwhelmed her.

He was playing with himself, and I was in a torture of throbbing. She had come geysers this evening, but we had yet to explode. But we didn't want to come without *her* come in the picture. So both us patiently let her rest, again.

Suddenly it occurred to me that she must be dehydrating. I suggested that he get her some water. He did, and she drank it, and for a moment my health-nut thinking took over.

"You guys should always keep a bottle by the bed." They chuckled, but I wasn't kidding.

We played with him again for a while, and at that point, he was holding himself back. He was waiting for the right moment.

So was I.

Then she and I did something lesbian-classic: she straddled me as I lay on my back, and we pussy-bumped each other. Now I was right on the furthest of the edge. The feel of her clit hitting my clit was perfect. I needed to come, *right now*. But still, I wanted to wait for her!

Then he decided to join in. He wanted to mount her, doggy-style. She pulled herself up to receive him. That frustrated me, because now she wasn't *on* me, but I was also much more excited. They were fucking right above me! Their genitals were inches from mine! I played with myself underneath them, and my groin felt the heat of their groins.

Then it happened. She squirted *right on my clit!* And he came too, without a condom, because he was in his beloved.

He also dripped on my clit!

I came like a tornado.

Yes, dear nurses and AIDS counselors, I did go to the bathroom and clean myself up. I got their secretions all off me before any got inside. I poured on the apple cider vinegar, that I carry in a vial to kill germs, just as though I'd turned into a salad.

And I reminded them to always keep water for her, right beside the bed.

And after those health concerns were dispensed with, *yes,* I was quick to respond to their question: I'd be very, very happy to see them again! Any time; *just call.*

I drove back through the darkness and scent of the sea with endorphins joy-riding all through me.

GOOD MORNING AMERICA, FROM ONE OF YOUR "ESCORTS"

I am a self-proclaimed whore and a rebel.

First and foremost, I want to make one thing clear: I sell myself for nobody's profit but my own.

I only work when I want to. I only see who I want to. I make all the rules. I keep all the money. And that makes all the difference.

I think that puts an iron cork in the anti-prostitution agenda. Isn't the exploitation of women the biggest issue there?

No one exploits me.

I don't have a pimp. I don't work in somebody's brothel. It's true I'm an "escort", but I'm not an *agency* "escort". No madam or manager lords over me, sending me out, taking big cuts, telling me who to see.

I'm completely and literally self-employed.

Actually, *nothing* exploits me. Not even Corporate America. When I wake up in the morning, it's not because an obnoxious alarm clock has startled my brain from its nest. I don't have to "report" or "go in" or "show up."

I wake up whenever I want to. I wake up whenever I'm ready. And after a while, when I feel like it—like, say, after a cup of coffee—I get around to checking my voicemail.

Usually I'll hear a couple of messages that were left in the middle of the night. My greeting explains that I don't respond late, but the callers don't seem to have listened. They want so much to get a call back that they just don't care what it says.

Usually, I ignore them.

I seldom hear any messages left extremely early in the morning. But by mid-morning, there are often a few.

Um, yes, my name is Tom, and I'm interested in learning more about your service. You can reach me at *******.

Hi, ****! This is Joe. I'd love to get together again. Any time today would be good. Let me know if that works for you. Call me back at *******.

Hey, ****. It's Ken. Are you free any time tonight? Call me back when you get a chance at *******.

As I listen to it all, I also listen to myself. I ask myself two questions. Do I *feel* like working today? Do I **need** to work today?

The first question addresses what I call my inner rhythm. I usually work only when that thing deep inside me tells me it's okay to. If it says no, no, stay away from it all today, then I'm not likely to work. The second question addresses my financial situation. If there's something I need or want right away that requires money to get it, and I don't have enough money saved, that need competes with the rhythm to decide me on whether to go for the money. The rhythm almost always wins out.

Obeying the rhythm keeps me happy and healthy. Financial solvency matters a lot, but it's usually the lesser concern.

Even if I don't want to see anyone, however, I always respond to the messages. That's just plain good customer service. Clients have always told me that whenever they call other numbers, sometimes they don't get called back. *Jeez.* My peers can be so unprofessional! I decided early on in this business that except for the very late-nighters, I would return all the calls. I've never regretted that decision. Because of such niceties, I get told I'm preferred.

First I call back the regulars, the clients I know and trust, who want to make me wealthy that day.

If the rhythm has ordered me not to work, I tell them sorry, no, can't see you today, but I'd be glad to see you another time, soon.

14

After they hear that, they might call another girl. Or maybe they'll wait to see me. If I'm lucky, they'll commit to an appointment for tomorrow. If not, oh well, no big deal.

If the rhythm has given me a green light, then I set up the times to meet with them that day.

Then I take a deep breath, gather my courage, and dial the numbers of the "info call" message-leavers. Those are the absolute strangers. Those guys want to know what I "offer" and "how much." Calling them back makes my stomach clench up.

My response to unknown callers is like a balancing act on a tightrope. I must step through such chats very carefully. Everything I say is a probe. Yet everything they hear must be sweet.

Much of it is making a guy understand, without a word of self-incrimination, that I'm the most amicable and sensual girl he's ever talked to, who won't make him sorry he gave me his money. That's a real song and dance, an extremely important achievement of rapport, yet it's only a small component of this dicey conversational mission.

While not skipping a beat of my friendly-girl tempo, I listen and listen to everything about him. I attune to his breathing, his chuckles, his pauses. I reach past the facade or the social acumen or however he's outwardly packaged. The truth lurks between and behind his expressions, and I'm going to find it, or I'm saying good-bye.

I ask casual questions that are critical tests. On the strength of this phone chat, I'm sizing him up. Is he a cop, or a creep, or some other impending disaster?

None of them are ever aware of my prodding inquisition. All they hear at my end is the voice of a cheerful free spirit. I'm all chitchat, breezy questions, and laughter and flirting and warmth.

At the end of our conversation, however, I have to be feeling the beginning of trust, or we won't be talking again.

If a feeling of *okay* evolves in the talking, maybe I'll make an appointment with him. Or maybe I won't, just yet. Maybe I need to chat with him more. Maybe *he* needs to chat with *me* more. And some day soon, we will.

At some point I also check my email messages. These are from guys who saw my online ad, and are reluctant to leave me a voicemail at the number I emphatically post there. Emailing irritates me. Though it's good to be able to present myself in some flattering photos online, emailing is an extra, unnecessary step; I need to hear the men's voices. They should need to hear mine.

Give me a number to call you, I type back to them, over and over. *I realize you're afraid to do that*, I also want to type.

No excuses! They've got to take the plunge, and have a real phone chat with me. I need to have more than this cyberspace bullshit to figure out whether they're worth it, or safe. *Stop typing, guys!* I want to peck on the keyboard. *Pick up the goddamn phone!* I'm an in-the-flesh woman, not some **virtual** whatever, and I'm referred to as a *call*girl so you'll *call.*

It can be hard for a wife to coax her hubby from his monitor. Well, we working girls have a similar problem.

Sometimes, by late morning, there aren't any messages yet. If I won't be working that day, that's fine, that's even a relief; but if I do want to work, then not knowing by eleven o'clock or so what I'll be doing later, sucks. It means that my day is on hold, as yet completely unplanned, a question mark scratching a hole in my brain.

I can't remember what it's like to get up in the morning and know, each day, precisely what I'll be doing. That's the only thing I envy in people with regular jobs. They know what they'll be doing and where they'll be at, from the moment they wake up until quitting time, or even bedtime.

Some days are frustrating stretches for me, unstructured and uncertain. Sometimes I'll find myself enduring a day where I really want to work, but nobody calls for a solid appointment until nine o'clock that night. I've waited and waited and waited all day, and finally, that late, the blessed call comes, but I'm deflated from the drag, the long-drawn-out suspension, and at that point it's torture to get myself up, and get myself out, and going.

And just the reverse can happen. Three or so clients might all call at once, and they all want to see me at the same time. No can do, of course. So I end up seeing only one or two of them, and I lose out for sure on the third, and I try not to think about how, if only their schedules had allowed for it, I could have spread out the times and gone to see all of them, and earned *every* fee that was offered me that day.

My business is catch-as-catch-can.

Such a lifestyle can get edgy and aggravating, but really, I shouldn't complain; it's actually very worthwhile. I make lots of money. I charge two to three hundred dollars an hour. I earn six figures a year. But I only have to work part-time, and only on the days that I choose to. I enjoy the financial freedom that everyone dreams about. I take breaks and vacations whenever I want.

Prostitution is the perfect employment for a mother or an artist. My kids are all grown up now, so whoring no longer serves me as the poor single mother's solution. But now I'm committed to my writing, and just as it used to terrifically cover my far-flung single-mom bases, now my whoring promotes creativity. It gives me financial security. It enables a lot of free time. There's always plenty of money, so I'm free to work on my projects. I should mention that right after I roll out of bed, pee and put on the coffee, I get on my laptop and write.

I'm deep in composing and editing, before even half of my first cup is drained.

I check all my messages and make all my calls during breaks from the writing, which come as they may.

Then, later on in the morning, when the clock is inching near noon, if I plan to be working that day, I get myself off the computer. I draw myself a bath.

My baths are extremely important. They're not just the means to get fresh, shaved and clean; I can sense that they're also a ritual. A shrink would probably call them my "transition."

They always have to be bubble baths. I couldn't tell you why. I just have to be covered in voluminous froth. I need to hear it gently popping, all around my body.

The water has to be deep, and as hot as I can stand it, and all modern lighting has got to be off; daylight or candlelight is all that will do.

I bond with my body in the bathtub. I admire the good parts, taking comfort from them. I acknowledge the bad parts, hoping no one will mind them.

My face, hair, breasts and legs are the good parts. My lower abdomen and butt are the bad.

I have a very pretty face. What makes it even better is that my face still looks quite young. On both sides of my family, there's this amazing genetic luck. Right into his or her seventies, everyone tends to look youthful. Even my passed-away father, with a heart condition that killed him, looked a dozen years less than his actual age, even when his health was failing.

I feel I should get a facelift. When I reveal my approximate age, you'll know why. But everyone, friend or family, insists that I don't need one.

My hair is always at least shoulder-length, the same length it's been since my teens. It's the billowing handfuls of tresses men love. It's baby-fine, which disqualifies it from much styling, but that doesn't usually matter; my hair possesses goodness on its own. It's naturally wavy and bunny-soft to touch, and the color, dark auburn, is a pleasing post-sunset hue.

My breasts are really good. All mine, size C, and after three babies who suckled, they're incredibly well-preserved. I honestly don't know how my tits have stayed so nice. They're very well rounded and still quite firm, with just a few barely visible stretch marks from nursing. My years of pectoral workouts in gyms have helped them along some, I guess.

My legs are long and shapely and perfect. I soap them and shave them and kneed them, all the way to my pubes.

My gut is a disaster. Whatever my babies didn't do to my tits is horribly made up for, down there. The best thing I can say is that none of the damage furrows up much past my navel. But in the downward direction, from my navel to almost my pubes, I'm all wrinkles, weird puckerings, and sags. I badly need a tummy tuck, and were it not for my prioritizing of my kids' financial shortfalls, I would have paid for the fixative knife years ago.

I'm comforted by the fact that most of my work is horizontal. Whenever I'm in that position, like right now in the tub, that ugly gut skin sinks inward, and almost disappears. Except for when a guy's going down on me, of course. In that situation, his eyes are just inches from that mess. I cover it up with my well-tended, colorful fingertips.

The problem with my butt is the opposite of most: mine is way too small. My sons laugh about it, and call me "flat-ass." They scold me for genetically causing theirs to be diminutive, too.

From the compliments of clients and other men in my life, I've gathered that when I'm bent over, then my butt looks good. Then I'm told it has a sweet little curve. But whenever I'm standing upright, in my mind I hear "flat-ass!" So when a client indicates that he wants to admire my backside, I turn around and arrange myself in a leaning, right-angled pose.

Guys who are "ass men" want "bubble butts." I'm sure I must disappoint them. But guys who are partial to legs, tits, hair and

Woman Whose Calling Is Men—Book One

faces will always be glad they called me. As for the worst of me, that stretched-out lower ab skin, well, I do what I can to hide it. Hip-high crotchless panties work wonders! The guys are distracted and mobilized by that amazing surprise of a view, and above it, my gut is pretty much covered.

Twenty years old and firm-tummied, I am not. According to some things I've read about sex work, I'm supposed to be way, way over the hill. I can tell you, that's absolute crap. My status as an older callgirl has never been a problem. It's even been a plus.

How old are you? I ask the young-sounding prospects on the phone. *Twenty-something*, they say. *Oooh, you're just a baby!* I coo in response. *Do you like older women?* And nine times out of ten, they say *Yes, oh, yes, I do!*

How old are you? I ask the ones who sound more mature. Their answers range anywhere from thirty to seventy-five. *I'm in my mid-thirties,* I tell them. And nine times out of ten, they respond, *Good! I don't want a kid.*

I'm older than my thirties. But people guess thirty-six or so, and sometimes even less. And when I first started out in this business, everyone guessed me at about twenty-eight, but I was over a decade older. So why should I tell my ***chronological*** age to inquisitive guys on the phone? Other than my inadequate web photos—which are faceless for the sake of discretion—these guys have not yet seen me. I don't want to tell them my ***years*** age, because they're going to picture a woman much older than I ***look***. I tell them the age that I ***look like***, as opposed to my age ***in years***, and it feels like no worse than a white lie, because, when they finally meet me, I look like what they're expecting, and they're happy with what they see.

I hope you're all getting this, ladies. You don't have to be twenty to do well in this business. You can be much older than twenty, and even much older than thirty, and tell everybody the age that you ***look***. You've only got a problem if you ***look old***. It matters not a bit if you ***are***. As a matter of fact, maturity in a whore is a good thing in this business, for herself and everyone else.

After I get out of the tub, I usually feel I should rest a few minutes. It's that rhythm thing, again. *Cool down, relax, ease into the mode.* I blot my hair and moisturize my skin in a languid, reclining position. Then I continue to sit for a while, in the hug of a big, soft towel.

Then I rise, lose the towel, and I'm a flurry of self-preparation. I moisturize my skin, fluff up my hair, lengthen my lashes, line my lower eyelids, and color up my lips. My cheeks are naturally pink from my bath.

Wow, I respond to myself in the mirror. I'm always amazed by that fix-up.

Less than an hour ago, I was dull and scraggly-haired. I was a wan, bespectacled writer, world-weary-looking and brow-scrunched.

And now I'm simply gorgeous. And I look as though I don't have a care in the world.

Both of those women are me!

Time to get dressed.

Where I live, to dress is ridiculously easy. My home is the greater Boston area, the heart of that infamous New England reserve and feministic murder of man-pleasing fashion. The style here is no style at all. I'm originally from New York City—the American mecca of chic—but I've lived in Massachusetts for so long now that my garb has evolved into a hybrid of the two disparate locales.

I'm like, okay, New England, I'll give you what you want, which is extreme understatement refined to an art. But I *refuse* to wear your drab colors.

So I always don something simple, yet in some small way prettier than the average local outfit. I have to be careful, however. I can't forget that my clients usually want me to dress with discretion. So no matter how fetchingly I'd like to be clad, I know I've got to hold back; I'm an outcall "escort", which means I go to them, and most of them live in the suburbs, and they want me to blend right in.

As I'm making my way to their doorbells, they want me to look like "the girl next store." No problem; I come wrapped in my plainest of ensembles, maybe just a simple pair of jeans; but I do get around all the dullness. I might have some bright-colored heels on, or a beautifully detailed blouse, or a gorgeously purple blazer.

New England men are the same way when it comes to lingerie. Only a few of them want something fancy. Most of them get ecstatic over simple thong panties and clingy little tops. Those crotchless things I mentioned are enough to stop their hearts.

Back in my early days as an "escort", I was very conscientious about good lingerie. I wore garter belts and stockings and all kinds of lacy teddies. But I didn't get a lot of adulation for it all. I found that most guys just want me to show them my naked body.

If they *do* ask me to come with sexy lingerie, sometimes it's so *they* can wear it!

But I'm only speaking for New England men, here. Other men might be different. One time, I went to see a guy who was visiting from the Caribbean. I was dressed in a classic, lady-like long skirt, something my Boston area clients are thrilled to see me arrive in.

This guy actually told me to leave! He told me he couldn't get interested in a girl who would show up in such dowdy wear!

So you dress in the way that makes you happy, and you adapt it to the preference of the men in your locale.

I pull on a sheer and clingy chemise. It's sort of an A-line, gathered under my chest; it draws the eye to my boobs. It drapes just below them, obscuring my gut, and just barely covers my ass; my legs taper long and naked beneath it...perfect! Everything good is accentuated; everything bad is concealed. Oh, how I love this chemise!

I've got on my crotchless decoy beneath it. If the client I'll be visiting takes off the chemise, he'll be staring not at my nasty lower gut, but at lace and the Wonder of Wonders.

I finish with outer clothing that's discreet but much better than dreary. I make sure I've got my cell phone and condoms. And maybe a "toy" or two.

I'm ready to hit the road.

JUST ANOTHER AFTERNOON OF TERROR AND JOY

It can be fun, especially if you like things like skydiving or hang gliding.

On my way to an appointment, I'm like any other on-the-road businessperson, dealing with the perils of traffic and trying not to get lost. Maybe I'm committing that controversial mind-split, driving while talking on my cell phone, or singing along with my music CD's. But that's nothing compared to the distraction created by my thoughts about where I'm going—especially if I'm meeting someone new.

If my tryst is with someone I've never seen before, and he's not in a house, he's checked into public lodgings, then terror is the term for what I'm feeling. Adrenalin is dripping inside me, working its poisonous jitters all through me.

Hotels and motels are where callgirls get "caught," and taken in cuffs to the precincts.

He didn't sound at all like a cop on the phone. He asked the appropriate questions, and sounded out-of-state; he guffawed with a sincere-sounding startled negation when, right out of nowhere, I said *Are you police*. Those were the traits that considerably diminished my fear of getting set up. Those were the noises that somewhat assuaged me, and made me decide that I'd go for this risk.

23

But I won't be completely at ease until I know him. I won't be at ease until he's paid me, and he hasn't distinguished our transaction with the chanting of my rights.

How would you like to be on your way to a meeting, hoping you look okay, anxiously hoping you'll make a good impression, and also clenched up with the raw, primal fear that you might get deceived and arrested?

I wonder whether people—people who aren't whores—can begin to imagine that terror. It's gut-wrenching, routine, and faced all alone. Protectors of the public are what we prostitutes *fear*.

I pull up at the hotel. It's a sweeping, three-star affair. When I go to a cheap motel, I *feel* a little cheap, even though I make the same money. I won't feel that way here.

I park and walk into the lobby. I approach the front desk people with a bright, friendly smile, and plenty of eye contact.

Don't act nervous. Don't ever act guilty. Walk proud; walk tall; you belong here.

Damn right I do.

But just to get me lost, just to lead me astray, just to get me gaping, impressed, at the vast banquet halls and theme lounges (so some day I'll book an event here, and make the hotel big bucks), the guest rooms are located remotely, in areas not apparent. These large hotels are strange mazes. Somewhere deep in this complex, tunnels of rooms spread out from the center in maddeningly different directions.

Which way should I go?

My client tried hard to be helpful on the phone; he described where I should turn once I got here. But the design of the place, and its hugeness and attractions, have all done their numbers on me; I've arrived, and my memory wavers; I'm a little bit overwhelmed. I'm probably going to go the wrong way, probably five minutes-worth of wrong way, and I don't want to be late. So I head to the desk for directions.

Somebody hands me a map of the hotel.

I realize I've just called some attention to myself. If I decide to go out the same way I've come in, these sentries will witness me leaving in an hour. If they're sharp they're going to peg me, and *know*.

Oh, well. That's why I jump around. From this town to that town to that town, and even that one over yonder. From this hotel to that motel to that hotel; I'm always a moving target, never easy to hit. By the time I work at this establishment again, a new slew of faces will be manning the desk. Or maybe the next time I come here, it will be on somebody else's shift. The point, and it's vital, is that these particular front desk people will never see me *a lot.*

Because of the map, now I'm orientated. I'm ready to face my next challenge, the big one. Now I'm heading straight for the lair of a man I don't know from Adam.

When I get to his floor, and I'm close now, scoping room numbers to his, my heart is a pounding hammer, and my stomach is knotted to the point of feeling sick.

Maids are all over the corridor. Their huge carts are parked just like trucks. Their invasions of rooms and their aggressive strip-downs make them look like they own the place. They also tend to look foreign.

For some reason, they always smile at me.

Why?

They smile at me, an attractive woman, more carefully groomed than the average female traveler, who's walking down this hallway all alone; I don't have any luggage, and I don't look at all wound-down; I'm clearly not a woman who's come here to rest.

They can see I'm not holding a key card. They can see I'm all peering and seeking, yet somehow bold just the same; I'm purposefully hunting for a room not my own.

So, why are they grinning at me?

Do they *know*? Are they *cool*?

Maybe they're beaming for the simple reason that their cultures made them randomly friendly. Or maybe they've been trained by their employer to welcome every face with a smile.

But there's something too real in their eyes.

Is it because they know what I'm up to, and they know I'm the highest paid female service worker this place will ever contain, and their culture has taught them to respect me for it?

*Or are they grinning because they know there's a sting operation going on here, and they know I'm a whore walking into her doom, and their culture has taught them I **deserve** it?*

Easy girl, easy. Stop it.

I return every one of their smiles.

I walk a bit further, and okay, here's his room.

By the time I'm standing there knocking, my fear has wrung me out; I'm like someone on the point of dying, who's reached the acceptance phase. I'll just deal with the detectives, if that's what awaits me.

I'm also like a soldier heading straight into battle. I'm committed to seeing this through. I'm now compressing the terror, so I can intelligently face the whatever.

He opens the door, and I feel a little shock.

The shock isn't him; it's the moment. It's the stun of two face-to-face strangers. No matter how well I plan it, no matter how often I do it, there's always this flash of *bizarre*.

We're both swallowed whole by it, weirded. But we're going to keep our cools.

I'm smiling, of course. I say hi. He does the same, and steps back. I step inside.

I don't give a damn about his age or his looks. The only thing that matters is what's in his eyes. And the language his body is roaring.

That roar is the loudest silence on earth. Your ears for it grow in a jail cell.

Well, his eyes are making me feel some relief. I see terror, mischief, hope and lust. And his body is doing the right stuff, too. It's tense, yet yielding, like a dog that's afraid, yet wants very much to be petted.

I can see that he's trying to hide his fear. He's trying to look relaxed. There's a tremor in his hands that betrays him.

I'd never see that in a cop.

A cop is all confident predator. The stealth of a killer emits from him. It's a vibe I'll never forget.

"How're you doing?" I start things, still smiling.

"Good. Nice to see you!" he responds. That means he's pleased with my looks. So now I can relax in that other, more minor relief I need to feel.

But he's still afraid I'm a vice cop. And of course, I'm still afraid he is. But I'm doing much better now. A cop wouldn't care what I look like, and this man plainly does. And also, his room has a lived-in appearance. There's a suitcase, and clothes on the hangers. And when I walked in, and eased past the bathroom, I got a keen sense of used, of steamed-up.

All of this is very reassuring, but I'm still a little scared. Maybe he's just a really good imposter-pretender-cop.

There's only one way to right things. I take off my jacket, and lay it close by. Then I open my arms, and say:

"Hug?"

"Sure!" he responds, and we have a good strong one.

And in that two-second moment, the terror dissolves. Neither of us feels any wires or pistols. There's just warm, nervous flesh, two scared-shitless people, needing to ease the dread.

Everything's going to be okay.

I think.

But now he might offer the money. That will tighten me up again. That's the illegal part of this meeting. That's when a cop would arrest me.

The "industry standard" is to "get the money upfront." I'm not going to do that. If he's a cop, that's like begging to be busted. And if he's just an everyday customer—and by now I'm almost certain he is—then demanding the money is an insult. It's like a sign that says: *I assume you're a dirtbag. I assume you won't pay.*

That's not a good way to keep a nice rapport going.

Back when we spoke on the phone, he sounded very decent. I could sense that here was a typical guy who would consider it unmanly to rip a girl off. So now that we're in here together, I'm going to show him that faith.

Most clients appreciate that. I think that's one of the reasons they tip me.

Suddenly I notice that this guy's made things easy. He's put my fee out, he's placed it in view. It's present, but I won't have to discuss it. It's five fifties spread on a table.

Okay, good. The hard part's all over. The paranoia's fading, the money's been dealt with, the rest of the hour will fly.

Men are so easy to please in bed!

I've been with over a thousand of them, and once we've gotten down to it, I've found that only a handful has presented any difficulties. And when I use the word difficulties, I don't mean what anti-prostitutionists picture when they think of callgirls' clients being bad; I don't mean my clients are violent or surly or in any way disrespectful; by my definitions, that's never occurred.

The few that have been less than easy to handle have potency problems, and are depressed over it. Or they've had too much to drink, or snort, and that's made them either clumsy or antsy. Or they need something I don't provide.

Most guys, however, potent or not, intoxicated or not, are able to enjoy what I do, and what I do is great blowjobs. I love to suck cock, and it shows. For many of my clients, the best oral sex they've ever had in their lives is when they've gotten with me.

If a guy wants me to, I'll suck his cock and lick his balls the entire time I'm with him. Often, however, they want a bit of everything. With me, "everything" is anything but Greek. No one is going to go where my shit is, not with penis, or finger, or *anything*.

I do let them kiss me a little, and touch me everywhere, and go down on me and fuck me with a condom. And I do make them feel they're good lovers, especially when they deserve it.

This guy, today, in this pleasant hotel room, is forty-nine, married, and from Pennsylvania. He's here for a convention (I forget his profession), and he's seeing me on a break. Our tryst will be a little abbreviated, because he's got to get back.

I ask him to make himself comfortable. My request is a subtle scold. He answered the door fully clothed, and he should have been down to a robe or his briefs. If his clothes had been off, that would have been an immediate reassurance that it was doubtful he was a cop.

I've heard that certain piece-of-shit cops will *do it* with a girl and *then* bust her, but that's just pretty damn rare.

He eagerly complies with my wishes. While he quickly undresses, I peel down in slow motion. I make just a bit like a stripper. He watches me, transfixed. Now I'm down to my see-through chemise. I've sucked in my gut, of course.

He steps up to me, naked, and feels me. He's ecstatic. He's thrilled. He's speechless. His tremors are back, worse than ever, but they're no longer caused by fear.

Guys *love* to be with a strange woman. It's a male gear that never stops turning. It's the reason "escorts" make great money.

He's rock-hard. We lay down on the bed. I can tell by his prostrate, belly-up position that he doesn't want to do much to me; he's waiting for me to do everything to him. Good. That means I won't have to *flower*. I won't have to open for him. I won't have to sexually bloom for him.

That thing that I call *flower* is the most complex part of my job.

I hover by his chest and lean over. I suck a nipple. I'm testing the erogenous waters, waiting for a response. He moans a bit; good, he likes it.

People are different about their nipples. Some guys feel absolutely nothing, and look bored, still waiting for the fun to start; but others go berserk, and want me to bite them there, and to even ferociously pinch them. Most guys enjoy a nice full-body tingle, caused by the pressure of a tiny, firm nibble.

This one's acting average.

While my mouth's on his nipple, my hand moves down his front, and stops just short of his pubes. It goes up and then down again slowly, a few times back and forth, dispelling bad tensions that collect in a belly.

I'm also at it to tease. His cock is like a hungry pup, begging, up on its haunches: *please*.

I keep on stroking his belly, and then with no warning, my hand goes to his cock. It's the nicest surprise of his week, and he gasps. My touch is gentle, especially on his balls, respectful of his male vulnerability. We are, after all, perfect strangers; I want him to know I won't hurt him.

Unless he requests me to.

Now I move down and get on with his treat. I get close enough to inspect his pubes for signs of disease or uncleanliness. As usual, there are none.

I don't use condoms when I suck cocks. I've gone to a clinic and conferred with a doctor who specializes in sexually transmitted disease. He's told me that the AIDS virus can only survive internally. When it's in the air, outside of the body, it dies within fifteen seconds. The mouth is considered external. He's told me it's nearly impossible to get AIDS from unswallowed semen. He said that I'd have to have open oral sores.

Well I don't, and men want it "bareback." And there's no sign of herpes or syphilis chancres, here. And anyway, when I'm through here, I'm going to go into the bathroom, and gargle and swallow some organic cider vinegar that I always keep stashed in my purse. I'm going to slosh it on my lips, too. That stuff kills absolutely everything, and I use it every time.

So I go for him with my mouth.

Not a lot of my clients have been with a woman who sucks cock as well as I do. This guy's built average, six inches or so, and not inconveniently thick; that means I can easily slide him in all the way to the tunnel in my throat. Up and down slowly, squeezing hard with my lips, back and forth his cock keeps disappearing, way into the tight nether regions. When my lips are touching his pubic hair, because he's in to the hilt, I reach out to his balls with my tongue, and lick them while squeezing his cock with my throat.

He's losing his mind with pleasure, but he's also intellectually amazed. He lifts up his head to watch.

I can't stay that way for long; my airway's completely blocked. So I come up for air, quite literally. While I'm catching my breath and soaking him with the saliva that always flows from me when I deep-throat a cock, I tongue-stroke him from the tip of his head right down to that erogenous place below his balls, and up a bit, circling all over his balls, and down again, same thing, and then all the way up, stopping for a moment when I get to the tip to go round and round and round, and aiming for the sensitive underside with a perfectly placed bunch of flickings.

Then I swallow him whole again.

"My *God!*" he's almost screaming. Clearly, he won't regret this.

I squeeze him like a too-big bite going down. While my tongue, once again, is getting busy with his balls.

While I'm at it, the gag reflex kicks in, but I taught myself a long time ago to just field that mechanism, diffuse it. Deep in my abdomen, something absorbs its force. I've always known how to do that, since before I became a sex worker. For as long as I've been sexually active, it seems, I've always been determined to excel at giving head, and to refuse to let gagging interrupt it. I've never once even begun to throw up; all that gets spewed is that river of saliva, which lubes things generously.

I've read somewhere that fellatio is the ultimate act of female sexual slavery. Two hundred and fifty dollars, waiting for me on the table, tells me that isn't so; for me the act is my valued and very well-paid-for performance.

This guy has good control of his orgasm. He's holding it back for his money's-worth of pleasure. That's good; that means I won't have to keep stopping, in order to keep him from coming.

I can concentrate on my job.

While I'm hard at work on him, he starts doing something they almost all do. It's something I like, and even crave: he gently fingers my hair, which causes my scalp to tingle. He massages my neck and shoulders and arms. He does this because he appreciates my service, and maybe because he enjoys the feel of my ultra-soft hair and skin.

So there we are, mutually pleasured.

Then his hands fall away, and incredibly, his cock gets even harder. I can feel his balls tighten up. His moment is at hand. I suck on him firmly, way up and down, making sure all the while that my tongue hits that groove, while my hand cups and strokes on his marble-taut scrotum. His limbs stiffen up, and his pelvis starts thrusting; his own primal rhythm begins; it's time to let his body take over. All I have to do is stay on him.

In my life I've seen thousands of orgasms, but each one is glorious, a wonder.

Why is it that so many only feel God when they're gazing at horrible death on a cross? Or only when they're bruising their foreheads on mats? Or only when they're mulling over holy laws? Or meditating, or crying?

No, God is here, in this ecstasy! In this unspeakably heavenly explosion!

Right after, he's swooning in endorphins. He's spread out, all dazed and spent in his mess, which I only would have swallowed if he were my lover. I've let it spill everywhere.

I rise. "I'm getting you a towel," I tell him. "Don't move now; just relax."

I always instruct them not to move, after. A lot of guys are in a pitiful hurry to sacrifice the subsequent blissfulness, and jump up to wash themselves off; somewhere they've been taught their ejaculate's dirty. I'm annoyed by that kind of thinking. A poor guy ought to be able to kick back and enjoy his own afterglow. I'll do the clean-up for him.

This is something I even do when I'm in a guy's own house. I'll find the bathroom; I'll wet the towel; let me take over, *relax*.

It's also time for my gargle. So when I go to the bathroom for the towel, I take my purse along with me.

I return, as promised, with a moistened guest towel. I've made sure it's perfectly warm. I gently get him spotless, and I wipe the bedding, too.

After a few minutes he sits up with a smile. He's sorry, but he has to go now. I can see that his mind's on his next scheduled mission. He's got to get back to his conference. That's my cue to start dressing.

I've only been here half an hour. My fee is by the hour. But sometimes, like now, with this guy, I'm going to make an hour's worth of money in only half the time.

And he doesn't care; he's pleased to give up every dollar. Now he'll return to the drone of his day refreshed, stress-relieved, and better able to focus. And maybe he'll look around at his colleagues, and feel more than a little bit smug.

*What did **they** do during the break? I'll bet I had the most fun!*

I've been told by many a working client that after he's been with me, his associates are baffled by his mystifying smile.

While I'm gathering up the money and we're saying our good-byes, he heartily assures me he'll be calling me again, as soon as he comes back this way.

We don't leave together. I go first. That's mostly for the sake of discretion, but it's also to break things off. Our acquaintance is meant to be only *in there*.

I walk back through the maids. We resume all those sweet wordless greetings. My heart goes out to them now. I think of the cleanings they have to do, and how, as with me, their work is performed for strangers. They purge away dust, lint, litter, loose hairs, used sheets, semen-streaked towels like the one I've left behind, tub scum, toilet filth…I consider their low pay.

I consider how awful some people think my work is. How much "worse" it must be than a maid's.

I think of the pleasure I give. And I think of the money I make.

And I feel so good I could shout.

THE WORKING GIRL'S DAY CONTINUES

My first trick was handsome and sweet.

It's mid-afternoon on a weekday, a time when the calls can be frequent. When I get in my car in the hotel parking lot, the first thing I do is just sit there, making my front seat a phone booth. I go for my cell phone and check my voicemail.

It would be wiser, in terms of surveillance, to make any calls while I'm driving. A retired-cop client once told me that. It was several years ago when he said that, but he might still be right. He said scanners pick up a lot less of your talk when you're on the move, in traffic. In order to hear all your business, cops have to be tailing you, up close behind you.

These days, his advice might be useless; I don't know whether cops have the wherewithal to pick up on digital frequencies. For caution's sake, however, I always assume that they do.

But right now, I don't feel like dealing with driving while I'm making my business calls. Wouldn't the bastards appreciate that? My putting of driver safety first?

So I sit there cell-talking, with my frequency immobile, maybe easy for them to pick up. It doesn't matter to me. In a moment I'll be leaving this small town, moving beyond their jurisdiction. If they've got the means to do it, the local fuzz can listen all they want to my cell chats with men about my measurements and fee; I don't give a damn. I'm content to just perch here, resting, maybe surveilled, but not caring. Whatever I say here can't hurt me, because I'll be gone in a flash.

A typical "escort" won't brush with cops much. If she's lucky, she never will. But she could, and if she does, it's awful. It's a total psychological collapse of her world, and then she has to rebuild it. I know that because I went through it. Once.

My obsession with police is the wisdom of the busted. It's the angry will to never let it happen again.

It's funny…I watch *Law and Order*. I love all the cops on all the versions of that show. I've even had wonderful dreams about them! But out here in the real world, I hate cops.

It hurts to have to feel that way.

There are three new messages. The first one's from Rhode Island. It's a guy who's responded to my Providence ad. I don't know him, and he's sixty miles distant; those are two good reasons to not see him today. But still, I courtesy-call him. I tell him I'm not available, but I want to say hello. I'm letting him know he's important.

I get him talking. I get him talking *a lot*. If I go to Rhode Island I cross a state line, which worsens the offense. And besides, my work is a felony there. Here in Massachusetts, it's only a misdemeanor.

After a long, long listen, I decide that he sounds okay. I encourage him to stay in touch. I leave him all warm and worked-up about me.

I'll hear from him again.

Another of the messages is from a guy I know, and he's right on my way home. He wants me to come right over.

Perfect!

After I call him and tell him I'm coming, I pull down the overhead driver's side mirror and run my brush through my hair. My lipstick is on way too heavy.

Before I left the hotel guy, I applied a lot in his bathroom—I was compensating too much. I wanted to walk out of there fresh-looking, not looking like I'd lost all my lipstick in the criminal act of a cock sucked for pay.

I blot it. I check to make sure my condoms are where they belong, easy to grab in my purse; this next guy likes to fuck. I

34

have one more message to listen to, but that will have to be on the road.

There's money to be made, and he's waiting!

I start up the car and pull out into traffic and wait til I'm cruising the highway, and then I retrieve the last message. It's another repeat customer; he also wants to see me right now.

Well, I'm already on my way elsewhere, and also, I have an appointment tonight, with yet another regular. But I could fit this one in.

From deep in my stomach, the rhythm thing speaks up:

No.

This guy is very young, he's in his early twenties, and as always, as all of the guys in his age group, all he'll want to do is fuck. He'll want to fuck the whole hour. No conversation, no leisurely glass of wine, no pampering rub of my feet or my back; just fuck, fuck, fuck, fuck, and plenty of suck in between. I've already sucked off one guy today, and I'm about to have sex with another. And the guy I'm going to be seeing tonight will expect me, as always, to respond like a nymph. Should I be getting with a horned-up kid, too?

I said no.

I call him and sweetly inform him that I can't make it today. How about tomorrow? He'll call me back then, he says.

Yeah, right. We'll see. You can never be sure of that with any of them, especially the youngest ones. As a rule they don't have much money, and when they do, it burns holes through their pockets.

It doesn't matter, the rhythm thing reminds me. *You're making plenty without him, and your well-being comes first.*

Okay Mommy, or whoever you are.

I drive on.

It's easy to find the guy waiting for me, because I've been there several times. He lives just a few towns over, between my town and the hotel's, in a sweetly positioned, upscale housing tract.

His house is rather large, a comely new Cape, on a half-acre rise in a group of other plots, behind a whitewashed corral-style fence, on a curving, beautifully tree-lined lane, with unspoiled woods everywhere. There's a hearty sense of pilgrims and wilderness, of fresh air and wood stoves and skylights, and cable and computers and designer kitchens, all perfectly coexisting. I travel down lovely, gently hilled roads, exactly like his, to get there.

I park in his driveway and stroll to his door. I don't have to worry that he's nervous about watchful neighbors. This guy is single and self-employed and solvent, and he enjoys his good fortune with good-natured rebellion. Unlike a lot of his peers in these places, he couldn't care less what the neighbors will think.

He's a laid-back, easy-going client.

He admits me with a cheerful face, and takes my hand and leads me into his tasteful-bachelor crib. In the open-concept main gathering room, there's a big, soft, plush leather couch. I love to sink myself into it; I smilingly plop myself there. On his gleaming, costly, hand-hewed coffee table, a bottle of light beer awaits me; he always has one set out.

He's a nice-looking guy, fairly fit, but his attitude is the best thing. He's worked hard for years, and it's paid off, and he exudes great satisfaction. A happy-go-lucky simplicity endows him. Neither marriage nor divorce nor fatherhood has claimed him. He's still rather young, not quite forty, still free as a bird, yet successful, and he positively glows.

I think everyone would like to be him, for at least one shining moment.

He's so busy with his business that relationships fail, but that doesn't bother him….yet. He can afford to be with good callgirls, and he deeply appreciates our fit with his life.

How different this is from a while ago, when I knocked on the door of a hotel room, with my stomach all knotted with dread. Guys like this one take the edge off all that, and mellow my days like a summertime breeze.

He wants what clients call the GFE: The Girlfriend Experience. He wants a full hour of romance and passion. He wants me to *flower* for him. He calls me a lot because he knows I'll deliver.

Intimacy with strangers is easy for me. I can't begin to say why. Before I became an "escort', I was intensely monogamous. I was no doubt a "good girl." I remain so, in committed relationships. But I've found that it's also incredibly easy for me to be a sex worker. I can walk into a place, face a strange man and, even if he's initially defensive, soon I have him relaxed and content, and warmly reciprocating.

I don't know how I can do this. It just comes to me, like mothering or writing.

And guys like this one make it so sweet. Good karma comes off him like a fragrance. It's great to immerse myself in it. We make out on his couch with much care for each other's comfort. Then we retire to his solid-oak furnished, pillow-top mattressed bedroom. We make love just like a chance meeting. There's erotic intrigue, even though it's been planned.

And whenever my soul isn't tethered to a lover, this luminous guy makes me come. I don't know how we do this. But we do, even though it's not love, even though I would never begin to imagine that he'd ever let me clutter his self-absorbed life, and I'm going to be glad to leave him, just like when I leave all the others, and I'm not going to miss him and cry for him, as I would if he were my man; and I'd never do it with him for free.

But while we're together, it's lovely. He's imparting a ray of his destiny to me, and I'm happy to let it in.

As I'm getting back into my clothes, he puts three hundred dollars next to my purse. I only charge two-fifty, but he always gives me more.

We say our good-byes, with warmth but dismissal. He wants me to go now, as much as he previously wanted me to come. Those are my feelings exactly.

I head home.

It's a little bit after four. My evening appointment isn't til seven, and that's good; I need time to unwind.

In some ways, my job is so easy—being with men is so natural for me—but the driving I do exhausts me. By the time I get home from my next appointment, the one I've made for tonight, today I'll have driven well over a hundred miles. That's typical mileage for one day, and I really hate to drive.

Oh, I could hire a driver, but I don't want to have to pay someone, and I don't want to have to depend on someone who just might not show up.

And besides, what kind of guy would be endlessly available to drive me somewhere at noon, and then maybe again after that, and then maybe again that evening, every time, every day that I'd need it? It would have to be someone who's *always free*, and I find that kind of suspicious. *Where's his life?* I'd be wondering. Why doesn't he have one? I couldn't feel comfortable about someone like that. I wouldn't want a partnership with someone like that.

So I drive myself around.

The driving is tiring, just ask my back, yet I know that's not the worst drain. Emotional exhaustion is the big thing; today has been a perfect example. At the hotel, adrenalin riddled all through me. And later on, a prince in his castle delighted me. This roller-coaster gamut from terror to joy is my constant, daily routine; I don't even think about it. But my body lets me know what it's doing to me.

I badly need to get home, and rest.

I think about some of my peers, some women in my business, who degrade themselves and degrade the work by allowing drugs and exploiters to control them. That's how they cope with the same things I deal with: the paranoia and stigma, the fleeting liaisons, the aloneness and lack of societal support.

Their weakness enrages me. It causes the feminists to think we need "rescue."

What we need is advocacy.

As I drive, I reflexively check for more messages. There are two; I reluctantly call them.

Sometimes I'm really, really sick of having to be my own front person. I don't feel like talking to anyone right now. But then my principles tell me I should. *Respond to each call, even when you're not available. Introduce yourself. Qualify them. Build rapport. Reel them in. Invest in future transactions.*

It's like any other business.

And I'm a corporation of one.

Suddenly I realize I'm starving. I pull up to a fast-food window. I order the healthiest-looking thing. I drive on, devouring, trying not to be messy, and I tell myself to work out tomorrow.

There's no way I'll get to the gym today. All I'm good for is a nap. That's okay; I don't feel guilt; I worked out yesterday.

I get home. There's no man living with me right now, and no kids except for their visits; but my Yellow Labrador greets me, and of course he's ecstatically wagging.

He's the loveliest, noblest creature on earth. He even exceeds what a horse does to me. Years down the road, after old age has killed him, I'll realize he was one of the big things, right up there with my children.

Right now, he needs a walk.

I oblige him, and then we come in and lay down. He sprawls on the rug by my bed. I know that when I wake up later on, and swing out my feet toward the floor, they'll connect with his great head. I think he arranges himself so they will. He'll instantly rise from his sound doggy slumber, happy to have been struck, alert to be my extension, and eager to follow my lead.

Sometimes I take him with me to appointments. He's content to wait for me out in the car. If it's warm out, I roll down the windows.

Clients laughingly call him my "driver". After I leave him, he jumps into the front seat. He sits in my scent, in a rod-straight position, with his eyes locked onto the door I went in. He waits with the focus and patience of something beyond human ken.

That makes me forgive all his dog hairs.

Right now, his breathing is helping me relax. So is my naptime read. Always, before my snooze overtakes me, I study a magazine. It's always a good one, a news one, the kind that informs me and melts in my head and takes shape again in my writing. Then the print starts looking like symbols from space, and the whole thing falls out of my hand.

I'm gone.

Half an hour later I open my eyes, and feel myself physically rested. But I'm also profoundly depressed. I'm not quite aware of it, though. I tend to be one to not face it.

My life's been a train wreck since I was a toddler, when my mother had her first stroke. Too young, I had to find far too much courage. I had to learn to rely on bravado. That's fine...until bravery becomes like a drug. Sometimes, it's wiser to throw down that armor, and allow myself the pain.

But I'd rather stuff myself.

In denial of depression, I do very stupid things. To be specific, I compulsively eat. Food has this wonderful, buffering way of displacing the buildup of hurt.

But then, of course, I gain weight. And when I gain weight, I'm self-loathing. Round and round and round I go, and always, I stop at the same destination: face stuffed or not, I'm depressed. I'm depressed because I'm lonely. I've had this little problem since my mother dropped dead, when I was six years old.

Being in love lifts me out of it, and I'm between lovers right now. That's not a good place for me. But I've always screwed things up badly. I've always picked the wrong man.

So as much as I hate it, I'm living alone, again.

If only the dog were enough.

I'm not hungry; I ate on the way home. But aloneness is sucking me into itself, opening doors on the blackness and shoving me into the void. Snacks make it all go away. They're totally nutritionally useless, but they ground me, they keep me from disintegrating, and here comes the impulse to GORGE, GORGE, GORGE, like the hug of a fat foster mom.

My need is even stronger than the lust of the men I service, and far easier and cheaper to slake.

STUFF IT. STUFF IT IN. NOW.

Yummy stuff. Good stuff. Crunchy, gooey, sloppy stuff.

Doritos. Onion dip. Ben and Jerry's. Ummmm. I can jam it all in right now, in one sitting. I don't care that the onion and ice cream don't match.

Suddenly my phone starts ringing.

The urge to gorge falls away.

It's a working-girl friend of mine. She's called to say hi, to see how I'm doing. That's nice. I say fine, how are you? But I know her better than that. She doesn't really care about me. She's hoping I'll throw her some business.

I give her the number of the kid I refused. Maybe he's still looking. We hang up so she can call him.

I don't have to give her any business. But I don't see why I shouldn't. I advertise well, I often have extra, and didn't she just save me from a snack binge? But her greatest worth is that she knows my big secret, because she's in on it, too.

You can seldom be honest about what you do with anyone but clients and other people in the business. Whore secrecy increases my aloneness. It actually causes something worse than aloneness. It makes me isolated.

When she calls, she eases that hurt.

Some day, I'll regret my generosity. Some day I'm going to find that every client I give her, she maneuvers to keep to herself. She bites the hand that feeds her. She tries to make inches a mile. I'm going to discover she's unscrupulous and greedy; she thinks nothing of stealing from me. She does it because she can. There's nothing, no authority, to stop her.

But for now, I call her a friend.

She calls me back in a moment, to say she got sent to his voicemail. She left him a message, and hopes he'll respond.

I'm glad that she's called me again. I launch into a discussion of all kinds of whore things, stuff I can't share with anyone else. It passes the time. We laugh about things. Wonderful belly laughs.

Then I tell her I have to go now; it's time to get ready for my evening appointment. We hang up, and my mind goes to what I should wear.

The compulsion to binge has slunk back to its hole. It loses its power when I'm focused on work.

Whew. But that was a close call.

As I rummage around in my stash of work clothes, I'm thinking, the next guy I'm going to has seen my chemise too often. It seems that I wore it last time I saw him. I think so; it's hard to remember.

I lay out another sort of flattering confection, a baby-doll, gauzy thing. I dig in my sexy-underwear drawer for a fresh pair of crotchless panties. Then I stop.

This guy, I've suddenly remembered, prefers that I show up kind of musky. Okay, I'll keep on the panties I've worn all day.

Most guys, as you'd guess, want their "escort" to be fresh and clean. Some actually want the illusion that she hasn't been around. I can easily provide them with that feeling; my look is naturally wholesome, my lifestyle is health-and-fitness, and my hygiene habits are good. But once in a while I encounter a guy who's turned on by the concept of multi-used whore.

That's how this next guy will be.

When I'm with him, he wants a detailed description of everything sexual I did that day or week, with every single guy. He wants to hear all my "stories." They make him as hard as a rock. He wants me disease-free, as anyone would, but if I smell a bit earthy, that's good; in fact, he requests that from me.

But I'm *not* going to show up with my privates unrefreshed. Musty crotchless panties are one thing…an unclean vulva is something else. I've peed several times today. I wipe myself well, but still…and there's spermicide left by a condom. And there's a sour taste from the vinegar I swabbed there after I was with the last guy.

I strip naked and go into the bathroom. I lean over the bathtub and turn on the faucet. I get it all warm, step in it and squat, and thoroughly wash myself down there. I douche with lots of plain water.

I grin to myself while I do this. I think back to the days when I lived with my second husband, the father of my last child. That was before my debut as a sex worker.

He was always in a hurry. He couldn't stand to wait. There were times when I'd be trying to change from harried mother of three little boys to cool, calm, pretty lady, trying to get myself presentable, readying for our night out.

He'd get himself huffing and puffing, and then he'd yell through the bathroom door: "Don't fill up the tub, now! Just give yourself a whore's bath!"

Was that a prophesy?

He could be an abusive fuck, to everyone but his own baby. He shoved his stepsons around like the trash, and that's why I had to leave him.

But sometimes he could be funny, and now, so many years later, I remember the comedies.

GOOD PORN, HAPPY TIME, SAD TIME

Together we would tell our secret stories! And I would find a place for my weird self.

The blinds have all been shut tight.

I'm luxuriating on the floor in my evening appointment's living room, on a stuffed down comforter on a carpet just as thick, sprawled in front of an incredibly large TV that takes up half the wall. He's put lots of huge pillows behind my head, to ensure that I'm comfortably propped up to watch. On the screen, a naked, very vocal girl is getting "done" by a girl and a guy.

My client's a married fifty-two year old. He's told me in the past that his wife won't watch porn. She won't have it in her house.

That's something I have trouble understanding.

Well, tonight she's away, and the forbidden has taken over. Her husband's down between my legs, he's earnestly licking me. He's not bad at it, he knows to be gentle, and he knows the right places to hit. I'm breathless, I'm plateauing and ready to come, but it's not because of him; it's the porn.

I absolutely love good porn.

I've seen a lot of porn. I've seen the old standard: the girls on their knees, they're sucking, they're allowing the semen to spurt on their faces. I've seen them getting ass-fucked and doggy-style fucked. I've seen them getting double penetration. And I've also seen something, in a lot of that porn, that far too many women may never acknowledge: I've seen women intensely enjoying themselves. In porn films, I've seen women having real orgasms. Before vigilant cameras that patiently shoot, I've seen them ecstatically letting themselves go.

I've seen men or other women working on them, giving them lengthy cunnilingus, and sending them palpably soaring. And I've seen women riding the men, or having the men ride them, and getting off with ululating cries. I've seen women squirting all over the other actors.

When these women are portrayed in a sexy progression from shyly smiling and fully clothed to helplessly, writhingly naked, porn scripts satisfy, in men, their fantasies of sexual conquest. But there's plenty there for women to appreciate, too. There's plenty for women to relate to. A lot of the actresses are shaking with spasms of authentic erotic response. Their submission is not to the filmmakers, or to the actors (or actresses) who "do" them. Their submission is to their own pleasure. To call these women "victims" is absurd. Their inner thighs are shining, they repeatedly vaginally gush; a few of them even can jettison their come.

I know their enjoyment is real, because I'm an orgasmic woman. I'm also a sexual professional. Just as a cardiologist can see heart failure on faces, I recognize genuine orgasms.

Some women in porn still fake it; lots of porn is still phony and contrived. In some films, the women are clearly excited, but throughout it, they never quite come. To encounter what you want to see, you have to watch a lot. When you do find a good porn video, if you're a woman I predict that you'll cherish it forever.

I define good porn as porn in which the women truly get off. Such porn is helpful to me. I've seen things in porn that have aided me, greatly, in achieving my own orgasms. Whenever I find myself stuck on a verge, I think of those eroticized women—those actresses in orgasmic extremis—and that sends me right over the top, every time. So do my memories of women who scream in motel rooms next to mine. Or the women who come in the **HBO** sex shows. Or the women I've seen as clients, who get off with me and their men.

Right now I want to come when the girl on the screen does, and so I hold myself back. Times like this, when I witness female sexual passion, are the only times I ever have to hold my orgasm back. Any other time, even with the man I love, I always have to work a bit to get there. But right now, I could come in a heartbeat.

She gets there—and it's authentic. I can tell by her face, which has forgotten the camera, and her belly, which spasmodically heaves, and her wails, which have signature rhythm. Now my orgasm shatters me, too.

I'm always amazed by this phenomenon, this fact that another woman so easily makes me come, just because *she's* coming. I love my fervent response. I'm not gay, but the empathy gets me. It instantly takes me there.

My client's all smiles; I've done what his wife won't, and wow, what a thunderous flourish. I've only been here a few minutes, and already, such sexual drama! It's the girl on that video, I tell you! The second I walked into this house, I could hear her. I was wet before I hit the floor.

"So, what's new?" he lustfully asks me. He's masturbating. He knows that I know that it's time for some stories.

My tales are *his* romp with the empathy. He hears about what I do to other guys, and it clearly makes him crazy. I only have to sit here and talk, while he does himself slowly, then with gusto, then with frenzy.

For once, he's got a companion, a woman beside him who gets it. And while he's hearing my stories, he's watching those tremendous sexual scenes at his theater sized down for a house. He's thrilled, he's in voyeuristic heaven, with someone completely accepting, someone who loves it like he does.

His semen is very copious for a fifty-two year old man.

"It's been a while," he says.

He's got that sad little look in his eye, that look that makes me consider the fact that so many people have marital partners, and yet the sex is dead.

I get him cleaned up, and then we kick back. He fast-forwards to a scene he knows I'll enjoy.

In a moment, I'm excited all over again. I kind of become the girl in the film. My eyes and ears are fixed on her lust. I rub my clit while he fingers me. Once again, I time myself. I merge with the other woman's passion. Once again, I'm amazed at the power. I actually have to stop touching myself to keep my orgasm in check.

When she announces to the world that she's going to come, it all breaks lose from me, too.

Jesus.

"*You* should be paying *me*," grins my client.

But he's actually honored to give me his money. To have all these girls in his living room, moaning, and one of them's real flesh and blood....*Oh God*, his face beams: *life is sweet!* His saddened expression is gone. He looks like a loved child on Christmas.

And I'm just a little bit awestruck, myself. Usually, when a client gets me to come—gets me to sexually bloom to the max—I never do it more than once in a meeting. It takes a lot of energy to give it all up. Enough is enough, this isn't my lover, I never do encores for anyone less.

But if a client's like this guy—if he throws in some really good porn—here I am getting off twice. I can't believe it.

That's why I don't understand all the women who refuse to watch any porn.

Fifteen minutes are left of his hour. He asks me to suck him a bit. I lean over and mouth his soft cock. I get him completely hard again, but he's spent, he won't come twice. He's perfectly happy with that. It's so good for him to just lounge here, contentedly watching these orgies, getting sucked, feeling free, getting something he needs, rebelling against his restrictions.

I suck. He rubs my back. I feel good. I'm going to get hundreds of dollars again, and all is right with my world.

When it's time for me to go, he gives me fifty dollars less than my current fee. That's because I've known this guy for years. When I met him, my rate was only two hundred, and two hundred it will remain. You can't raise the price on a regular customer.

That's okay. Two hundred just to enjoy such great porn, with such a familiar person, is fine. And I didn't have to drive far. He's only twelve miles from my house.

We say our good-byes with affection.

On the way home, I discover new messages waiting. Of course there are; it's night. The lonely, horny late shift has begun. But for me, the day's winding down now. I'm not a nocturnal person.

If I've just had a busy day like today, and even if I haven't, any guy who calls after nine P.M. is likely to lose out with me. He should have called earlier, and set something up. I'll go out as late as ten if it's been planned. But *only* if it's been planned. I won't go out late on a whim.

I call them all back and tell them so. Sorry.

I know they're going to take their money and spend it on other girls. That doesn't bother me. I've taken home $750 today. I've made it in less than three hours. That's a fine sum of money to me, and I earned it in a miniscule expenditure of time. I could make even more, but so what?

That's right, atta girl, the rhythm thing speaks up. *Greed and workaholicism will burn you out in no time. And then where will you be?*

Besides, I know they'll all call me again. They're challenged by my refusals. The more I say no, the more often they call. It's like any other flirtation.

And sooner or later they'll all give in, and learn to do things my way. They'll learn to call in advance for appointments.

I get home, and again, I walk the dog. We come in and I take all my supplements, being extra careful to remember the kind that cleans out my urinary tract. Then I dress for bed.

My favorite thing to wear to bed is a long, Victorian-style nightgown, prettily ribboned and lacy and ruffled, just as cover-me-up as you please.

I get under the covers and continue my reading, right at the part where I dozed off before.

The urge to gorge away loneliness starts ominously stirring. I'm deep in a captivating article, but my read is getting sidetracked by persistent little nudges. I want to rise, fill a bowl, and take it into my bed. Wouldn't it be perfect to munch while feeding my mind?

Once again, I get saved by a phone call.

It's Greg, a special friend of mine. He urgently needs my attention.

He used to be a client. He used to buy my underwear. We'd meet up, and he'd be wearing the panties that I sold him the time before. He'd be eager to unzip himself and reveal them to me, all lacy beneath his blue work pants.

Then we became good friends.

Greg loves me with the worshipfulness of somebody "different" who knows I completely accept him. I accept his cross-dressing, and all. He admires me for helping him come out to himself as a passionate bisexual. I don't feel I've done much to deserve it; all I can take any credit for is being nonjudgmental. But to someone like Greg, that's precious.

Before he met me, he knew he was bi, and he also had a feeling that he wanted to be a female. But he'd never told a soul. He'd barely even told himself. He was a tough, strapping, macho kid, from a working class, macho family. This was just too big for him.

Then one day, he responded to my ad. When I responded to his message, he haltingly, shyly disclosed to me on the phone that he wanted to buy my panties. He'd pay $50 for a pair. Would that be okay with me?

"That's all you want to do?"

"Yeah. I'll meet you at the ***** rest area. You know where I'm talking about?"

"Yeah, sure."

"I drive a tow truck. Will you sit with me in it for a while?"

"Uh, now, wait a minute. I don't do "car parties.""

"No no no no. I don't mean that. Not at all. I mean, will you just *talk* with me for a minute? Right there, you know, with people all around, a safe place. You know, just talk. Not dirty talk. Nothing like that."

"Well…"

This was really different. I couldn't figure him out. But what was the harm, I decided. He couldn't be a cop; he wasn't proposing anything illegal. And he was right, we'd be meeting in a very safe place. And all I had to do was hand over a pair of $8 panties, and they didn't even have to be new. For this I'd get fifty bucks. He was asking for only a few minutes, so he wouldn't take much of my time; I could easily catch him to or from an appointment.

And that's how I met Greg.

When I joined him in his truck the first time, and sold him the first pair of panties, he had very little to say. He just sat there, quietly smoking. He stared straight ahead, and he held my underwear. But I could tell that my presence was important, somehow. For me to just be there, a witness, was something he needed a lot.

His lack of conversation was a little unnerving. But after a few more of those underwear transactions, I understood that his wordlessness was caused by a state of self-awe. This big, tough twenty-nine year old in his big, tough, idling truck was coming around to a truth about himself. His silence was pregnant with it. He didn't know how to put words to it. He didn't know how I'd react.

After a few months, he'd bought so many lace panties from me that I had to go to *Victoria's Secret* and get myself some more. And now he was asking to buy my lingerie. He was offering me really good money for it. Now he gave me $200 for all the old lingerie I could sell him.

The next time we met, he was traveling in full costume. He was dressed in my sexy goodies underneath his drab work clothes. He was joyful and excited to show me.

Then he paid me to come over to his place to watch him get dressed up. He had sex with me, wearing my old lingerie. It had to be uncomfortable for him, because he's a pretty big guy. Though I'd sold him only outfits made of stretchable fabrics, they expanded to the ripping point on him. But he didn't seem to care.

His dress-up appointment was nothing new to me. I'd bedded cross-dressers before. Yes, there is such a thing as hetero transvestites. They want to get with a woman. Dressed as one. Actually, they're everywhere, hiding their fetish from everyone except us working girls.

I know guys who wear their wives' clothing, and their spouses haven't a clue.

But Greg was different from the rest of them. I wasn't just a hire to him. He repeatedly told me that he was in love with me. He kept telling me he loved me because I helped him come out to himself. He said that he wore my lingerie because he loved me so much. It made him feel close to me.

I knew there was an Oedipal aspect to his feelings. His mother had abandoned him when he was three years old. He knew I was older than he was; I knew he was transferring his love of his mother to me.

A guy who's been hurt by his mother as a child is likely to grow up to be a hater of women. Greg hadn't turned out like that. Instead, he was compensating. By becoming the female he missed, and also by yearning for me, he found a deep satisfaction. His feelings for me never caused problems. He demanded nothing from me. He seemed to be content to adore me from a distance. As long as he could share his secret with me, and don my sexy old stuff, that seemed to be enough for him. He asked for nothing more, and like any other client, he was always happy to pay me.

The turning point came on a terrible night when I was very upset. I was living with a guy who had become routinely abusive. I knew I had to dump him, and that hurt me unbearably. I was driving around sobbing, unbearably angry and sad, and suddenly my pager went off. It was Greg.

He wasn't calling for an appointment. He just wanted to know how I was.

Strange.

As a rule, I don't disclose my problems to clients. That would be a professional breach. I'm their personal service, not the other way around, and any crying on shoulders is supposed to be *theirs* on *mine.* That's what they pay me for. If I were to switch up those roles, the business aspect would blur. It would diminish my professional distance, and possibly give clients the illusion that they're boyfriends, no longer required to *pay.*

But my guard was down when Greg paged me. I was hysterical. And I guess his adoration had gotten to me, and also his incredible timing, because then I did something I never, ever do; I responded to his page in my raw, distraught state, and did absolutely nothing to hide it.

I needed to cry to him, and did.

Greg may be a bisexual cross-dresser, but just the same, he remains very macho. When he's feeling intensely protective, he's just as testosterone-driven as the next young working-class guy. He listened to my pain over the cruelty I'd just been put through, and he imagined an awful scenario even worse than what had occurred. Greg wanted to kick some ass. He wanted to physically hurt this guy who had caused so much hurt for me.

"I'm so in love with you, ****," he said. "You've done so much for me. You mean so much to me. I'll do anything for you. *Anything.*"

"I want you to call me tonight," he continued. "Call me if he does *ANYTHING* more. You'll call me, all right? Tell me you will."

I thanked Greg for his concern, but I knew I wouldn't call him. I couldn't imagine a client crossing over that close to my life. But I was grateful to Greg for listening. I was grateful to him for caring.

He told me a few days later that he had gone to the edge of my town that night—almost an hour from where he lived—and sat the entire night in his truck, waiting for my distress call. He'd been worked up and ready to kill for me.

That's when I made him a friend, not a client. I knew that in Greg, I had found a real treasure. He would defend me to the death if he had to. And he would never demand to get paid for it. Greg would never even demand to get *laid* for it. He would help me out of sheer unconditional love.

After that, he metamorphosized. Greg got into my business. He saw hetero couples and gay and bi men. His "type" was a rare specialty, and he made more per hour than I do. He was called by clients who wanted, for a potpourri of reasons, to get with a well-hung bisexual male. He still drove a tow truck, but he moonlighted in my work, and saved up a ton of money.

After a couple of years, he had enough saved for a sex-change operation. Greg wanted to identify completely as a woman. He found a good doctor for the process, and started the preoperative regimen of female hormone shots.

Well, he's calling me tonight because he's devastated. He's so depressed that he's crying. I've never heard Greg sobbing before. He may be bi, he may want to be a woman, but just the same, he's true to his upbringing. I've only seen him conducting himself in a distinctly masculine way.

Something must be terribly wrong.

"I can't have the operation," he tearfully explains.

"Why not?"

"The hormone shots are fucking me up. My blood pressure's off the charts. The doctor says if I keep up the shots, I'm going to die. He won't give me any more."

I know that Greg must be down beyond words. For some time now, becoming a woman has been his life's major focus. His pain must be equal to that of a woman who wants to become a mother, and has just been told that a pregnancy would kill her.

Dear God. Poor Greg. I comfort him as best as I can. But there really are no words. He's deeply, desperately mourning. He's grieving for a huge part of himself that he thought he could give visceral life to, and now he's found out it can never be born.

After we hang up, I feel a sadness as big as the world. Right now my defenses are down so far that every emotion is jagged, every mental picture is focused. The urge to displace them with a snack, or even a good belly laugh, has no power when my mind rings this clear.

All I can do is feel.

Times like this, I used to remember my mother. I used to remember her mini-strokes, her final-days warnings to her six-year old daughter to "*Move! Look out! I'M FALLING!*" And then she'd crash to the floor.

But these days, I see the towers.

On the evening of September Eleventh, I had a long-standing appointment with, of all people, a firefighter. We decided to keep our appointment. We spent most of it tearfully embracing.

He was deeply upset about his peers in New York. Likewise, I was a mess. I had slumped on my coach the entire day, shaking and broken and riveted. I had desperately needed to shut the scene off, yet I couldn't turn away. Until it was time to see the fireman, I couldn't even get up.

For one full week afterward, I couldn't sleep in my bed. Whenever I was home, I was crumpled on my couch, where I could languish in front of my only TV.

This was my city, my country, my horror. I embraced it maniacally. I was like some grief-crazed mother who gathers up and clutches every piece of her blown-to-bits child.

I was glued to the TV.

I cried with the agonized foreknowledge, days before it was scheduled to arrive, that the cover of the next *New Yorker* magazine would be a stunning rectangle of coal. When my tie to the City finally came in the mail, with its cover the color I had known it would be, I was chilled, after moments of staring at the black, by a ghostly outline of the towers.

Most of the business world had seized up, but I became exhaustively busy. The need for my sexual service—a perpetual need in the best of times—had abruptly intensified. Games were cancelled, vacations were cancelled—what was a guy to do? TV had utterly lost its allure as the means to men's bliss of escape; it was constantly beaming the unspeakable. It was ripping out everyone's heart.

So men called their favorite whores.

When overwhelmed by the shock of death, men often head right for the life-giver, sex. It's common for me to have appointments with men who have just interred a parent, or seen carnage on a highway.

After Nine Eleven, everybody was calling. I should compare notes with flag-makers.

The firefighter was the only client who wept. Other clients I saw were much more conventionally "manly." They were tactile, not weepy, in revealing their distress. So many clients called that I could barely catch my breath; men sought me and pulled me around themselves as though I were a blanket on a fatally frozen night.

Even those regulars who were normally light-hearted seemed to seethe with a newfound intensity. No one was calling me just for fun. There was a deeper need to everyone now, a sad and fierce desperation in their groping.

And I was glad to oblige them. My appointments became my short breaks from the pain.

Several years have passed since those soul-rending weeks. But what's time to a wound that won't heal? Every time I feel any kind of heartbreak, mine or someone like Greg's, I remember the towers falling. I see them dropping out of their place in the sky.

The rhythm thing stirs inside me. *Shhhhhhhhhhhhhhhhhh.*

Mommy. Mommy-Goddess. Please. Take me to sleep now. Please.

I drift off feeling held.

FEAR AND COMPASSION

Maybe we can embrace our whores…take one more giant step in the
development of a humane consciousness.

Go back even further in time. Nine Eleven is two years in the
future.

I'm on my way to a client.

This client has never spoken to me. He has no idea I'm
coming. I'm to be a surprise.

I don't know this guy from a hole in the wall, but I'm feeling
sufficiently secure about him. Even my edgy companion, *Fear*, is
keeping reasonably quiet. She always jumps into the car with me,
and on most trips she constantly pokes me. She nags me to focus
on the stranger I'm going to. She wants to keep me thinking about
how he was on the phone.

On this trip, however, she's not too bad.

This trip will be different because I've never conferred with
the man I'm about to see. Someone else spoke for him—called
me for him—and he called himself his boss.

As I listened for the first time to this "boss" on the phone,
Fear leaped up and screamed.

***"It's a set-up! A police set-up! NO! DON'T GO! DON'T
GO!"***

The one time I'd gotten arrested, the cops who deceived me
were just like this guy. The cop who called me persuaded me to

believe that he was a local businessman who wanted me to entertain his client.

Fear told me not to believe him.

When I asked him whether he was a police officer, he said, "Trust me. Trust me! I'm not a cop."

The novice in me made me stop listening to *Fear*.

"Trust me," the bastard kept saying. "Believe me, I'm no cop."

Over and over he lied.

When I got to the designated hotel, this "businessman" assailed me by a bank of elevators. He wore a strange little smirk. He led me on to an elevator, made the big doors shut tight, got the thing moving upward, and pushed an envelope at me. He said it was my money for a "blowjob" for his client.

I reflexively took the envelope, but right then, I knew this was trouble. New customers *never* talk like that.

The doors opened on a high floor. Suddenly, he reached out and grabbed me. Roughly. I was flung into a maintenance room. I will never forget the violation of that shove.

The "client," the man he wanted me to "blow," was waiting for us in there. He chanted me my rights.

They took me down to the precinct. The liar fingerprinted me, and sat me down and told me that it's wrong to do what I do. He tried—with no success—to get clients' names out of me. He coerced me to sign a "confession." He said I'd be in the news if I didn't.

He could see I was green and scared shitless, so he hadn't bothered to cuff me. But he did make me sit in a jail cell for a while, even though I had money for the little-bitty bail. He wanted me to feel like a criminal.

He sent me home with an "appearance slip" to present with myself at the courthouse.

My sense of being a criminal was new. Before I became an "escort", one time I received a little more public assistance than I should have, even though it wasn't enough for even my family's basic needs. There had also been a few bounced checks, all of them very small, all written at the supermarket, in order to feed my kids. Other than those minor transgressions, this was the first time I'd ever been charged with any kind of real-feeling crime.

So, because of my not-too-bad priors, the judge released me with a measly fine of two hundred-fifty dollars, and an order to get tested for AIDS.

The biggest punishment, to me, I felt, was the horror of my arrest.

So I'm conversing today with this man on the phone, this man who says he wants me to get with his friend. A thousand red flags are unfurling. That's exactly what that fucking cop had said he wanted me for!

I'm making nice, I'm playing him, and I'm assuming until convinced otherwise that he's playing me. I'm thinking he's another cop who's hoping, just like the last one, that I'm stupid. He's hoping I'm going to let him deceive me.

Fear keeps brandishing fiercely, but I don't let the guy see.

Though she's my best and most indispensable friend, no one ever meets *Fear*. I refuse to introduce her, not even as a quiver or an icicle in my voice. To be cool, the queen of cool, is to come across as warm. I act interested, amicably interested, asking this stranger one question after another, drawing him out, getting him to go on and on so I can scrutinize him, size him up, and finally decide about him.

Usually the callers are what they say they are: honest customers. Most of them are harmless, eager to enjoy me, and to sincerely pay me my fee. But all it takes is one slip-up.

Socrates is credited with the genius of evocative questioning. But shouldn't merit go to the wariest of whores?

I've got him going on about the business he's in. I politely elicit the details of his work. It's stuff that could never be recalled by a man who spends his days at a precinct. I have to admit that he's telling me exactly what I need to hear. But *Fear* keeps jabbing me anyway, needling me to make him divulge even more, to paint me a vibrant picture of himself that can only be produced by someone truthful.

This man continues talking with the ease of the perfectly honest. I begin to relax. I begin to think he's okay.

Fear isn't convinced, however. But then, she never is.

Now I focus on the particulars. I'm not going to see this man; I'm going to see his associate. So now I must learn about *him*. I'm told he's a widower.

"About a year ago, he lost his wife in a car accident. He blames himself for her death."

"Oh my God! Why is that?"

"He feels he was so caught up in his work that he wasn't giving her enough attention. Because of that, he thinks she lacked the will to pull through. He feels she died of a broken heart."

Someone is trying to get past *Fear*, attempting to move from my heart to my head. It's my other friend, *Compassion*. This bit of information has compelled her.

At first, *Fear* holds her back. Always *Compassion* must wait, restrained, until *Fear* is finally somewhat assured that it's safe to let her proceed.

Fear is jagged and spiked, a hideously ugly woman. She must almost always be hidden. *Compassion* is sweet and gorgeous. All of my clients can sense her, like gently lapping waves behind an ideally located beach house. The prospective client now under discussion, whose tragedy has been described to me only secondhand, has already won her attention. I can feel her warmth spreading through me.

Now *Fear* slumps down in resignation. She knows that *Compassion* has won. *Fear* knows that at this point, if I heed her at all, it's going to be too late.

"He's one of the nicest guys in the world," the prospect's boss continues. The boss seems pretty nice, himself. I'm certain of that now.

Always, I listen for the predatory stalk. Always, I listen for the sound, or the silence, of undercover lies. I've decided that nobody's lying to me, here. Nobody's hunting me. This guy is just a good person, he's not some cop out to get me. He respects and endorses my purpose. He wants to engage my service for somebody he cares for. He's a perceptive soul, close to the widower, a good judge of his colleague's readiness to finally embrace the option of having a little fun.

I'm told that, since his wife's death, the widower has avoided all women. He subsists in a guilt-ridden shutdown, denying himself all pleasures and burying himself in his work.

But now it's time to release him from pain. He's recently been heard to say that he might take a woman up on it. That got his boss seeking me.

This caller has been sizing me up, too. He wants only the best for his friend. By now I can tell that the man I'm being sent to is no obscure employee. He's someone very special. My truthfulness is as crucial to this caller as his has been to me. I must look as good as I say I do. My photo on the web must really be me. And I must be as nice as I sound.

I'm glad it was I who he contacted. So many women in this business are mercenary liars. So many are indifferent and callous.

I assure him that my looks won't disappoint, and that I'll make his friend as happy as I can. But privately, I'm worried. I'm pretty but hardly perfect, and in the course of this conversation I've learned that the man I'm about to encounter is a fashion photographer.

Jeez! So he's used to impeccable bodies!

The worst thing of all is that his deceased wife was a **Victoria's Secret** model.

Oh, boy. Will I measure up? Parts of me will. Other parts won't.

We finish up our talk with location, time, and where I'll find the money. There are mutual reassurances, and the deal is verbally sealed.

After I hang up, *Fear* is just a faint buzzing, way back in my head.

I'm all anxious preparation. And I'm feeling some misgivings.

What if this guy has been misjudged by his procurer, and I'm not a welcome surprise? If that's true, he'll turn me away. I'll have driven an hour, round trip, for nothing.

On an everyday, routine basis, he gazes upon the flawless planes of the bodies of young models. What if he finds my extra eight pounds repulsive? And that mess below my navel...! God.

And what about my age? I'm older than most models. I've been told he's forty, and that's good. It means he's no cocky youngster. But what if he dreams of the young and the perfect, and will part with grief only for a treat just like that? If he feels that way, he'll reject me, and that won't make my day.

With regard to my looks, my self-image is fragile. One disparaging glance can affect it. I think a lot of women are like that, but, given how I make my living, it's especially destructive for me.

Just the same, I remind myself, I've got my trusty all *Compassion.* Her beauty is exquisite and flawless. Men al' gravitate to her. She's the one thing that never fails me. Sl much a part of this mission already. I know from experi' the moment we arrive, she'll start performing her magi<'

She'll look into this client, and she'll loosen his soul. She'll bring it over to me. She'll tenderly bare it to me. She'll show me what to do.

She's the strength of good friends, good caretakers, good counselors and good whores.

I pull up at the place he's supposed to be. My heart pounds like it always does when I'm dealing with the unknown. But this is different. This time, it's not the thought of cops or creeps that has *Fear* heating up my blood. It's not her hard adrenal grip. It's more like the blind date jitters.

I'm at a pretty Victorian cottage that's used as a setting for country-style shoots. My client's been lovingly tricked; he's been told to come here for an assignment. He awaits the busy convergence of models, equipment, and crew.

I'm all that's shown up today.

I turn off the ignition. I ease out of my car. As always, I can sense the furtive appraisal of eyes from inside the house. It's afternoon. I'm aware of the sun on the lines on my face. Self-consciousness makes me feel flustered and harried, but I deliberately slow myself and stroll to the driveway-side door.

I don't have to knock; he's already there.

He's clearly confused.

"Where is everyone?" he asks me.

Hey! This is good! He thinks I'm a model!

As I step over the threshold, I make myself broadly grin. "Well..." I respond, "I'm all there is. I'm the only person who's going to be here." My huge smile remains, and I'm hoping he sees the conspiratorial glint. I'm hoping he'll catch on quickly.

He doesn't. He's completely bewildered.

He's a lovely looking man. His boss had said as much. He's English; he sounds it and looks it. His face is both patrician and boyish, an irony that appeals. His hair is pure silver, but that's all that age took. He's impressively tall, but he has a certain presence, something height only accentuates. Shortness would not have diminished him.

He's only spoken once, it was just a simple question, but already I'm sensing the thinker, and the pain.

I'm heavily counting on my great big smile. It's not a fake le—I don't fake. What I seem to do well is turn anxiety into ives, like the palpable flush on my face right now. It could be -hither glow.

I have to tell him why I'm here. Will he be receptive, or will he be put off? Smiles almost never put off.

But I'm here because someone else sent me. I'm supposed to be a pleasant surprise for a man very steeped in grief. Timing is everything, I've always been told. Is this the right time for this man to enjoy me? Is he ready to lose himself in arms not his wife's? If the timing here is wrong, then all of this is futile. When he figures out what I'm doing here, he'll see my smile as an insult, my proffering as an offense.

I repeat: "There's no one else coming." I want him to get the gist of that; we are, and we will be, alone here.

Since I entered the house, we've been keeping the distance of the just-met. We're not quite standing still. We're shifting our weight from one foot to the other, releasing our tension through our soles. This nervous little dance is familiar to me. It always occurs when I meet someone for the first time. I'm afraid he's a cop; he's afraid I am. We circle each other a tad, like bold but frightened cats. He's afraid of getting arrested, and he's also caught up in the terrified excitement of calling upon the Goddess. Her emissary has arrived, and he's freaked.

But for this man, none of that's true. This man believes I'm merely a model who's here for a routine shoot. So he's not afraid, he's just agitated. He's wondering why there's no crew. He's here in his element, eager to go at his craft, and that, I now see, is my challenge. That may be hard to break through.

He's a wounded man. He shields himself with his work.

To disarm him, then, will be *my* work.

I make myself utterly motionless now. I ground myself in this unknown place, deliberately quashing my unease. My glow is even stronger now, filling the space between us with a concentrated warmth.

I was born with bedroom eyes, and I fix them on him now. I pull on him with them. He can't look away from me; he forgets that he should.

I watch him begin to understand.

"Oh! Well!" he flushes, and there's a little smile.

"Your boss said to tell you that he and the folks at the office sent me."

His smile gets wider now.

Ah! Good! He likes what I'm telling him! Relief spread through me like whiskey.

We're still about two feet apart. His face has turned pink and his eyes now have fire, but suddenly he's all graciousness and British decorum, he's offering me a tour of the place. I'm happy to oblige him.

The cottage is meticulously true to its style, adorably appointed and much to my taste. I relax in his need to help me see where I am.

As we retire deeper into the house, and he shows me the sitting room, I discreetly search out what's important. The money? There it is, in an envelope that has "Crew" written on it, just as I was told it would, right where I was told I'd find it. And where shall I encourage this man to sit down? Or lie down? Here's a good place to begin, here where the light is sunless, on this large, soft, comfy-looking chair.

Here, I decide, is where I'll first touch him.

I don't instruct him to go to the chair. I allow him to gravitate there on his own. He's worked in this house before, so it's his familiar ground, so for now I'll follow his lead. But soon this place will be mine to maneuver. He'll want me to take over, as most of them always do.

I wait for the perfect moment for our roles to inevitably switch. When the moment comes, I, the visitor, invite him to sit.

He lets himself into the chair, and I arrange myself in front of him, facing him, on an opportune ottoman. That way we're pretty much eye to eye, and our faces are inches apart. My knees are sandwiched in his.

As the instruments of transition, my hands reach out to him. I place them on his shoulders, and then I begin to knead.

I'm enjoying the feel of his luminescent shirt. It doesn't seem to me that very many men ever wear shirts this lovely. But maybe they do, and I just haven't noticed. Maybe I see the beauty of this man's shirt only because he himself is so beautiful.

"Have you ever modeled?" he asks me. His look says he thinks that I should have.

My confidence now takes wing!

I explain that I considered it when I was younger, when models were all sticks, and that the modeling agencies all told me I'd have to lose some weight. I didn't want to. I was at my best weight already. If I lost any more, I knew that my body would ⸱come like a boy's. So I ditched all thoughts of modeling.

He's loving the shoulder massage. My hands work toward his neck, and he sighs. "It's been so long since anyone's done this. To feel someone's touch...."

Then he speaks of the loss of his wife. True to the codes of his gender, he tries to show little of his pain. But his pauses are bottomless canyons.

My fingers are squeezing muscles from his neck to his chest. To reach around to his back, I lean closer.

"You're beautiful," he says.

My face grows hot and my stomach tightens. A blushing little smile is my thank-you. I'm often told this, but each time I hear it, I love it. Every time I hear it, it's a new affirmation. It's especially good coming from this one, this professional imager of female perfection. I'm afraid he'll change his mind when he sees me with my clothes off.

"I'm not as slim as a model," I tell him. It's a warning.

"That's not important!" he suddenly blusters. "It's the inner person that counts."

He laments, for a couple of moments, about fake breasts and swollen heads. His tone is very disdainful.

But I'm glad for his little outburst. Now I don't have to worry about not looking perfect. He relaxes again, under my hands, and I relax, too, from his words.

I say: "Let's get you somewhere where I can make you feel even better."

Soon we're in a bedroom, by authentic antique iron bedposts. I'm down to my baby-doll underthings, and once again, he's making me feel good. He's complimenting my breasts.

Back when I first discussed this encounter, listening to this man's boss, I knew that I was being considered for a mission of delicacy. I knew that if I landed in the presence of this man, and succeeded in making him happy, a deep sense of job satisfaction would follow.

Yes! To make a lost man feel alive once again, after death's incarceration of his soul! To open his inner jail cell, and witness his first bold steps to freedom! To watch him begin to love himself again, reaffirming his worth to woman!

To be his first big breath of fresh air!

Few things in this life are sweeter. That's the reason I take such risks.

After that introductory tryst, that client and I became very close friends. His name is David. Our relationship is platonic. David didn't want to pay for his sex, and I never made him my boyfriend. I loved him, but I wasn't "in love," so I wouldn't do him for free.

I either do it for money or I do it for love, and there's no sex at all in between. I don't have casual sex with friends—that is, not for free.

David concluded that that's okay. "To be friends with you, sex or no sex, is all that matters to me."

Whenever he describes what I've done for him, David sounds a lot like Greg. He tells me I set him free. He appreciates me for it, and has sworn his friendship to me.

I feel honored.

And David has confided something earth shattering to me. His work as a fashion photographer is only a sideline. It's actually just a front. His real profession is soldiering for the British military. He's a Special Forces Anti-terrorism Specialist.

When we met in the late nineteen-nineties, he was working in the States as an undercover agent, watching the movements of the States-based cells of the Irish Republican Army. That's what he did when he wasn't behind a camera, shooting away at models, letting the world think that's his real job.

David was hiding out here. As a participant in a mediation effort between the Irish and British extremists, he was at risk of being murdered in England by proponents from either side. Attempts on his life had been made several times.

His wife had been a tragic victim of his work. That was no car crash that killed her. She was blown up by a car bomb meant for David.

The man who brought us together, his "boss," is David's American military liaison.

Immediately following September Eleventh, David got reassigned. He got pulled from the IRA maelstrom and sent to the Middle East. He's been based there ever since, on anti-terrorism missions he can't discuss, in countries he can't disclose.

We stay in touch by email.

He's told me that stopping the mass slaughter of innocents is all that he lives to do. It consumes him. It always has.

Now *Fear* forgets her own mission sometimes, and collapses into a trembling heap, thinking about our friend David. She gratefully weeps for her hero in the war zone.

She knows she's met her better.

Compassion emails with David, and endlessly takes notes.

PEE DRINKER, TOILET SLAVE, CHICKEN ARMS, AND LILY PAD MAN

What I liked was getting this insider's view, this secret story to tell.

"Would you pee in this cup so I can drink it?" he says.

Oh boy, I think. What a surprise. Even for an old hand like me. When he told me he wanted to "taste my essence," I thought he just wanted to lick me.

Wrong.

"No, I can't do that," I'm quick to respond. Yet my tone is resiliently friendly. I'm alarmed by this news, his need to drink "gold," but I know he's a very sweet guy. I'm shocked, but I'm not feeling hateful.

He's a longhaired old hippy, he's fiftyish, but he looks only thirty-five. He smokes dope. He seems to be someone who got left far behind, to quietly mellow and molder. He's never been married, never had kids, never had to join the Establishment. I guess that's why he looks young.

His gentle face and Jesus hair make him look a little bit mystical. He lives by himself in an authentic log cabin, heated by fire and built in 1860, with innumerable cats and one dog.

I've been here before, and I like him. He's my kinda people, a caring sort, back-to-the-earth. He loves animals.

But now he wants to drink my pee.

Later on I'll realize I should have seen this coming. He surrounds himself with too many beasts, the kinds that mark territory. His sweetness is almost self-effacing, like an extremely groveling dog. For a moment I wonder, is he going to ask me to dominate him, too?

But no, he's not showing any signs like that. I don't think he's masochistic. He's simply what he's been telling me: he's enamored of my *essence*.

For most men, female essence is vaginal. Well, this one wants something more than that. He wants something much more *inside*.

"There's nothing more beautiful than a beautiful woman's essence," he joyfully continues. "It's the biggest compliment I could ever, ever give you. Please let me give it to you. Please let me drink your essence."

There's something not quite horrible about this. There's a certain visceral worship. I guess I should feel kind of flattered.

Or maybe I'm being way too understanding.

"I really don't think I can do that," I tell him. "I'm sorry.... it's just too weird."

"Um...." he responds, while he's clutching the cup, with a pleading, puppy-dog look. "Well...would you let me watch you pee in the toilet?"

"Well..." I consider. "Well, all right," I decide. "I guess that would be okay."

And then I realize the light beer he gave me was more than a friendly gesture.

"Remind me, where's the bathroom?" I ask him.

He leads me there right away.

I sit down on the toilet. Cats are rubbing my shins.

"Could you spread your legs more, so I can really, really see?" The puppy is begging me.

"Okay." And I'm thinking, *He's just gonna look.*

I spread. He kneels. My beer pee splashes down. Suddenly the cup is beneath it. He quickly retracts his prize. I violently snap shut my legs.

The cats scatter.

The opaque plastic cup has an inch or so of yellow. He lifts it to his mouth, and he tips it. He empties it in an instant.

"Ahhh, that was delicious!"

His smile is pure lunacy.

"I can't believe you did that!"

"Can I have some more?"

"No!"

"Please don't be angry with me," he implores me. "I just wanted to taste your essence." He's standing up now, but his head's bent. He's regretting that he's upset me.

"It's okay. I'm not mad."

And I'm not. Freaked out to the max, certainly. But there's no staying mad at someone who thinks I'm so great that he wants to imbibe my pee.

I guess there's such a thing as innocuous crazy.

****

Only one guy with a "golden shower" fetish has ever got me to pee on him. At least a dozen clients have asked me to do that, and my answer has always been no. Except for this one guy. He managed to talk me into it.

He had that pleading-puppy appeal, just like the one who snuck a drink. And he wouldn't stop begging me. I saw this guy often, because he lived close, and he just kept wearing me down.

Well, in the end he thought of a plan that I figured I could live with.

He rented an adult potty chair. He removed the pail underneath it. He placed it on top of a bunch of garbage bags, so my pee wouldn't permeate his floor.

I figured I could stand to pee on him that way, because I wouldn't *see*. His face would be under the chair.

He gave me two strong diuretics: a beer and a diet coke. Then he massaged and kissed my feet, relaxing me as I drank it. We were taking our time, so I'd drink it all down, and my bladder began to fill up. I knew that my need would get urgent. With that magnitude of an urge to go, there was no way I would seize up, once I sat down on that throne.

I got both cans pretty empty. He rose, and went to the chair, and laid himself down on the floor, and arranged his face under the hole. I was right behind him. The reason had nothing to do with his fetish; I had to relieve myself, *now*.

In less than a second, I was making his day.

I don't know whether he drank it. As I've said, I couldn't see. Thank God.

But it wasn't the golden shower that made this guy memorable. It was something a thousand times worse, something that made me stop seeing him.

I knew by the end of our first appointment that this guy was masochistic. He was single, late thirties, a commercial fisherman, and masculine and cute. He was the kind of guy who might easily get women to talk to him in a bar. But something about him was a little bit, well, *soft*.

I'd been around enough as a sex worker to quickly pick up on that vibe. I knew that this guy wanted torture. He was looking for a very cruel mistress. I knew it even better than he did. I could see it was the underlying reason for his call.

He couldn't explore this with the girls in the barrooms. He couldn't have them whip him, viciously pinch his nipples, and encore by peeing all over him. What would his fishing buddies say?

They'd probably drown him at sea.

So of course, that's why he called me.

I don't have a problem with mild domination. Role-playing comes easy to me. I'm a little bit submissive, myself—that is, when I'm with my lover. So in clients, I can relate to the need. I can give them the bossiness they're craving. But when their requests get extreme and disgusting, then you can count me out.

Each time I went to see that guy, what he wanted got more self-demeaning. He wanted humiliation. He wanted to be treated like dirt. For his orgasm he'd always jerk himself, but he couldn't get off unless I'd gotten much meaner than any of the times before.

On the appointment before the appointment when I peed on him, he came when he got me to talk about doing it.

And the next time, we progressed to the real thing, the potty.

How much worse would he get? I should have been asking myself that.

And here we were, again.

"I want to be your toilet slave," he was telling me over and over. He murmured this while he adored me with hands that were good at massage. I had demanded the rubdown.

"Please, please, Mistress, let me be your toilet slave," he repeatedly, pathetically begged me.

"Yes, you're my toilet slave," I hissed.

"Please, please, Mistress, tell me I'm your toilet."

"You're my toilet, you nasty little slave." I listened to myself, and a little red flag unraveled. The massage felt wonderful, enough to daze me out, but where was this verbiage going?

Wake up, foolish. Forget the joy in your muscles. Something not good is developing.

I decided not to say "toilet" again. I ordered him to massage my legs, and then my butt cheeks, like always. Then I tortured his nipples for a while. Those were things we did every time.

But when it was time for him to get himself off, he brought it all up again. He kept telling me, over and over, that he wanted to be my toilet.

He was taking too long to come.

"Tell me Mistress, *please*, that I'm your toilet. Tell me you'll shit on my face."

There it was. It was out. *Fuck!*

He was jerking himself like crazy, but he wasn't ready to come.

I couldn't say I'd shit on his face. My stomach was starting to turn. But he begged me and begged me to say it, and finally, I had to face it. His cock wouldn't spew until I told him the horror he wanted to hear.

"Please, Mistress! PLEASE! Tell me you'll shit on my face!"

"I'm shitting all over your face, slave."

He exploded all over his bed.

I was all done with Toilet Slave.

****

There's a nice little guy in Rhode Island—he lives either just inside or just outside the city limits of Providence, I can't remember which—and if he happens to read this, and he recognizes himself, I hope he won't be offended that I've placed him in a chapter with a toilet slave. I've thrown him in with such characters only because this chapter addresses a question that's put to me often: *What's the most unusual experience you've had as a prostitute?*

In a sexy-sweet and heartbreaking way, this guy qualifies as one of my answers.

Back when I knew him—I won't travel that far now—he was twenty-six years old. When we spoke on the phone for the first time, and I decided to see him, he told me his door would be unlocked.

"Don't knock, just come in," he instructed.

That was the only way he prepared me for his shoulderless torso and tiny, bent-up, useless arms that looked just like chicken wings. He couldn't open a door.

That was the only way he prepared me for his one-and-a-half leg status. He'd also been born with one of his legs terminated at the knee.

Whenever I put his prosthesis on him, and he was able to stand, I could see he was undersized. He stood only five feet tall. But just the same, in spite of everything, he was a very handsome guy. He was Italian-American, with a face like a Roman god. And his cock was normal-sized. And always very hard.

Just like any other young stallion.

Having sex with him never repulsed me. Quite the opposite, actually. He knew a position that works for someone who doesn't have much for arms. We'd both be on our backs, a straight line of flesh with a head at each end, with our genitals connected. Or I'd get on top, and lean close enough for his locked-up hands to touch me.

If you get **HBO**, have you ever watched the drama series, **Carnivale**? Think of Samson, the midget boss. He's a charismatic little bugger, isn't he? I remember an episode where Samson's ex-wife, a stunningly sexy and normal-sized woman, is confiding to a friend that she misses him in bed.

Well, I don't miss my deformed little client, because I never miss any clients. But just the same, I know what she meant.

"Please lock the door on your way out," he'd tell me.

Next morning, a caretaker would unlock it, coming in.

****

At about the same time, I saw another guy with unusual physical traits. He hadn't been born deformed, and he wasn't disabled, but he'd done something terribly outrageous to himself, something that drastically altered his skin.

He had gained, and then lost, over four hundred pounds. He hadn't had the skin-clipping surgery yet.

The skin on his middle hung down past his knees.

72

He was thirty-two years old, and personable. He was very emotionally honest. He was good at communication. We spoke on the phone for over an hour before I went to see him. I liked him as a person long before we hung up.

He confided the traumatic emotional reasons for his over-eating insanity. But now he had conquered his grief and his demons, and for a while now, his diet had been healthy. He had taken off the mountain of weight, and he felt like a brand-new person.

He wanted to celebrate that. He wanted to celebrate that with a woman. But he wasn't presentable, yet. He'd been ordered to lose just a few more pounds before any surgeons would slice off the skin flaps. And then he'd have to spend more time alone, healing up from that.

Well, he wanted to celebrate *now*. He didn't want to wait any longer.

He'd never before called a prostitute. He'd done it now, because he figured this: a prostitute wouldn't judge him. She wouldn't care what he looked like.

He was absolutely right.

He had called several numbers before he called mine. He hadn't liked the way he was treated. He refused to have someone come over, and see him in this strange state, unless he could establish a great rapport first, in a long conversation on the phone. No one he'd contacted had been willing to talk much.

Until he contacted me.

When I got to his house, it was nighttime. He was hidden beneath a long robe. He took me around to the back, out to his cedar deck. It was chilly, but he obviously wanted us to spend the appointment outside. He had candles lit, and wine, and even a little food, all graciously spread on the patio table.

He sat me down and gave me a blanket. Then we drank and talked for a long time, just like on the phone.

He had a pleasant, intelligent face. It hadn't been affected by the downward pull of fat. There were no sags there from the meltdown. You could look at his face and not be aware that here was a person whose skin down below had been stretched to the point of deformity.

The robe he was wearing prevented me from seeing the huge loops of loose skin that started below his chest.

Soon it was clear why he wanted us outside. He gestured toward his hot tub. That's where he planned to finish our tryst.

I don't recall taking my clothes off for the water. I must have felt comfortable in front of him naked, with my saggy gut skin in view. By comparison, it was nothing.

What I do remember, what I'll never forget in a million years, is this: when he got into that tub, and sank down inside it, his skin floated up all around him. He looked exactly like a man on a lily pad.

I stepped in to join him, and I wasn't repulsed. He'd done such a good job of preparing me...now it was obvious, why. And there was actually something rather nice about this. Maybe I'm just adaptable to the point of being surreal. But the darkness, the candles, the wine, and this smiling dude literally floating in his skin, were somehow exquisitely peaceful. The gently undulating petals of dermis were not something disgusting. They were part of his metamorphosis. I was witnessing the flutter, the physical unfolding, of someone's profound self-renewal.

I felt rather honored to be there.

TRADING

A lot of women trade sex for some advantage…I have a right to look
square into it.

All types of men call prostitutes. The business is an absolute
leveler, a truer democracy. A working girl sees clients in just
about every profession.

And sooner or later, she and a few of them are going to barter.
They're going to trade off their services, whichever of them she
needs.

The word "barter" might sound kind of negative to some. It
might conjure wretched images of female desperation. A sexually
bartering woman could be one who's miserably married. Or she
could be a single woman, intolerably poor, who's bedding a man
she doesn't love in order to get his help. Or she could be coerced
into whoring. Whatever her bad situation, she's fallen into pure
desolation, maybe in a scene of outrageous exploitation, with that
wrecking ball of the soul slamming at her, that thing called
"survival sex."

But the feeling is radically different for the independent
"escort". To barter, for her, is simply a choice, and never the result
of despair or coercion. It's just another good option. "Trading" is
just an additional way she can get her life nicely wrapped up.

The first guy I did a trade with was a CPA. I badly needed his
know-how—I didn't want to shirk Uncle Sam. But at the same

time, I didn't want to reveal to the Uncle the truth about what I do. Its prohibition might cause me some problems! So I sought out the help of an expert—one aware of my true occupation.

That would be a client, of course.

Sam is one of the sweetest guys I've ever met in my life. Divorced, in his fifties, gently handsome and successful, he could be narcissistic, but he comes across as caring. He's one of those guys who I feel would give the shirt off his back in a heartbeat. He's probably very well off—I'm sure he has wealthy clients—but his manner makes me think of someone non-materialistic.

Depending on the time of day, he either has me go to his house, or to a decent motel near his office. Fellatio is Sam's only preference. That's after I fulfill his first request, which is a sexy caress of his body with my breasts. The whole thing is over in minutes.

But prior to that, he sets up a prelude, and that goes on for a while.

Wherever we meet, he always brings fresh strawberries and topping for their dipping, or some really good cheeses to sample. He always has a bottle of wine. A couple of times, he's taken me to lunch. Sam is a person who understands that the lead-up to any good erotic encounter is just as important as the act itself, and deserving of time and care.

And when we finally get down to it—wow! He's always overwhelmed and ecstatic. He always makes me feel like an angel, lit down from the heavens just to thrill him.

Most clients respond on a level like that, but Sam seems even more pleasured. He's loving and joyful and grateful by nature, and that gives him deeper sensations.

So after I got to know Sam, I felt it would be easy to turn to him about taxes. In the end, Sam himself brought it up. He asked me adroit, concerned questions about how I was handling things.

Before I became a sex worker, I worked as a personal trainer. So as an "escort" I'd invented a "cover" profession: fitness seminars and consulting. I kept careful records to back that all up, and I acquired a bunch of deductions. I used my mileage as a write-off—there were so many drives to those "consults"! I also had some motel receipts. Sometimes clients had me reserve motel rooms in my name. Those rooms were a perfect deduction, because "fitness seminars" have to *be* somewhere. I also subtracted all my meals on the road—a traveling "consultant" has to eat.

I wrote off part of my cell phone bill. I did the same with my computer. I maintained a deductible website on fitness.

On a very different website, in a huge chunk of cyberspace about bodies, but not fitness, I advertised my *true* consultations. I did so under an alias, of course. I also advertised incognito in a paper, and let me tell you, did that ever cost me, up to ten thousand dollars a year.

But Uncle Sam would never be told about *those* ads. The only thing deducted would be the measly cost of my fitness site.

I fabricated all the receipts for the "fitness services" rendered. I'd bought a receipt book just for that purpose.

And I've done so every year since. I know I should get some small-business software, but I'm pokey about those things.

The most critical thing, every tax year, the thing that matters the most, is that the amounts I write on all the receipts are the same as the deposits I make at my bank.

And Sam always does it up right for me, with the formulaic expertise the IRS requires. A couple of times, his bill has come to more than a session with me, but he says one tryst is enough.

That's quintessentially Sam.

Now I'd like to share some information that really blew me away. In the government-issue handbook of tax laws, there's a section on illegal professions. It lists all the things an illicit taxpayer is expected to report, and what he or she can deduct. It's exactly the same as for people with legal jobs. The message is very clear: the IRS could care less about what you do for work—you could be a hit man or a crack dealer, for all they care—as long as you pay taxes. You're expected to pay taxes on that hit fee, and you can deduct the cost of the bullets. You can deduct the meals, the car rental and mileage, and the lodgings you put yourself up in while you murderously stalked your mark!

Well, that's all very fascinating, but I'd never put "sex worker" on the line by "occupation." That could most certainly backfire somewhere, even if the IRS doesn't care.

Someday in the future, a long time after I'm gone, when the feminists have stopped being stupid and have decided to fight for our rights, an "escort" might dare to write "sex worker" on that line! And feel free to deduct her *real* advertising costs!

But I'm in the here and now, where an "escort" has to hide what she is, and Sam helps me out with that. I currently owe him a meeting. He knows he can trust me to show up and "pay," whenever it's convenient for me.

Besides Sam, another of my favorite trade-off guys is a local nurseryman. For several straight springs in a row, he's provided me with zillions of flowers. He's enabled me to have gardens for free, everywhere I've lived.

One of those years I got married, and he was my free wedding florist!

All I have to do for this guy is join him for a few minutes, off to the side of his acreage, in a comfy little room that he uses for his breaks.

This guy was in his late thirties when I met him. Every spring, it's been the same. I drive to his nursery and park my car discreetly, way out there by the break shack, where huge greenhouses surround me, and seasonal Mexican workers. The place is a gardener's paradise. I see thousands and thousands of six-packs of ready-to-plant baby flowers, and hundreds of baskets of gushing mature ones, every variety and hybrid of annuals, acres of them hanging and tabled all around me. It's a sweeping panorama of the proof of spring's power, it's the glorious cornucopia of the birthing of summer, it's an enormous concentration of blooming and promise, and I get a little bit giddy.

This is stuff you pay a fortune for retail, and I can grab all that I want of it, for free.

He lets me take all I can fit in my car—front seat, back seat, floors and trunk, and dangling from hooks by the ceiling. This is the one time I wish I owned a pickup. What I do get in there is amazing—enough to make a beautiful season, enough to make my gardener's soul surge high with fulfillment and joy.

In dollars and cents, market value, what he gives me has got to be at least five hundred dollars, every single May. Sometimes I go back a second time, and visit his shack again, and load up my car again, for a son or a friend with a yard that needs a facelift.

And all I have to do is spend twenty minutes or so, back there with him in that shack. That's less time than choosing my flowers.

He's married. He likes to point out that every single night, he goes straight home to his wife. He talks about his friends with their disastrous affairs and divorces.

"Why don't they just do this?" he laments. His eyes get puppy-dog sad when he says that. I'm touched by his regret for his peers and their families.

I'm the way he gets just a tad of forbidden fruit, without the catastrophe.

We merge our own particular strains of spring fever. We exchange some delightful fruits of nature. Flowers and sex: they're not very different. Ask any botanist.

Ask any poet.

Ask any feminist *herstorian.*

"We're helping each other out," he says, with his warm and simple smile. I can tell that's his regular attitude, his everyday philosophy of familial give-and-take.

How I envy his wife.

Well, I don't have a good husband like that one, but I sure have a wonderful garden every year. I leave his place so damn happy. Oh, if you could only see me with my carloads of beautiful flowers! I vacuum out scads of petals! Oh, if you could only witness all my gorgeous summer marvels! They grow and spread all around me, they trumpet their rainbow colors, they inspire my gardener's passionate care, and obtaining them all cost me nothing!

Talk about awesome job perks.

Once I traded with a mental health counselor. He was also an MSW—someone who's earned a master's degree in social work expertise. I was hard at work on a project at the time, a how-to for whoring professionalism. I asked him for a copy of the *Code of Ethics* that social workers must follow. I wanted to fashion something similar for "escorts".

This guy always seemed strapped for money, so I offered him a deal. If he ran off a copy of the *Ethics* for me, I'd shave twenty bucks off our next meeting.

He was happy to oblige.

So the next time I went to see him—in his airy, comfy, plant-filled office with a couch for his clients to emote from—the coffee table in front of our tryst held a folder with the stuff I'd requested. It was next to the box of Kleenex.

It all ended up on the floor, because we ended up on the coffee table. But that's another story.

Another guy I traded with was an electrical apprentice. I had just bought a house. A new barn graced my property. Its builders had put in some lights, but no heat. I wanted some heat installed in the loft—electrical would be fine—because visiting sons and friends liked to stay there. I'd hung some insulation.

I knew just the client to call.

He not only put in the heat for me, earning himself two trysts—he also showed up as a witness for me at my extremely infuriating divorce trial. The guy I was divorcing was hoping to win half the equity of my property. He deserved absolutely nothing. He hadn't contributed a dime to its purchase, he'd only lived there for two months, and he'd mostly just gotten high there. My client agreed to testify that the ex had messed up the lighting in the barn when he attempted, stoned and stupid, to change it.

In exchange for his testimony, of course, my client would get a third tryst.

Well, the judge never called him to the stand. There wasn't any need to. I had done a good job, pro se, of demolishing my ex and his lawyer on my own. Long before the trial, I'd been well aware that could happen. So I "paid" the electrician upfront. I knew he'd be stuck in the courthouse all day, missing a day of work, whether the judge wanted to hear him, or not. Therefore I owed him, regardless, and I "paid" him two years in advance.

Soon after I bought that property, several different clients were in and out of there, working on it for me. A professional sheet-rocker did a room for me there. A landscaper came over and raked and edged and shaped. One guy dropped by with some furniture for me. Two talented handymen did all sorts of things.

What I owed them, however, was never done there. I always left home to "pay" them, always at our usual spots.

Only my lover gets to bed me where I live.

One day, the electrician and one of the handymen were both working there at the same time. Each one guessed, correctly, that the other one was a client. It was a little bit awkward, but funny. Everyone got a chuckle.

Before I let any of them come over, I would carefully consider how safe each one seemed, in terms of revealing my address. That's a risky situation.

Some girls are idiotic enough to work right out of their homes. You'll never find me among them. Almost none of my clients know where I live. Even when they want to know, I keep that to myself.

But when I was an unattached woman all alone in her new house, with a barn that needed work and land that was almost an acre, I had a million "honey do" projects! My sons weren't around very often to help. All of them had grown up, and lived out of state, so they were only there for long visits, if that. So I decided to trust a few clients to help me. I engaged them in some trades.

I never regretted that decision.

None of them ever showed up uninvited. None of them ever stalked me. None of them extorted me. None of them ever got mad at me and fingered me to the police. Those are some of the risks you're taking when you let clients know where you live.

Well, these guys, just as I'd figured, were fine. They never caused me a problem.

I got by with a little help from my friends.

Sometimes, however, some clients have to be set straight about just what constitutes "trading."

For instance, once I had a client who wanted to see me often, but he didn't have enough income. At the end of one appointment, after he coughed up the cash, he asked me to stay for a minute. Then he manically brainstormed for future ways to "pay" that wouldn't require money. He went over to his closet and pulled out a bunch of backpacks. He wanted to "pay" with them next time. They were nice backpacks, they were rather well made, but I didn't need any, so I gently declined. Then he went somewhere else in his house, and came back with some pots and pans. They were a fairly good brand, and had never been used, but they were no competition for cold hard cash, especially since I didn't need any cookware. Again, I told him no.

This guy wouldn't give up. By the time I was itching to walk out his door, he'd assembled a huge pile of offerings. I didn't want any of it. He was disabled, unemployed, and desperate for my future company, and I felt really bad for him. But…we're talking about my *living*. We're talking about my time, which is *money*.

All right, I confess. I did let him talk me into seeing him, once, for two backpacks, the pots and pans, and some other things I could care less about, but no money, not one dime. He did throw in a used tire, which was something I really did need.

And that was the last time I responded to his calls.

Too much compassion, all expended on one client, will break me at the bank in no time!

Sometimes, some clients will ask me out to dinner, hoping that's a trade, just the dinner. They're hoping I'll have sex with them in exchange for a lovely meal. Well, that's not a trade, that's a date, and we're not dating. Clients all owe me my fee or the equivalent, and dining out doesn't qualify, not even if it's first-class.

Is dinner going to pay my bills? Or improve my home? Or help me in court? Or right me with Uncle Sam?

Nah, it'll just make me fat.

If, and only if, I have the time to be wined and dined, and I've decided I could use a little pampering, then I might say: "Sure, I'd love to have dinner, if afterwards, we have *dessert*." They know that what I'm proposing is their commitment to a transaction. They know no dinner will happen without their agreement to "dessert." And "dessert" will cost them the usual.

After they hear that, they all get the picture: to never confuse me with dating. Even if I do look like the proverbial girl next door. Even if they feel I'm the sweetest, kindest woman they know. No matter how wholesome and nurturing I am, no matter how sexually giving, what I'm doing for these men is *paid service*. I can't let them forget that.

One thing I've learned is that with men, almost *anything* is negotiable. And they tend to respect a woman who knows how to lay down the rules. And usually, they're happy to follow the rules. And maybe they're more than just happy; maybe they're even *relieved.*

Men like things definite, cut and dried, a deal.

That's why men like callgirls.

The only trades I've attempted that haven't turned out right have been with massage therapists. A few of them have responded to my ad with the offer of a rubdown for sex.

My first response was joyful, because I love a massage. Actually, I *need* my massages. I crave them from head to toe.

But whenever I've gotten with those guys, the massage has been kind of ruined by my mental number-crunching. I've kept thinking, we're both body workers. We both get paid by the hour. But I get paid a lot more. I've ended up lying there under the guy's hands, uneasy over what's fair. He's working so hard on my muscles, and soon I'd be hard at work on his cock. But it would be *only* his cock, so wouldn't that be ripping him off? But then again, what he did was legal, not something terribly fraught through and through with stigma and fear of STD's. So how much time should I get? How much time should he get? Round and round those thoughts have whirled, the concerns of a worker for herself and her kind-of peer, in a place where instead, I ought to have been relaxing, and feeling my brain melt to bliss.

Another problem with trading with masseurs was that I've felt a loss of control. In a trade the masseur sees my naked body, with all of its imperfections. He arranges my body before him, in just the way he wants it, in order to properly rub me. I haven't been able to pose this way or that, I haven't been able to make the most of my assets, or divert his attention from my flaws.

That's bugged me.

So I'd rather just pay for a massage. It's better to see a practitioner who knows nothing about my profession. Then I daze out, and enjoy.

I did get into a good rub-for-sex with a client who's not a masseur. He's a neuropsychology Ph.D., profoundly aware of the benefits of massage. His hands are almost as good as someone licensed. After I get him off, he spends a half hour on my muscles. For this we've agreed that he'll pay half my regular fee. With him I feel okay about things. I don't lie there mulling over the terms. And I arrange my body any way I want.

And if he takes more time for his pleasure, I remind him that if he does that, then he owes me the full price. I strictly perceive him as a client, not a fellow body worker, so I always feel free to chide him, and to be the one in charge.

Prostitution is comforting and sexually satisfying, a nurturing feminine role. But it's nevertheless a business. What an "escort" does is a service, and it always comes with a bill. It's a service for a fee, or a service for a service, and that's that, there are no exceptions.

That is, unless I start dating a client. Then I'm in serious trouble.

Like anyone else in love.

But I'll save those tales of upheaval for a section all their own.

Your Husbands Love You— They Tell Me So

Perhaps communication can fill the gaping wound.

I'm laying in bed in a motel room, naked. I'm with a regular client, and we're finished. He's somewhere in his forties and married, and as usual, he wants to talk.

He's pondering infidelity. The subject creases his brow. He says:

"Without any callgirls to turn to, we married men would be much more likely to run away from home."

He likes to make that point often. He makes it every time I see him. This time, as I listen, I invent an appropriate motto.

"I guess you could say that an "escort" is the married man's best friend."

"No," he immediately shoots back. "An "escort" is his *wife's* best friend."

Well, most wives would emphatically deny that, but still, I know he's right. After all I've learned as an "escort" about the polygamous, wanderlust nature of many men, I'm aware that yes, men *are* more likely to go home more often, and show a lot more affection, if their wives just back off, leave them alone, and allow them to get there "the long way."

But I also know how scary that prospect can be for wives. When husbands go home "the long way," all kinds of bad things can happen. The worst of those things is the dreaded Other Woman. And that's been my client's whole point. That's what he means when he designates sex workers as wives' invaluable buddies. A callgirl keeps a husband safe from falling into those clutches. A callgirl keeps the family safe from the Other Woman's home-wrecking ravage.

Ladies, we "escorts" do suck your husbands' cocks. And yes, we do fuck them, though with condoms. I know how much that must hurt you. I know, because I'm a woman. Like you I'm intensely monogamous, from my brain right down through my soul. I can feel it deep in my body. I can feel my monogamous nature as an etching into my genes, a code that will never scramble. My desire to merge with only one man is as real as the milk that's welled under my nipples, or the blood that's flowed from my womb. When I fall in love with a man, I'm blind to any other. Even when the novelty's gone. I don't even acknowledge that other men exist, except in my profession.

The custom, much-hated by American women, of Asian wives trailing behind their husbands with their eyes fixed on the ground, is emotionally apt, regardless of how sexist. I only think of the man that I love. I live him, I breath him, I cry for him, my love for him completely takes over my brain, and if Brad Pitt himself or Christopher Noth were ever to come after me, I'd be flattered, but they couldn't have me...their touch would feel like a sting. I'd spurn them, great looks and charisma notwithstanding, just because they're not my man.

But ladies, you need to understand something. Men just aren't wired like we are. Not mine, not yours, not anyone's. After their initial obsession with us passes, monogamy, for most men, is mind-boggling. For some men, it's downright impossible. In my dealings with men, I've come to accept that. That acceptance has been called Whore Wisdom.

But here's the most important thing, something I know is true, and I want more than anything for you to know it, too: *most of your husbands deeply love you. Even though they watch porn. Or ogle other women at strip clubs. Or ever get with a whore.*

I'm deep in the heads of husbands. They show me all that they are. Wives, for the most part, are not. You wives see only what your terrified mates feel safe enough to reveal.

Because I'm an erotic practitioner, your husbands can trust me as their sole female witness to the total male erotic dynamic. They show me what they need to show the women they love, but are afraid to: the dedicated mate and the erotic free spirit, both of whom are intrinsic. Men often struggle with that double identity, desperately hoping not to offend, desperately praying for results not disastrous. With me, they know they won't be judged. With me, they know they won't be maligned for any of their wanderlust leanings. With me, they know they're not hurting anyone. With me, they can just relax.

I have much to share with wives. I have useful information meant to bring more understanding of the sexually meandering behavior of many males. It may ease the feeling of betrayal in women when their men either literally or, in fantasy, "stray." I seek to ease wives' sense of threat.

When a husband secretly visits a sex worker, the only threat to his marriage is the rage of his wife, if she finds out. Most of the husbands I see as a whore would rather die than leave their wives.

Some men want to tell their wives about their sessions with me, just as they tell them about everything else. Not as a confession, but as a sharing, just another confiding. Yet because their women would be intensely enraged if they knew about their sexual adventures, those men lie or omit.

But those men don't want to lie. They don't like being deceitful. It pains them to be.

Sometimes I have to remind those clients to be a lot more discreet. Deep down, I think they *want* to get caught. I don't think it's because they feel guilty about what they're doing. I think it's because they feel guilty about the lying. What they're doing with me is something they *must*, but it makes them feel estranged from their mates. They ache for her knowledge and approval. They need her to say, *it's okay*.

Because of that need, they get careless. They get so careless that it scares me. Once, one guy had me go to his house while his wife and kids were at a movie. I asked him when the film would be over. In forty-five minutes, he said. The theatre was right down the road. He'd timed things so we'd be finishing up at about the same time they got home!

That was insanely on-the-edge. I informed him that I was going to leave long before he wanted me to.

You could say that that guy was obsessed with taking risks—it's true that some men are. Some men will gamble everything for a piece of forbidden fruit. But I think something else drove that guy. He always told me how much he wished he could share me with his wife. He called me a fun recreation—yet that wasn't digging at it deeply enough; I think he wanted his wife to know about some hidden facet, some part of himself she didn't see. So what if it was trysts with me? So what if it was sex? That didn't mean he didn't love her absolutely. It was just that he saw me as some kind of addition, some kind of cog in the wheel of his life. He actually pictured me out with his family. He wanted us all to be friends.

So I decided that he was a perfect example of a guy who sincerely wants to be honest about everything with his wife, especially something that makes him feel good, even if it is another woman.

But most wives don't want to hear that.

I've seen a few others like him. One guy did get caught. He liked to take me out to dinner as a prelude to the "dessert." He met me at restaurants too close to home. This was in Small-Town-America, where the night has a thousand eyes.

One night, his wife was out of town, but his stepdaughters, both grown women, were not. They spotted us leaving the restaurant. They followed us to the hotel, and watched us go inside. They waited for us to come out. He didn't notice them there, and they didn't want him to. They hid there, watching, and later on, they never said a word. But boy, did their mother get an earful, as soon as she got off her plane.

His marriage didn't end, but his trysts with me sure did.

Of his wife that guy always spoke lovingly. They were partners in everything: home-owning, child-raising, grandparenting—they also ran a business together. But his formerly beautiful soul mate had gained a lot of weight. It was caused by some heart medications. He knew that if she knew about his pursuit of pretty callgirls, her already wounded self-esteem would be irrevocably shattered. So for her sake, he dreaded getting caught, yet I think he also needed to fulfill an impossible dream. I think that he needed his beloved to tell him she accepted his trysts.

Well, she would never tell him that, but he slipped and slid in his caution just the same, because deep down inside, subconsciously, I think that he hoped she'd find out what he was up to, and understand, and permit it, and even give him her blessing.

That wifely permission is what some "cheating" husbands crave, even though they know that they won't get it.

And now I'll describe a very different type of client. That kind *does* like deceit. Those are the married who want the forbidden, and they want to *keep* it forbidden. They're determined to do something naughty, and then to mischievously hide it. It's a rebellion they need in return for their commitment.

Oh, that terrifying subject, commitment! Now there's a word that makes some men shudder, even the ones who *do* it. For a lot of men commitment is less about love, and more about feeling *beaten*. That's the big difference between them and us.

For us, commitment is easy. It's pure unadulterated love. For men it's love too, but there's something else there, a bad sense of *being defeated*.

Most men don't want to be conquered. It's written into their warrior genes that *they* should be in control. To let someone else take charge, even in an equitable way, can amount to a strong sense of downfall. Marriage, to a lot of men, is a way of getting conquered. Some of them just can't accept it. Not without a little insurgence.

I've known a lot of married clients like that, but one of them really stands out. That guy clarifies everything.

Back when I used to see him—I no longer do because I moved far away—he had a situation with his wife. The two of them led a promiscuous sex life. They were members of several of those notorious swap-clubs.

They would go to those places and get it on with people, right in front of each other. He said it was a wonderful time. It was open and honest extramarital sex, no lying, no omitting, no sneaking around.

But here's the thing that's amazing. Even though he went to those sex parties, he *still* had to sneak to see *me!* That guy was having more sex with more people than any client I knew, or know now. And except for the costs of the club memberships, that sex was totally *free*.

So why did he need to see *me?*

Because he had to have one little secret, is why. Something his wife didn't know about. Something she couldn't control. He needed it so much that he'd pay for it, even though he wasn't rich, even though his cock was sore from all the sex clubs they went to.

Boy, did that ever teach me. Some men just have to rebel. No matter how much their wives sweeten the pot! No matter how open the marriage! No matter what it costs!

Another example is President Clinton. I can't begin to tell you how I rue his choice of companion to thrill him in the Oval Office.

If Monica Lewinsky were an "escort", and the limits of their friendship were as clear as they are between most married men and their whores, she would have kept her mouth shut. She wouldn't have been giddy; she wouldn't have been lovestruck; she would have remained discreet. She wouldn't have gushed her secret to the ears of a spiteful woman. The United States of America would never have become a preposterous worldwide spectacle of petty character assassination, hypocrisy amongst officials, and sexual McCarthyism.

You might ask, why didn't Bill turn to Hillary for a blowjob? Well, why does a guy turn to a pastor for comfort, instead of his marital partner? Why does a guy go out with his friends, instead of being nailed to the house? It's all about needing something outside the box.

Men like Bill Clinton can't be stopped. They can only be divorced or accepted. My suggestion, for the sake of the survival of marriage, is to just let such men be. Just look the other way. Your jealousy and suspicious tirades will only increase their rebellion. Your nonchalance may diminish it. With the possible exception of the radically religious, who drown wanderlust in doctrines and become rigid, oppressive, and sexist, those men just can't be changed. The payoff is that they're likely to adore the accepting wife—the one who doesn't demand to know where he's been every minute of the day.

Pure fear is another reason for men's need to be deceptive. Not just their fear of the ravages of divorce. They're afraid that if their women get wind of what they're doing, then they'll start doing it, too.

Men's terror of that is well-founded. Think of the consequences. Think of how deeply monogamous we girls are. We tend to fall out-of-control in love with whatever man we're bedding. If that man isn't our husband, then our marriage goes out with the trash.

Husbands, for the most part, aren't like that. Most of them can fuck around and stay contentedly married. Clients have sometimes declared to me that as long as they don't leave their wives, that means they're being faithful. Those guys are bed-hopping everywhere, with sex workers and girlfriends galore. But they feel that they're true to their wives because they'd never pack up and move out.

Seriously. That's how some men define fidelity. But that's not the way with us women. We tend to want to bed just one man, and there goes the marriage if that man isn't hubby.

So our infidelities tend to be a lot more disastrous than theirs are. I know this is true. So many times, I've seen it. I've seen scores and scores of married guys who can't wait to jump on me, but they'd never desert their wives. When they're done with me, they go home. I've also seen some dumped husbands. They need to reach out to an "escort", a sympathetic stranger, from the suicidal depths of despair. Their wives have left home, or made them leave. They've abandoned them for a lover.

Those men are another category of clients who are married— and theirs is a very small group. A miniscule minority has called upon me as a result of their terminating marriages. The number of married clients who are soon-to-be divorced is so small that it's hardly worth mentioning. But a very big point is revealed there. In my experience, and in the experiences of all the callgirls I've spoken to or read about, almost all married men who see sex workers emphatically want to stay married.

Now ladies, please pay close attention to what I'm going to say next. There's a type of married-man client whom *you've* created, *yourselves.*

Not every husband is fucking around. Not every husband even *wants* to. But *you* can *make* him that way. Those of you who get nasty and whacko, and are constantly in his face, constantly ranting over cheatings you're afraid of that he hasn't actually committed, you're going to *make it happen*. You're driving him right to my ad. I can think of three clients, right off the top of my head, who have called me, met with me, laid their money down, and bitterly announced:

"God-*damn!* For *years* she's been accusing me of something I didn't do! So I might as well *do* it! I might as well *enjoy* it! Because she thinks I've done it *any*way! What the *fuck!*"

Control that fear of yours, ladies. Hold onto it like a big fart. Don't let it stink up your marriage. The man who's harassed seeks a fitting revenge.

And now I'll move on to another type, and this one distinctly disturbs me. It's the man who wants to erotically play with everyone *except* his mate.

Oh, boy. That's where a discussion of male eroticism gets murky. That's where I feel kind of helpless, reduced to a sad sort of guesswork. There are tangled whys and wherefores behind that split between the cock and the heart, and all I can do is wonder. Here I sense Western religion at its worst, mangling the psyches of both husbands and wives with its signature dualism. I'm forced to conclude that in America, that twisted-schizoid soul wrecker, that infamous Madonna/Whore complex, is alive and well and kicking.

I'll never forget my most exemplary client who was plagued by that sexual schism. I met him in a motel near Providence.

A lot of that city is Italian-American. Catholic churches are prevalent. In fact, the state capital resembles a cathedral. The only thing missing is a cross. I don't know whether this is actually true, but a Providence client once told me that the edifice was made sort of Vatican-looking because the city's run by the Mob.

Well, the guy that I saw on the day I'm describing was obviously Italian-American, and obviously Catholic. His features were distinctly Roman. A large gold crucifix hung from his neck.

But this was no Tony Soprano. He was shaking like a leaf.

Italian men tend to look like cops, so I was quite jittery, too. Especially since, as I've mentioned before, prostitution in Rhode Island is a felony. But it didn't take me long to see that this guy was more scared than I was.

Cops don't look scared; they look happy. You're their catch of the day.

The fright on this guy was extraordinary. He wore a jacket and a tie and a look that said successful, yet he'd lost all his self-assurance. He was so scared he'd gotten preverbal. The room was cool, yet his forehead was sweat-soaked. He was much too young for a heart attack, but he looked as though he might have one. One glance at his cross and his wedding band explained it.

The poor guy was standing before me in pants-shitting terror of God.

I don't know how I managed to get him calmed down. My usual personable efforts, I guess. Then he found his voice and indicated that he wanted me to suck him. And oh, he wanted it **bad**....

He wanted it so bad that he was doing something unbearable—he was morally fleeing his lifestyle. According to what he'd been taught since First Communion, when he was barely more than a tot, he was committing a terrible wrong. He was offending the Father, the Son, and the Mother of God, and the Sacrament of Marriage. He was failing his wife, the whole Family.

He had to.

"I haven't had a blowjob in eight years," he sighed.

I almost asked why, but then it hit me: *He's been married for that long*. His wife was "a good Catholic girl." There was nary a blow, and never would be.

Dear God. I just don't get it. I consider the come of my man something sacred. It's his deep-down bodily nectar, my lover's beautiful juice, the joy I'm determined to pull from his body with the seeking, sucking, bottomless passion that powers my worshipful mouth.

I swallow every spurt. I lick up the last drop. It's a lovers' holy communion.

I blissfully taste him and smell him, way back in my throat, in the tender hours that follow.

I can't believe there are people, in the sanctified bondage of marriage, who are cheated of that beautiful physical love, for all of their wedded lives.

My devout Catholic client departed, all grateful and grinning and sated, to trudge to his wife and his church and Confession.

I left that motel sadly chuckling.

Though I despise all Western religion, and it no doubt hates me, I have to admit that my wallet's not complaining about the messed-up way things are. But my intellect isn't so happy. That part of me is appalled. How can a guy who loves getting his cock sucked wed himself forever to a woman who won't do it? To a woman he wouldn't even **ask?**

People shake their heads at the "moral depravity" of a sex worker like me. Well, I shake *my* head at *that.*

In some eras and some cultures, there's been less broken thinking, a bit less hypocrisy. Prostitution has sometimes been allowed as a legitimate "social safeguard", an erotic diversion for married men who need that sort of escape. Such cultures recognize, like the client I mentioned, that some husbands might abandon their families, were it not for what whores provide. So down through the patriarchal, woman-hating, Madonna-Whore-mind-fucking centuries, sometimes we whores have been valued.

Almost.

Accordingly, I harbor the hope that contemporary wives might come to see sex workers as a marital aid. Their husbands certainly do.

We "escorts" can prevent the agony of wives like Clara Harris, the convicted Houston murderess. In the summer of 2002, she hysterically slaughtered her husband with her car.

At her murder trial she insisted that she had briefly lost her mind, and that it caused her to lose control of her driving, and fatally run him over. She said that it wasn't just because of his cheating. It was also because of his horrid declarations. To hear Harris tell it, the way her husband treated her was catastrophically belittling. He had openly, repeatedly compared her to the preferred charms of his lover.

I can't think of a cruelty more crushing. Even the strongest of women would be stricken. Imagine being told, by your life's emotional pillar, the father of your children, the man whom you've trusted for decades, that the other woman has a better body, makes better love, and *fuck you dear, I'm all hers now*.

We can assume that behind Mr. Harris' lack of mercy, his mistress hovered in triumph. She had obviously maneuvered for his loyalty. She had obviously ruined the marital home with an arsenal of powerful seductions.

And now a father rots in his grave. And a mother is rotting in jail.

We prostitutes never do that. We don't do what mistresses do. We are absolutely not home-wreckers. We harbor no motive to induce married men to insult, neglect, or abandon their wives. We sex workers serve our purpose, collect our fees, and send women's husbands straight home.

Often, we even bolster our clients with marriage-saving advice. We know that they want to hear it, we know that they love their wives, and we're happy to help out. Those of us who are truly professional understand that's part of our job. I believe it's high time that wives knew that.

To wives, and legislators, I propose this: decriminalize our work, but jail any one of us who steals someone's husband. Send her right down the river. Make home wrecking by a hooker a charge that would stick. I doubt any whore would be inclined to do that, but just in case I'm wrong—how's that for playing fair?

And I ask that you wives play fair, also. Some clients have asked me to speak up for them. They want me to squarely address the wives who deprive their men of sex.

To those of you wives who come under that heading, for whatever the reason may be—you're old, or religious, or hormonally challenged, plain tired of him, or whatever—to those of you who don't want to have sex and haven't done it for years— please don't punish or divorce your men when they seek it somewhere else.

Husbands don't lose their need for sex, just because you do.

Leave the poor guy alone. Let him go get what he needs. Please don't condemn him for it.

That's just so insanely unfair.

And don't worry. What he's doing with us won't change anything. (Well, it *will* make him easier to live with.) We give him what he's called us for, which is safe sex, as in condoms and no strings. Afterwards, he goes home. He's on time for dinner or mowing the lawn or whatever you want him there for.

He's a good boy. Especially after we've done for him that thing that you don't want to. Not one grouchy word from him today!

Oh, and by the way—if what he spends on us pisses you off, you can always turn it around. You can use it as a bargaining tool. You can tell him you're going to the mall. You can tell him he owes you one. You can tell him it's *your* turn to spoil yourself, and he won't have a leg to stand on.

One more thing. I think it's you wives who should contact us "escorts". *You* should locate our ads, *you* should call us, and *you* should set your husbands' appointments. You should send your hubbies right to us with a hug and a kiss and a pat on the ass.

If you were to do that, your husbands would exalt you. Giving a man that much freedom, and that much understanding, is the only way you'll ever "whup" him. Have you ever heard the expression, "If you love him, let him go?" It's very wise. Give him that freedom, and he'll bounce right back. He'll be more in love with you. Maybe he'll even be as crazy about you as he was "in the beginning." Do you want your man to be nuts about you? If you cook like a pro and suck even better, you're definitely on the right track. But the way to sustain his absolute worship is to allow him to play with other women.

If you do that, he'll be in awe of you. He'll respect you for your strength, adore you for your generosity, and revel in the sweet relief of not having to lie or omit. It will deepen your bond beyond words.

Why? Because you accept him! All of him! Even his lust for other women! That's true partnership.

He may even dump his drinking buddies. With a mate like you, what's he need them for? You hang out with him, you check out the babes with him, you comment with him about them. You may feel jealous of their hotness, but cheerfully, good-naturedly so. Maybe you even go to the strip joints with him. At *your* suggestion, not his!

Astounded and impressed, he'll lay his soul at your feet. He'll also be a little bit nervous. *How can she be that strong*, he'll be thinking. *What's going on with her? Does **she** want to fool around?*

Of course not, you'll reassure him; you're doing all this because you love him, you understand him. And isn't it cool to share *everything?*

It's good when a man's a little mystified. It focuses him right on you. If you don't make him just a little bit scared, you'll seldom have his full attention. Men are only absorbed when they're challenged. Your cheerful throwing open of that door on other women will rivet him so profoundly on *you* that he may even forget about the treat that awaits him.

But remember the client I mentioned, the one with a wife like that, who still had to have a secret. There will always be men like him. Maybe *your* man is like him. What're you going to do, pay a divorce lawyer over it? Become a depressed single mom over it? It's better to gently accept him, and indicate you don't mind. As a result, he'll still sneak around, but I would bet probably *less.*

I know, I know, I'm proposing something hard. But isn't it true that the best things don't come easy? Like maintaining, forever, the rapt attention of a husband? You have to go right to the edge.

You may read this and say: *I don't need to do those things. My man wants only me*. Oh, please. That's only true if he's extremely testosterone-deficient, or obsessed, to the point of imbalance, with religion or his work. Or if you've just met, or you're newlyweds. And maybe not even then.

It's probably true that your man *loves* only you. I believe that most men, when they're ready, can easily commit to one woman. But they *lust for* a lot of women. That's the big difference in men. Even the most placid, flaccid married male will furtively ogle other women, and that's the least way he'll "cheat". Yes, I'm talking about that snoring lump in his favorite over-stuffed chair. Does he have a penis? Are you certain he's not gay? If so, then no matter how much he loves you, and no matter how docile he seems, you can be sure that he thinks of other women.

Whenever I've read articles about traditional polygamous Mormons, I've noticed that at least one of those particular men of God eventually 'fesses up. If someone's decided to be unabashedly truthful, he'll eventually come out and freely admit that his polygamy isn't religious. He simply wants sex with more than one woman. He takes several wives because he *can*.[1]

Accordingly, on the HBO series, *Big Love*, I can sense that simple truth lurking. Though Bill, the drama's polygamous Mormon husband, seems sincerely, endearingly pious, and he refers to his support of three wives as the way that he serves God, he nevertheless seems to be somewhere quite natural, in a purely sexual sense. This man is profoundly responsible, and his exhaustion is the main point, but his male sexuality is obvious, also. For all his triple husbandly stresses, and for all his commitment to faith, Bill bed-hops around his wives' compound with the ease of a bull or a dog.

Wives should stop axing their marriages if it's only because "men are dogs." Arf, arf, whine and bark, whatcha gonna do? Negotiation, not condemnation, is what will make things work. If he's *not an abusive fuck*, and he *works very hard*, and he's also *a really good father*…you're going to divorce him for seeing "escorts" now and then? Come on.

Women need to face one critical fact: they will not change the sexual ways of the male. It will not happen. Women who try to stamp it out are only going to get lied to. Deceit, and not understanding, will be the glue that holds their relationships together.

The "I don't want to know" policy may work for a lot of women, but it's never worked for me. I've always trawled for the truth with my men, even if it hurts me. Even if it *kills* me. How else can partnership truly prevail? If he wants an extramarital thrill, I want to know about it. I want to be so inside my man's head that I know about *everything* in there, even the stuff hard to take. But he'll never let me see it if he knows I'll pitch a fit, or worst of all, try to change him.

Every once in a while, a woman leaves a message on my voicemail.

"I'm calling because it's my husband's [or boyfriend's] birthday. I want to give him a present...a session with an "escort.""

I believe that those women have the best shot at happiness with their men.

Those of you women who refuse to do that tend to hate whores with a passion. You hate us because we're the flesh and blood proof of a truth that you can't accept. That truth is the sexual wanderlust in men, and your helpless failure to stop it.

I've used the word "failure" because that's how you feel, but I don't believe that you should. Many of you haven't failed at anything at all, when your husbands call on me. Often, it has nothing to do with you.

They love you.

With some men, it's a lose-lose situation. If they're neglected by their women, of course they're going to cheat. But they're going to cheat if they're *not* neglected, too. Why? Because they're addicted. They're addicted to a woman's attention. When their woman's not around, they can't bear it. They've got to go get a "fix."

What can you do about men like that? Leave them or live with them. But you're not going to change them.

Your hatred for whores won't change a damn thing, either. It will keep you all miserable and spiteful and divorced, and keep "escorts" down and oppressed.

Isn't it better to understand that we're all in this thing together?

PART TWO

CROSSING THE LINE

Health Nut,
Fitness Buff, Callgirl

Sure, I've suffered a heavy loss of chastity, but what
kind of society is this that equates my acquisition of
sexual experience with a loss of purity?

Since the earliest years of my life, black pain has threatened to
waste me. I've always been aware of its terrible power, and I've
learned to aggressively fight it. Over and over and over again, I've
jumped up and fiercely grabbed hold of my mind, sorted and
rummaged inside it, and carefully, purposefully shaped it. I've
scoured and polished and painted in there until it's positively
shone.

Because I knew that if I didn't do that, if I never reached in
and rearranged things, and plugged in a really good attitude, and
accepted that it's all about being self-made—-I'd probably die
very young.

I guess that's the mission of a motherless child.

In the beginning, when I was little, long before I learned to
self-strengthen, a whole lot of bad things happened. My
developmental years were catastrophic. I was surrounded by
grownups whose eyes betrayed pity. My little-kid world was so
damaged that people grew silent around me. Their heads would
sadly shake.

I was a child whose birthright to security had been torn away and permanently trashed.

In some ways, however, my conditions were fine. They were even enviable. No one ever physically or sexually abused me. No poverty stole my dreams. No disease restricted my childhood, and neither did classic calamities, like a hurricane or a fire. On the face of things, I was fortunate. I was a white child, and pretty, the offspring of cultured people. I was heir to every social advantage.

But I was extremely emotionally beat-up. Severe instability wrecked me. Dreadful tragedy, unbearable loss, devastating rejection, and nonstop uprooting: those were the demons of my childhood.

If I could make that horror an entity, if I could give it a face, I'd make it a grand master of cliffhanging yo-yo, endlessly flinging me away on a string, dangling me over the edge of the world, with a sociopathic sneer.

As a preschooler, I was perceptive. I was acutely aware of my young mother's despair. From my toddlerhood until the day of her death, her demise repeatedly crushed me. She was always in terrible pain.

I can only remember her pain. I remember my panic and guilt-ridden anguish, all in response to her downfall, which I endured when the loss of a teddy bear should have been my most terrible trauma.

There was her first, permanently disabling stroke, the one that toppled her suddenly and cruelly from her prime. Then came her agonized divorce from my father, who had decided he preferred a fully functional woman to his newly crippled wife. What followed was her ruin from paralysis and heartbreak.

In the end she was felled by her worst cranial bleed, the one that killed her when I was six.

Frequent separations from my father were what followed, and a permanent parting from my only full-blooded sibling. Compound rejections by fickle caregivers were additional shocks to my mangled little life.

To everyone who took care of me, I was dispensable. I was the commitment they could rid themselves of when life got a little tough. One of them wanted to keep my brother, but didn't want to keep me. That's how I ended up losing my sibling, on top of everything else.

Between kindergarten and my senior year of high school, I got moved around so often that I attended *fifteen* schools. I was always the scapegoated "new kid." Other kids sensed my aloneness, my smashed and broken defenses, my desperado groping for the fragments of my self. They often closed in and attacked.

As a young adult, I deepened that painful-life pattern, inflicting it on myself. Many years prior to becoming an "escort", I bonded with undependable men. I tolerated horrible marriages.

I finally broke free and faced the outcome, single motherhood.

I was poverty-stricken, bereft of child support, and as usual, much too alone.

My father had been gone for a long time. He had made himself scarce, financially broken, when I was just nineteen. He dropped dead soon after I turned twenty-one. He never saw any of the grandchildren I gave him, starting at age twenty-three.

He had once been a successful and responsible dad. In spite of his desertion of my mother, and his absences caused by his work-related travels, he had always been loving and attentive to me.

While I was growing up motherless, and my vacillating guardians were bouncing me around, my father always wrote to me and called me. And whenever he materialized, he took me on special excursions. He enchanted me with presents. He would bring me a doll from every single country his business caused him to visit. Those dolls were gorgeous creations. They were dressed in the traditional costumes of their cultures. Eventually, I owned about thirty of them.

My traveling father provided my guardians with more-than-adequate child support payments. Unlike my mother, who was absolutely gone, somehow my father seemed there for me, even when he physically wasn't. He was alive. He was in touch. He never failed to think of me, even when thousands of miles away. He would always remember to find me a doll.

He made me feel important to him. I remember the thrill of his loving attention, whenever we were together. I remember the annual Easter Parade, on Fifth Avenue, in New York. I was dressed to the nines in some fancy, flouncy, little-girl Easter dress. I remember the billowing layers of yellow, and pinafore, petticoat white. I felt lost in the promenade of thousands, and yet people noticed me. Strangers were snapping my picture. My father was beaming with pride.

When I was a child in grade school, he'd return from his travels and stay for a while at home, in his Manhattan apartment. During those times, he'd have me visit. My father would take me to diners' clubs where he schmoozed around with his friends. I remember the bartenders saying, "It's okay for a kid to be here, but you'll have to keep her six feet from the bar. That's the New York State law." So Daddy would cheerfully sit with me, that far from the bar.

By the time I had turned fifteen, his business trips had dwindled, so now he could have me move in. I had stayed with him on all my school vacations when he wasn't on the road, but I hadn't actually lived with my father—not since before he left my mother, back when I was four. Finally getting to cohabitate with my only living parent was the best thing that could have happened to me.

Eventually, however, my father's business floundered, and so did his cardiovascular system. When I had barely reached young adulthood, suddenly he was dead. So were all of his assets. Emotionally, he left me in shock. Financially, he left me with nothing.

After all that I'd been through growing up, as a tragedy-stricken, motherless, tossed-about kid, my emotional health was tenuous. The loss of my father seemed to be the last straw. It was as though I just snapped apart. I became self-destructive. I wasn't attracted to alcohol, drugs, or any kind of dangerous activity, yet I found a sure way to wreck my life; my ruinous path was bad relationships with men. I seemed to hurl myself at abusers and losers. Even after I rid myself of them, their negligence poisoned my life. The two fathers of my three children were both of no help to me. One was a totally deadbeat dad, and the other one only involved himself sometimes, only when our child lived with him.

I ended up subsisting as a dismal statistic. I eked my family by. I grappled and bargained with the never-ending pressure of attempting an impossible mission. I was trying to raise a family with no support at all. My status was common, yet subtly scorned: I was poor, divorced, and female, with "brats."

I endured the triple impact of no child support payments, no parents to help out, and total estrangement from my sibling. To top it all off, I lacked earning power. With those multiple disadvantages, my single-mother status was exceptionally bleak. I was trapped in the desolation of a failed, yet inescapable, survival operation. Emotionally and physically drained in a dangerously chronic dejection, I hopelessly acknowledged, and hopelessly tried to negotiate, the nonstop onslaught of living expense, on my own with three mouths to feed.

Having not been raised in poverty had ironically proved a disadvantage. I had always lacked the cold pragmatism of a money-hungry, working-class kid. The assortment of people who raised me had all been fairly well off, and they had all been very well-educated. They were highbrow intellectuals who despised single-minded materialism. In the wake of their lofty influence, I learned a bit late that such thinking works only for those who have a trust fund.

After my father, a documentary filmmaker, went totally bankrupt and died, I failed to realistically face my destitution. I kept right on poetically majoring in English. It was the early nineteen-seventies; I kept right on protesting the Viet Nam war and the outrage of racial injustice. I kept right on with my nurture of insecure men who would eventually tear me to pieces. I kept right on with my screaming for equality for women. I focused on the violently downtrodden women—-but certainly not on myself. I, of course, came from privilege. I was impervious to dire disadvantage!

I was impassioned by every worthy cause but my own. And I believed that money's not important. Such is the naiveté of a kid who grew up with enough of it. A born-poor kid, untouched by elitist idealism, would most likely have been materially galvanized by the demise of her only parent. She would have nailed herself to some kind of lucrative career track, no matter how much she loathed it. She would have avoided all infantile and penniless men. She would have left all the protesting to those who could afford it.

But that just wasn't my thing.

Later on, as a single mom, I paid a high price for my practical unpreparedness. In order to feed and shelter my family, I was forced to hold two or three low-paying jobs. I was seldom available for my kids. I was in terrible need of a clone. I had to be in two places at once—at home and at work—and I had no choice but to pretend that I was.

That desperate delusion made for tragedy at home. All of my children were boys. All of them were getting big. Damaged already by the negligence of their fathers, in the darkness of my work-related neglect they became aggressive lost souls. "Juvenile delinquent" is the uncompassionate term—and the memory that will pain me forever—for what my young sons were becoming.

In those wretched years before I learned "escorting", I worked as a substitute high school teacher, and as a waitress, and as a home health aid. I subjected myself to a depressing assortment of additional low-paying jobs. I held those jobs not consecutively, but collectively. At night I came home late, exhausted, to the festering wounds of my absence and my poverty. To a chaotic and shabby apartment, ruled by my neglected boys and their friends, and visited by police and truancy officers.

My relentless strife with the unbearable had grown to be a real threat. I feared for my mental and physical health. In response to the stress my body became like a water-bloated balloon. My emotional outlook was increasingly grim.

I was terrified of becoming so overwhelmed that I could no longer properly function. What would happen to my kids? Would they end up without their mother, as I had?

Eventually, I managed to pull myself up. I created one liberating light in my life. In the mid-nineteen-eighties I forced myself into the health and fitness movement.

That call to healthy living redeemed me. It was instinctive. It was the mastery of flight before the crash.

I couldn't afford the cost of a health club, but I joined one anyway. I couldn't spare a minute of time for such things, but I made time, just the same.

My involvement in fitness saved my life. I've always declared that, and now, as I actually type out those words, I can see that my claim looks exaggerated. It's not. When I started working out, I was a desperate girl in her thirties, nearing some kind of breakdown. Exercise turned me completely around.

I had never been in sports or in any activity that causes prime physical fitness. Now I had joined that fraternity, and I was learning the most beneficial lesson of my life. All that I needed for a sense of well being had always been within me, right there inside; it had simply never been tapped. In order to feel good, really deep down strong and good, I didn't need a bottle of pills, or a drink, or a cigarette, or an illegal drug, or a fattening snack, or a sitcom, or any other kind of escapist "help" that exists outside of me. In order to feel deep down strong and good, all I needed to do was learn how to properly stimulate my heart, my lungs and my muscles. And to keep that good thing going, all that I needed externally was pure water and the right kinds of foods. That was *all!*

But in order to perpetuate that good thing, I had to lay on the willpower thick. I had to *continuously* work out and eat right.

When I realized how great I was feeling—and looking—that wasn't such a hard thing to do. For a long time, I never pigged out. I can't say that working out stopped me forever from compulsive eating behaviors, but it sure cut them down a lot.

Eventually I experienced another great truth, the one behind anyone successful: self-discipline is the only true path to fulfillment. I had already learned something about that through my labors in college, and sometimes in parenting. But seeing that truism working in fitness—in the immediate, glowing rewards from my body—that was the most uplifting!

Ever since then, I've maintained that strength of will. Though poverty and disturbed young sons are years behind me now, I still get to the gym. I visit my temples for the rites of endurance. My DVD player is a shrine of sorts; with workout CD's, I pay homage in my house. When away from home, or bored with the gyms, I turn industrial parks into power-walking lanes. I strap weights to my ankles, and strategically pump and swing barbells as I go. Sometimes I even jump-rope. And if I spy the right pavement— smooth, with a challenging upgrade—and the weather permits and there isn't much traffic, then I pull on my rollerblades.

Security guards sometimes oust me from parking lots. Passers-by tend to smile; sometimes they simply stare. The obese ones and the smokers emphatically look away. Everyone who sees me reacts. Exercisers are a common sight, but I'm probably considered a spectacle because I'm a lone female and I'm bold about it, I don't care how foolish I look. I'll Taebo-kick or barbell-pump or jump-rope anywhere. My workouts are my lifeblood, my indispensable fuel, and as a whore I've found the will to conquer my fear of getting out there and doing it alone.

Years before I became an "escort", and I was learning devotion to exercise, I experienced, for the first time ever, a profoundly upward spiral. I had always been terribly aware of downward spirals, or vicious circles. I knew too well how one bad thing leads right to another, and another. Exercise took me completely the other way.

Having a vitalized body vitalized everything else. Improved circulation made everything in me work and feel a lot better. My newly toned muscles worked miracles: my organs were now much more supported and aligned, so my headaches and bowel irritations diminished. My posture improved so much that, even though I was a grownup, I actually grew half an inch.

In the punishing midst of my poverty, aloneness, and uncontrollable children, my spirits would sometimes improbably soar. And I had become somewhat calmer. Exercise, and the addition of stretching that I had learned to make time for, was soothing to my mind. I was virtually living the mind-body connection. In one long stretch, I could feel my anxieties loosen. After ten long stretches, my stress would feel malleable and easy to subdue.

After a couple of years of this regimen, I attempted to glean a living from my newfound healthy lifestyle. I found work as an exercise instructor. That was a bright addition to my otherwise spirit-killing roster of jobs. I interspersed my drearier employments with shifts at various health clubs. I studied hard, and passed the difficult multiple-choice exam, to become certified by the American Council on Exercise.

With that credential under my belt, now I could legitimately present myself as a professional fitness instructor.

I enjoyed myself in that work. I designed new club members' workout programs and taught them how to effectively use them. People looked up to me. People wanted to *be* me. They admired my disciplined leanness, my well-tended muscular tone, and my buoyancy honed from daily cardio workouts. Doctors, lawyers, professors, CEO's…everyone, including the prestigious, persistently approached me with eyes that beseeched. To me they turned over their tired, flabby, lusterless selves. I showed them how to put the bloom back into their smiles, and the lilt back into their gaits. It was deeply fulfilling work.

It paid five dollars an hour.

I attempted to establish myself as a personal trainer. When enough clients sign up for that coaching, a fitness instructor's low income can greatly, though gradually, improve. I had little success. People generally take years to get around to joining a health club. After that expenditure, few are willing to pay out even more for much-needed, yet much-resisted, pricey one-on-one training. The building of a lucrative clientele from a crowd that reluctant takes time and reliable cash reserves.

These days, I think I could pull it off; I now have the resources to enable me to. I just might go back to work in the gyms, and promote myself as a trainer.

When I was a poor single mother, however, I had neither the savings nor the time to succeed.

Along with my devotion to exercise, I eventually developed a passionate interest in supplemental nutrition. I learned that *intensely augmented nutrition* would help to keep me strong. I began to consume, and I tried to distribute, some nutrient-dense "super foods."

The first of those marvels that I tried to promote is a naturally growing type of blue-green algae, a primal food rich in amino nutrition. One's mood and one's energy level perceptively improves after swallowing a few freeze-dried capsules. Its internal cleansing properties and its bolstering of the immune system have all been clinically evidenced.

I continue to take algae capsules every day, and I plan to for life. I make sure that my loved ones are getting theirs, too.

My repertoire of "super foods" spontaneously grew. I learned of natural antibiotics extracted from foods and herbs, and natural energizers and antioxidants, and many more nutrient sources that strengthen the immune system and prevent or heal illness. I took each of those remedies when I felt that I needed them, and I could sense, with a growing satisfaction, my mind and my body respond. I became less susceptible to colds and flu. If I did come down with something, I got over it remarkably fast. I successfully treated my urinary tract infections without ever turning to a doctor or a drug store. I aided and eased my intestinal tract with cheap and simple, old-fashioned remedies that far too few people know about these days. I supplemented with natural aids that are native to the gut: intestinal flora, called probiotics, and capsules of digestive enzymes. After adding that stuff to my system, my symptoms of Irritable Bowel Syndrome vanished.

I was approaching forty. I had much more energy than most people that old. I childishly bounded up stairways, while other mature adults trudged. Despite my travails as a desperately poor single mother, I looked young, acted young and felt young, and people refused to believe me when I told them my actual age.

People insisted that I had to be in my mid-twenties. They demanded to see the birth date on my license. When I showed it to them, they were bowled over. Some of them seemed pissed off.

Well, I had thought that I could never afford the health-food-store well being-enhancers, but I saved my spare change, sacrificed things, and found that after all, I could buy them. I had noticed that low-income people could always find money for their cigarettes and beer; I could find bucks for my health.

Some of the brands of nutritional supplements can be sold by individuals. I tried to become a distributor, but it never got profitable. Just as it went with the personal training, I was continually frustrated to find that, in distributorships which offer self-improvement through nutrition—where people are invited to buy supplements, and invest in their well being—most resist, and close up their wallets. This is true even when they perpetually gripe for relief from their various ailments. Most continue to take whatever their doctors prescribe, even though their trust in doctors is becoming quite shaky, too—even though they've grown sensibly weary of scalpels and toxic pharmaceuticals.

I observe American medicine with an increasingly cynical eye.

In order to maintain their moneyed lifestyles, and to pay for the high costs of being in practice—such as huge malpractice insurance premiums—medical professionals depend, heavily, on the persistence of mass chronic illness. Intentionally or not, they count on the terrible prevalence of the process of disease. Though I'm certain that American doctoring careers must surely attract the altruistic, I can sense, just the same, that many in the health field avoid teaching people preventative wisdom, and even avoid developing their own proficiency in it, because the long-term result—a healthier public—would greatly diminish their income.

I'm plagued by that suspicion.

One night, I was watching *ER*. On that sovereign of medical TV dramas, I witnessed a conversation that chilled me to the bone.

The arrogant Dr. Romano was complaining to Dr. Weaver. He was annoyed about a vending machine in the break room. "It's all raisins and rice cakes…what happened to the candy bars?"

His conscientious colleague replied: "We're trying to set a good nutritional example for the patients."

Said the show's God-complex M.D.: "Big mistake! America's poor eating habits help to keep us in business!"[1]

In both principle and retaliation, I gravitate to traditions and fields that fly in the face of such mercenary "care." All that I study enables self-healing. Along with my commitment to exercise and my attempts at super-nutrition, all of the following rivet my interest: holistic awareness (the mind-body connection), Asian medical practices (most of which tend to be intrinsically holistic), therapeutic massage, healing meditation, healing breathing, and ways to detoxify our environment and consequently, ourselves. Maybe the future holds a lucrative place for me in one of those wonderful fields. Maybe some day I'll be a licensed naturopathist. For now, I'm content to absorb from all areas.

I want to become highly knowledgeable in the process of natural healing. Though I've never been able to profit from it, and I don't know how I will, this much I'm sure of: I'm appalled by the American system of professional medical training. It empowers its practitioners to diagnose, surgically remove and chemically treat disease, but it provides little or no education in the means to show patients how to prevent illness or to naturally heal themselves. So often, I've either witnessed or been told of doctors who perform as brilliant diagnostic detectives, and who command an impressive repertoire of post-diagnostic therapeutic prescription. Some of them possess a beautiful gift for the plying of surgical tools. All of them seem to be wonderfully trained in how to fix bodies that come to them broken. But ask these invasive gurus for the simplest advice on how to eat or breathe right, and—with the exception of cardiologists, to whom the solutions of diet and exercise are as obvious as the sun—most of these physicians become helplessly dismissive. Most of them shrug and refer us to their receptionists. Their non-medical front desk sentries might, and only might, have a list of nutritionists, or some such, to call. Meanwhile, the main man goes off to examine his next patient for symptoms of disease, and the only thing he knows, for absolutely sure, is where his "script" pad is waiting.

Medical researchers and their heaviest investors, the pharmaceutical companies, all rally to the curative cause of meddling with DNA. I appreciate their mission to eradicate genetically caused disorders and disease, but I'm aware that profit, and only profit, is the motive of the backers. From the monetary perspective, cellular manipulation is greatly preferred to inspiring healthier lifestyles. The former might make drug companies richer one day; the latter might render them bankrupt.

Meanwhile, every time I watch commercial TV, I find myself wanting to scream. Every other ad I see is a ploy to get me drugged.

To my great relief, however, I've discovered a handful of rebel physicians who defy that dismal status quo.

I always to subscribe to the advisories, in monthly newsletter form, of that foremost American authority on natural and preventive health maintenance, that renegade alumnus of Harvard Medical School, Dr. Andrew Weil, M.D. I give his best-selling book, *Spontaneous Healing*, to everyone on my Christmas list who hasn't already received one.

Recently Dr. Weil was on the cover of *Time*. And now he has a health column featured in there.

I also subscribe to the writings of Dr. David G. Williams, M.D., the founder of *Alternatives*, an informative series of newsletters on unconventional healing. Dr. Williams is a Baby Boomer with the energy and passion to immerse himself in diverse, often primitive, cultures, and even jungles. He literally searches all over the globe for natural preventatives and curatives *that work*. Those medicines also tend to be *cheap*. His efforts have been fruitful. He conveys all his findings to the public.

Dr. Williams tends to have knowledge of things before others in the medical community. For instance, he knew as early as 1992 that inflammation, not high cholesterol, is the worst cause of heart attacks.[2]

Dr. Julian Whitaker is another revolutionary M.D. Dr. Whitaker's contribution is largely an understanding of how to most effectively consume natural supplements—particularly in which combinations. In pamphlets that he publishes from his Whitaker Wellness Institute, he offers a wealth of professional advice on how to best absorb the vitamins and herbs that people increasingly try. Whitaker is a supplement industry watchdog. He seeks to dismantle the make-bucks-fast mission of herbal suppliers who are in the business just to get rich, and who might throw together inferior or useless herbal concoctions.

Doctors Weil, Williams and Whitaker are clearly in nutritional supplementation for the virtue, not just the bucks. I thank and admire them. They forego the ease of convention, and endure the malice of their threatened colleagues, to forge for the public many ways to self-heal.

I, too, have defied convention. When I became a prostitute, I found an alternative way to be.

My prior quest to master self-healing profoundly impacted my beginnings as a whore. Becoming a whore was perfectly in keeping with my attraction to alternative medicine. Becoming a whore was perfectly in keeping with my devotion to physical fitness. People don't associate whores with health, but the blending of whoring with a healthy lifestyle is precisely the path I discovered.

Immediately, "escorting" healed me financially. But then I saw that being in sex work could heal me in other ways, also.

As I strengthened myself through the identity of whore, I began to intuit the power of the primordial sexual priestess. At first, I merely sensed her. Eventually, I actually read about her. With the aid of the writings of feminists who have freed up the hidden archives of our prepatriarchal past, I learned of her ancient glory. I learned that thousands of years ago, before the global takeover of patriarchal religions, before the catastrophic oppression of Goddess and nature and women, priestess-whores were the official and highly exalted healers.

I joyfully internalized that beautiful truth.

I had begun to examine the writings of several enlightened sex workers. One such is Nina Hartley. She exemplifies and clarifies the priestess-identified sex worker. Hartley states: "I believe that sensual pleasure (self-generated or shared) is a meditation, opening a direct path to the life force, i.e., 'God.'"[3]

Hartley is a registered nurse. She's also a world-renowned porn star. She recently published a book entitled *Nina Hartley's Guide to Total Sex*.

Another lady of singular radiance stands out among activist whores. While most of the activists mundanely campaign for the basic right to work, Cosi Fabian stirs me with the ancient and the hallowed. Regardless of whatever any law may disallow, she perceives her whore status as holy. She identifies with the *Qadeshet*, or angelic erotic priestesses, of our prepatriarchal ancestors' temples. She recognizes whoring as sacred.

As a whore, Fabian utilizes her American right to practice her own religion. Her astounding, groundbreaking, and loving creed of faith is showcased at the front of this book.

Back in my early days as an "escort", Fabian and Hartley and others were making me aware that I was far from alone with my perceptions. With the aid of those "outed" whore thinkers, I understood that when practiced correctly, whoring is a healthy rebellion. I began to see a parallel between the rebellion of self-empowered whores, and the rebellion of people who attempt to self-heal. I began to see a parallel between those who better themselves through whoring, and those who get much better health by defying conventional medicine.

Indeed, that marriage between healthiness and whoring has been noted by the doctor of a whore. Fabian remarks: "Even my doctor, who was initially horrified by my career move, has been impressed by the extraordinary improvement in my...health."[4]

Another example of parallel between whoring and healthy endeavors is a certain plight shared by the patrons of each business. Those who hire prostitutes and those who buy nutritional supplements are both at high risk of getting ripped off.

In 1994, Congress passed a law called the Dietary and Supplement Health and Education Act. This act deregulated the supplement industry. The result? Just as it goes with the prohibited service—the service of prostitution—the production of nutritional supplements is now without mandated rules.

When a consumer opens a container of herbal-remedy capsules, he or she can't know whether the processed plants inside it were taken from a potent batch or a useless, inferior harvest.

> There are almost no standards that regulate how the pills are made, and they receive almost no scrutiny once they are, so consumers never truly know what they are getting. Companies are not required to prove that products are effective, or even safe...some herbs do work, of course, yet the absence of effective manufacturing standards in the United States means that even then consumers can't rely on commercial formulas.[5]

Likewise, prostitution—because it's illegal—is endemic with ways of getting away with disappointing the clients. Though the passage above is about plants, not women, anyone who's hired different "escorts" can relate.

When the profession is practiced correctly, prostitution is more, so much profoundly more, than just a mercenary act. Just like the superior medicinal herbs, which are sold not only for profit but sincerely to promote better health, whoring can be an inroad to an ancient healing power. That power is healthy for both "escorts" and their clients. When practiced with the right principles and corresponding attitudes—*by women who have reclaimed the holy priestess role*—whoring enables self-healing.

Prostitution brings self-understanding. Like cornucopias flowing with highly potent herbs, principled prostitutes foster well-being in themselves and the people they service.

In the nineteen-sixties, psychiatrists tacitly affirmed that truth when they routinely referred their patients to the famed New York City callgirl, Xaviera Hollander.[6] Likewise, Cosi Fabian affirms it, today. Her awareness has evolved into a sharing, an outright evangelism.

> For years now I've been teaching in small groups and large halls. Time and time again a woman will approach me, often in tears of gratitude, and say, "I always knew there was something else. I've had dreams...." In my classes I have watched women expand their minds and spirits, reclaim their strengths, and find their creative talents, all in the name of the Sacred Prostitute and her goddesses.[7]

In holistic-health oriented feminism, I've discovered a similar leaning. The author and psychologist, Chellis Glendinning, has been a spokeswoman for that Goddess-grounded faction of healers. My favorite books by Glendinning are *Off the Map*, and *When Technology Wounds,* and *My Name is Chellis and I'm in Recovery from Western Civilization.* You can glean just from reading those titles that here we have someone who's profoundly unhappy about patriarchal achievements, and how they've defiled the earth.

Glendinning has written of the strong evidence that women were the original healers. She describes the takeover of medicine by men, which began around the time of Christ, as the "patriarchal assault."

> The change was particularly disastrous for women. Called allopathic medicine (meaning treatment opposing, *allo*, the suffering, *pathos*), its "heroic" treatments of drugs or surgery assaulted the delicate balance of the female body, rather than catalyzed its natural tendency to heal itself. In keeping with patriarchal politics, the new medicine viewed the female body as sick, dirty and in need of alteration. Moreover, it excluded women, the original and perhaps the most natural healers of all, from contributing to the healing arts. The results of these changes in health care

have been deadly for millions of women in modern times.

The techniques of allopathic medicine are based on the aggressive notion of countering the obviously diseased part(s) by cutting them out or eradicating the symptoms with drugs....Assaulted by these practices, the original healer has been transformed into the most likely patient.[8]

Glendinning has reported on the emergence of an "unofficial guild of feminist healers" who defy the present-day allopathic methods with therapies from the epochs before men took over. They are taking back the old ways. They are "psychics, herbalists, body therapists, energy healers, ritualists, midwives, dream-interpreters, and death guides."

Her writings have blown me away. For years before I read them, I was gravitating there on my own. Glendinning and others have made me understand that all my life I've been aligning myself with a worldwide resurgence of matriarchal wisdom.

But I also got involved with something radical, a truth way out on the edge, a *herstory* that scares off the majority of even the most radical feminists. Those women realize, but tend to ignore, the fact that the prepatriarchal priestesses were not only medical healers. In tandem, they were mystical prostitutes.

I had merged with *all that*. I had gone *all the way*.

And the more I learned about those priestesses, and their healings, and their holy pagan sex, the more and more logical it seemed to me that I, a proponent of natural healing, had also become a whore.

In the wake of becoming a whore, I felt driven to seek out my peers. I found them, all right, in a most common place: in books in a large public library. I found Fabian, Hartley, and many other activists for the basic rights of whores. And then, when I persisted in my rummage for the priestess-identified, I stumbled upon an endearing little book, entitled *The Harlot's Room*.

In an understated departure from the glowing assertions of Fabian, or the angrier defenses of others, its author delivers a clear stream of insight not sullied by the fury of activism. She serves up her memoir with the hit-or-miss, rambling manner of a diarist. She imparts, without any preaching, an amazingly striking truth: that once upon a time, under nobody's influence, she intuitively made prostitution the means to her self-healing.

Her penname is simply "Melissa." Since writing the book she's "come out" with her full name, Melissa Bank.

Her background is complex.

As it goes with the mentally or spiritually gifted, she seems to have been born with a perceptual difference. For Melissa, it was amplified empathy. Her childhood was ruined by a hypersensitivity to the physical sufferings of others. And then, when she was twelve, a horseback-riding accident caused a nasty concussion. In the strange and torturous aftermath, Melissa's empathic condition got worse. She severely felt other people's pain, to the point of becoming disabled. Then she developed psychic powers.

Clairvoyance can be a dubious gift. Melissa then suffered the emotional disruptions that seers are forced to endure. In addition to those troubles, she succumbed to an eating compulsion.

After years of psychiatric counseling, which hadn't helped her at all, Melissa, by then a young woman, decided to act on a recurring intuition. She would retreat herself into prostitution.

She'd had no prior experience in whoring, and was acquainted with no one in it; she couldn't explain her feeling of this strong, astonishing urge. She was certain, however, that she should whore. She knew, somehow, that whoring would heal her.

The first thing to do was to seek the right location. In a boarding house, in a peaceful London neighborhood, she found herself the right spot.

> The room is quiet, white, gentle. No one knows [I'm] here. It's beautiful.[9]

She was determined to only see people in her new self-employment, and to stave off emotional entanglements.

> [I] just want clients, not to socialize and be available to people...

At first glance, her withdrawal might appear to be unhealthy. It could be the isolation that often precedes self-destruction. But Melissa was on a positive mission, and soon she was remarkably content. Her prescience had served her well. As a totally self-employed sex worker, receiving her clients in secret, she gained, for the first time ever, a desperately needed sense of control. She was no longer forced to tolerate the discomforts of the buttoned-up, boxed-in, work-a-day world. She didn't have to answer to a boss. She didn't have to languish, "trapped in angles and ugliness," underpaid in an office or a shop.

She had deeply retreated to reduce her perceptual hell. She had decided to do this completely alone, no longer submitting to doctors and pharmaceuticals, and no longer subjecting herself, in her over-sensitive state, to a fulltime onslaught, in the world outside, of environmental pollutants, health-challenged people, and her devastating encounters with other people's suffering.

> A client is licking me. I've accidentally read about torture in [a magazine]. I feel the pain in my body but not for days after, as I used to. As a three-year old I had a diphtheria jab, and when my baby sister had hers I cried with her pain. Saw only four films before I was eighteen. Someone was burned in each one. I felt their pain years after. Here there are happy smiling faces on the pillows. Now I feel other people's pleasure, there's no pain.

In that cloistered and lucrative room, Melissa was able to negotiate her bizarre vulnerabilities. Her chosen convalescence—a therapy no doctor would begin to consider—was the giving and receiving of sexual pleasure, for both money and peace of mind. She had taken leave of the world, and yet she was assertively taking it on, through the narrow yet intensely illuminating portal of sexual intimacy with many. As a result, she was measurably, inexorably, getting herself quite strong.

> No one could take possession of my mind.

She intuitively sought a diet full of fresh fruits, juices, and fasting.

> ...eating is becoming unfearful and wholesome. I'm learning to control the cravings I had. The room is bare of stored food....and I can afford to eat beautiful food.

Melissa fasted for one day each week, and that was also her day off from clients. On the following day, she would resume her work, feeling refreshed from the fast, and able to tolerate the hints, that clients brought to her haven, of the outer world's toxicity.

> I feel my insides rested and clean and taste red grape
> juice. Some nicotined lips pass by.

Melissa's discovery of whoring-as-retreat was not the result of financial desperation, and not stumbled upon by chance. She had been filled with a mysterious foreknowledge, arrived at by herself, that the work is an aid to well being. Urged on by her gift of the sixth sense, she veered from conventional healing paths and headed for the ancient whore-priesthood. She fielded ambivalent comments made about her work by her clients, and she pitied all people in other jobs, knowing, despite its censure, that "working naked" is health-promoting. Working naked is natural.

Working naked was straightening her out.

> From the cupboard I take my drawing book from years
> ago. I turn to a new page and open my tin of oil pastels.
> I do what I feel. I do one complete apple. That's what I
> am and around me is free space. Flick through previous
> pages where I was a white and egglike creature,
> sometimes with drops of blood inside, crushed and
> hemmed in by other shapes.

Eventually, Melissa felt ready to brave the world outside. She felt strong enough to handle the empathies in committed, fulltime relationships. She felt healthy enough to withstand, fulltime, the assaults to her body of pollutants. She decided she would visit a clinic. She would go there because she was curious. She wanted to see how well she might fare on diagnostic tests.

After the testing, she was told that she had hypoglycemia, a recently-discovered condition, a blood sugar imbalance. She was told the condition had been aggravated by her serious childhood concussion. She was told that this was the physical cause of her years spent compulsively eating.

She was told to eat foods that she'd already been consuming, such as fresh fruits, and she was advised to deny herself things, such as alcohol, nicotine, and coffee. Melissa had already been strictly avoiding all of those things on her own.

She was told that her affliction was mild.

Privately, Melissa acknowledged that her disorder had once been severe. Now it was almost gone. She had accomplished that process of healing without any medical knowledge or aid.

She then went to see a New Age sort of analyst, who gave her a test called "aura diagnosis." As the woman studied Melissa's results, she informed her subject that she could see she possessed a "tremendous creative healing energy."

Melissa was hardly surprised.

I wonder whether that analyst, that contemporary of Chellis Glendinning, would have been awfully surprised to learn that her subject was a whore. Would she have shrunk from that discovery in shock, or would she have perceived it, correctly, as Melissa's constructive rebellion? Would she have recognized that Melissa had attuned herself to the Goddess, and had revived in herself, to get herself well, the ancient healer-whore-priestess?

Melissa dubbed her last chapter "Happy Ending Time." The reader is left to wonder whether she continued to whore.

I found out that indeed, Melissa does still whore. And she posts her revelations online. She sports her own "harlot" website. She's a sensual facilitator of healing and sex, complete with a web conversation: *newageharlot.blogspot.com.*

Melissa has certainly conquered her demons.

Any true whore has conquered her demons. That's the trait that renders her *true.* True to herself, true to the memory of matriarchal priestess, and true to the highest standards of the present-day service she renders.

Not all prostitutes are drug-addled car-hoppers who peddle themselves by the gutter. Not all whores are victims of a dire psychological background who feel at home in the grip of coercive, brutal pimps. Not all prostitutes are minors, or diseased, or underprivileged, or in need of any sort of rehab. But the general public, and most feminists, think we all are.

As she "struts her stuff" by the filthy curbside, the pimped and addicted streetwalker portrays, more keenly than anywhere else, the tragic and hideous ruin of women's original power. Not because she's whoring, but because she's *disgracing whoring*.

I am a *true whore*. That is to say, I love myself as a whore, and as a whore I love the world.

I love this lucrative helping profession. I do it not to feed an addiction, and not to turn money over to a scavenging madam or pimp, but only to take good care of myself, and only to take good care of my family, without having to leave my children to work for sixty hours a week. I do it for the money and the blessedly freed-up time, but I also do it because it feels right. This is vital, earthy work for a vital, earthy woman; it suits me.

I'm a tragic child turned tragic woman turned happy exultant hooker. I'm an English major turned divorcé turned single mother turned whore. I'm a fitness instructor turned nutritional consultant turned whore. I'm a writer turned whore turned whore-writer. Because of commitment to a man who wants me to stop, or else inevitable aging, whoring is a lifestyle meant for giving up one day. But I'll never give up its defense.

Whoring has empowered and enriched me. If I cower without a word for its advocacy, if I fail to tell the world about the good things whoring has done for me, then I'm endorsing what women have been pressed into doing for thousands and thousands of years. Hiding our truth. Hiding our brains. Hiding our bodies. Hiding our knowledge. Hiding our wisdom. Making little of our strengths.

No, I won't hide. Not in print.

THE MOTHER
WITHOUT THE WHORE

I went to graduate school at Boston University to study with Anne
Sexton. She committed suicide the semester I arrived. Anyway, what
would I have done with a degree in poetry?

A woman's start-up in whoring can be a sure sign that
calamity has struck. In the woman about to try it, desperation is
often the cause.

But that's not to say that her troubled condition will cause her
to tumble to doom. Her dilemma could be a kind of beneficial
wreckage. It could be the beginning of something constructive. It
could be the demolition that precedes a renovation.

The changes that happen in a woman who learns to "escort"
are the breakdown not of function, but of limits. If she's got what
it takes to become a "happy hooker," then she may somewhat
mirror the *Titanic* character, "Rose," who dashed, with a self-
annihilating purpose, to the gigantic stern of the ship.

Rose was despairing and hopeless. She was planning to throw
herself overboard.

And then she found out, after Jack showed her hope, that she
could open herself up to the horizon, and thrive.

That's how it goes for a joyful prostitute.

As a dangerously poor single mother, I learned that when
nothing permitted works out, the desperate can be driven to the

breaking of the law. And then, as I began my new life as an "escort", I was overcome with good feelings.

Before that, however, I was Rose without Jack. I was buried in pure desolation. The force that pushed me into the whore's life was grim. It was the need to uplift my wretched family. Or die.

The prohibition of whoring builds a thick and forbidding wall. Few women ever break through it. Only we, the initially hopeless, get desperate enough to smash it. Then lo and behold, we stumble onto an amazing and hidden truth: prostitution can be pure liberation!

The rest of the world is unaware of that truth, and declares whores a feminine ruin—we are "fallen." That word makes me burst out laughing. *Fallen?* After I learned sex work, I soared!

Before I became an "escort", however, my life was impossible. I was overworked, yet unbearably broke, and my children were neglected and emotionally disturbed. I worked both days and nights. I was gone from home sixty to seventy hours a week, earning little and leaving my sons all alone.

My absence was destroying my family.

My oldest son was teen-aged. My middle son was a preteen. Those two were badly damaged. They reeled from emotional woundings.

Their father, who had once been attentive, had recently gone through his second bad divorce. His first one had been from me. Now he was demoralized, doing a lot of drugs, and becoming apathetic. He no longer seemed to care about much, and that included his children. He had virtually deserted his sons. They almost never saw him.

The boys also had an ex-stepfather. Before I split up with that guy, he routinely emotionally and physically abused them.

The two of them were walking around with all that.

Last but not least, my boys had to deal with me. I was horribly overextended. I was guilty of neglect caused by way too much work. I was also emotionally exhausted.

The depressing limitations of my poverty were the crowning thorns of their pain.

My youngest child was elementary school-aged, and haphazardly cared for by the big boys. He had a different father— the guy who had mistreated his brothers. His dad was occasionally present in his life, but only in a fragmented way.

Neither father paid child support.

My eldest sons' father had fixed things so he wasn't required to give us a dime. He had managed to prove to the courts that he was disabled from a work-related injury. Though he lived in a neighboring town—just a local phone call away—the only support his sons got from him, and the only time they ever saw him, was when he dropped off a couple of cheap Christmas gifts.

My youngest son's father, who, when he had lived with us, could neither hide his resentment for his stepsons nor his sappy adoration of his own flesh and blood, was an okay dad when our child lived with him. But whenever our child lived with me, as he did now, his father was almost never around, and he never helped out financially. And he drank.

He and I had an agreement. We would take turns with physical custody of our son, and whichever one was keeping him would not force financial support from the other. That seemed fair in theory, but in practice it was not. He had only one child, and a family to help him out. I had to contend with the needs of *three* kids, and with no help whatsoever!

But you see, I was Superwoman. I needed to live up to the agreement. If I didn't, I'd feel like a feministic failure.

When my eldest sons' rebellious behavior was becoming really alarming, for a while I kept calling *their* father. I begged him to come over just to show them he cared. I implored him to simply show up when he could, and spend time with his sons while I worked.

Every single time I called him, he would coldly decline. He was obliging a woman he lived with who wanted him all to herself. His drugs were also affecting him. His stock response to my anxious calls was the most chilling string of words that I've ever heard spoken. He'd say:

"I've got my own life. Leave me alone."

Soon I gave up, and did.

I had no hope of paying for a full-time childcare provider. And even if I could have, I'm sure that the outcome would have been darkly absurd. My teenager and his preteen brother would have scared off the bravest of housekeepers or nannies. What my sons needed was a man. What I needed was a large enough income to pay for a qualified caregiver. I didn't earn a nickel's worth of income for that, and I believe that it wouldn't have mattered if I did; I don't think male nannies exist.

The early loss of my parents was taking a terrible toll.

If the nuclear family can be seen as a temple, mine had always lacked critical pillars. After a motherless childhood and an early adulthood torn apart by the death of my father, I was carrying on as a single working mother with not just the lack of the fathers' support, but also without any loving assistance from a maternal-grandparents team.

Single working mothers all around me were saying: "I leave the kids with my Mom."

I was acutely alone.

The paternal grandparents of my older two sons were alive, but they may as well have been dead. They had moved far away, to warmer weather. They sent ten dollars to each of their grandsons at Christmas, and another ten bucks on their birthdays. That was it. They never came north to see them, and never invited them down. They had nothing to say to me at all, no offer of help, not even a greeting. They were selfish and ignorant people.

My youngest son's paternal grandparents were also alive. They were somewhat more helpful. Thank God, they lived only about ten miles away. Sometimes, they availed themselves as sitters for him.

But only him.

Some single mothers have a sibling to rely on. My one and only full-blooded sibling lived in a neighboring town, but I never turned to him. I never even spoke to him. He was my closest living relative. But I'd recently found, to my horror, that that didn't mean a damn thing.

Since my brother had been seven and I had been ten, we'd been raised by different people. We'd even been raised in different states. Even when our father stopped traveling, and finally took me in, his children remained separated, because he didn't take in his son. I guess the prevailing opinion was that my brother seemed nice and secure where he was, so why uproot him from there.

Many years after our father's death, I would bitterly learn that our early unjoining had severely parched, in my brother, the depth of bonding and caring and loyalty that ought to exist between parentless siblings. I had moved to Massachusetts for a number of reasons, not the least of which was that he lived there. But later on I would be forced to conclude, from an agonized wakeup call, that he and his wife were attitudinally just a pair of "fair weather" relatives.

Well, these days we're talking, and sometimes we visit, but hell will freeze over before I'll ever find the courage to test their love again. I'm afraid of how badly they'd hurt me, again. My brother and his wife are charming and warm, and I'd even say exceptionally cordial, when they invite me to spend a little time in their home. But I know they're not dependable as real, down-home, always-stand-by-you family. They're not to be turned to in a crisis.

And they're not to be trusted with the truth. If ever I were to tell my brother that I've spent years as a sex worker, I'm afraid I'd lose him again.

The hardest thing about coping with that is I'm painfully aware that I wouldn't be like that. If my brother turned up at my doorstep, in trouble, I'd gladly open my home to him. I'd allow him to stay for as long as he needed. I'd let him impose on me, always. He could get in my way or annoy me, whatever. He could be someone radically different from me, and I wouldn't care at all. He's my family. I know I'd accept that. I would tell my spouse that he had to, as well. My brother would have to do something horrendous before I'd tell him to leave. He'd have to molest my children, or shit and piss in my food, or deliberately burn my house down, before I'd push him away.

Well, I bitterly learned that it's not in my sibling to go that distance for me. I found that he does have it in him to rid himself of me in a heartbeat. Guardian relatives did that to me, over and over, when I was a kid. So my brother upholds a family tradition! He does what he's been taught! When it's time to lighten his heavy load, his sister's the thing to dump off!

Back when I was burning away in poor-single-motherhood hell, my brother had recently done that. My brother had shattered my heart. I was feeling so hurt that I couldn't go near him.

And I didn't, for eleven whole years.

I sent him a perfunctory card each December, just as though he were nothing but a barely known acquaintance. I never went to see him, not even on Christmas Day. For all those years, that was it. Our children, first cousins, were growing up strangers. That caused me a lot of sorrow, but it kept me safe from having to witness the lack of my sibling's love.

I lived just eight miles from my brother. I was estranged, isolated, depressed, and overwhelmed. I was sinking into dangerous dejection. But I told myself that I'd sell myself before

I'd ever ask him for anything, again. I thought I was just being rhetorical. But oh, I should have known better! I usually end up pretty much doing exactly what I say.

During that time, my oldest son, Ayden, was a total party animal. He was an eager disciple of teenaged revolt.

He had once been a remarkably good-natured child. As a newborn, he almost never cried. Even when the doctor roughly yanked him out of me, and slapped his tiny wet bottom, my firstborn contentedly greeted the world with not a wail, but an affable gurgle.

At the age when most toddlers cling fiercely to their toys and roar at their playmates: "No! Mine!"—Ayden had been happy to share. By the time he started school, it was clear that he lived to have fun. All the other little guys loved him; my home teemed with merrily romping young boys.

When he reached his teens, however, and my single-mother apartment was yet full of his friends, the toys and bikes and *Legos* of yore became beer and pot and skipped school. That went on daily and nightly while I worked. I felt forced to reconsider Ayden's easygoing childhood. Maybe it had not been such a good thing. Maybe his fun-loving nature as a child had been a portent of this adolescent hedonism.

One thing was horribly certain. I was away from home far too often, and a very irresponsible teen was in charge.

I eventually turned to the Department of Social Services. I called the agency believing it existed for parents like me. I was a statistic it was funded to help. A family caseworker was assigned to me.

When he came to my apartment for the first time, I couldn't wait to get him inside, sit him down, and appeal to him for all the types of help my family needed.

I explained to him that the father of my eldest sons was formally unemployed, and that he'd been freed by the system from having to pay child support. Yet I'd heard that he worked off the books. Could that be investigated? "No," my caseworker flatly responded. It was the late nineteen-eighties, and dead-beat dads working out-of-sight jobs were not yet getting flushed out.

In the past I'd applied for a rent subsidy through the Section Eight Housing Act. For years I'd been on my town's waiting list. Acceptance would lower my rent to almost nothing, which would mean I could drop at least one of my jobs, and neglect my family

A WOMAN WHOSE CALLING IS MEN — BOOK ONE

much less. I asked my caseworker whether Social Services could speed up the acceptance process. "No," he firmly told me. "We have nothing to do with that."

My children spent their daytime hours well supervised, in school. Actually, that wasn't entirely true; Ayden kept playing hooky, and eventually, he would drop out. Night was the dangerous time, for them all. That was when all of my sons were alone. I asked my worker whether the Department could hook me up with state-subsidized, evening childcare. A tender-tough, *male* caregiver would be perfect—an actual "night watchman" for my sons.

"No, nothing like that is available," he replied. "You'll have to stop working nights." I countered his remark with the obvious: my supplemental jobs were indispensable, and night was the only time I had for earning that crucial extra income. If I sacrificed any of the jobs I worked--day or night—my shaky provider means would topple.

I kept on about this with my palms facing him.

He blandly stared at me.

I asked him whether the Big Brother Association could help me with my boys.

"No. Their waiting list is several years long."

Sigh.

Now I got ready to tell this nay-sayer about the scariest thing. My middle son, Jeremy, was at risk for injuries from Ayden.

Jeremy was intense and perceptive, a naturally responsible kid. He probably would have fared better if he'd been my oldest child. Indeed, if he were the eldest, the son that was always in charge, the whole family might have fared better.

As a student and a child athlete, Jeremy applied himself well. He always got decent grades. Even in the absence of adult supervision, he always got his homework done. Whether or not I was there to chauffer him, somehow he got to his practice meets and games.

He constantly harped at his older brother for his partying, school-skipping craziness. That annoyed Ayden a lot.

And Ayden was currently teaching his younger sibling about pecking-order abuse. Ayden had suffered most often as their ex-stepfather's scapegoat. Emotionally and physically treated like dirt, he was the kid that my most recent ex had obsessively mistreated. That had been the reason for my latest marital breakup.

129

And now my boy who had once been so happy, my boy who had once been my fun son, had internalized all that cruelty. He had begun to brutalize Jeremy. A frightening pattern of violence had developed. I saw painful beatings I was powerless to stop. I suspected that, in my absence, the attacks were even worse, and that Jeremy was afraid to tell me.

I asked my caseworker what could be done.

For the first time since he'd sat down at my table, he nodded his head in assent; he was programmed to do something about sibling abuse. He sat up a little straighter. He struck an authoritative pose. "You need family counseling," he said.

Yuh THINK???

The kids and I had already tried counseling—the kind that's provided for the poor.

I had specifically requested a male counselor. We had sat for a very long hour before a meek-mannered Masters Program student. He'd presided with an expression of stage-struck dismay. He'd asked his long list of "preliminary questions" and squinted at my children as though they were exams.

Uninspired and virtually twitching with boredom, my sons had eventually tuned him out. They had slipped off their chairs, all goofy-faced, and rolled in a wrestle at my feet. The only good thing I can say about that meeting is that their rough-housing didn't turn hostile.

On the way home, Ayden had opined about counseling. "It *sucks!*"

He'd been echoed by agreement from his brothers. He'd announced that he'd never go back.

And how was I to make him? I couldn't physically force him to go; he was a tough and strapping fifteen. I couldn't ground him for refusing to go; I was gone far too often to keep him in. I couldn't bend his will by denying him things; I had nothing to withhold.

If raising a teen is a power struggle, I had long since lost the battle.

"The Department won't intervene," said the emissary I'd summoned, "until Ayden puts Jeremy in the hospital."

And what did "intervene" mean?

"Your violent child would be removed from the home."

Can't help you with this. Can't help you with that. His negative responses were like inner tubes with slashes. They sank when I grabbed them while drowning. But I could count on the Department for one thing: the forced separation of my children.

Yeah, like my brother and me.

I stared at my hands. They were clenched in my lap. My caseworker glanced at his watch.

His final words were like the punch line to a sick joke.

He advised me to turn into a full-time mom by quitting all my jobs and getting on welfare. Despite the impending welfare reforms, he'd submit, on my behalf, an urgent and fruitful plea. He believed that his office could convince the state that the violence, delinquency and substance abuse of Ayden, coupled with my work-induced neglect, made us critically needful of public assistance.

I knew from experience that life on welfare would be a financial suicide. I'd tried it once, back when the kids had been little. A stay-at-home welfare mother of three got—monthly— some food stamps and a few hundred dollars. That amount was the same, **with or without** a Section Eight rent subsidy, and I was **without**. That monthly handout, which was supposed to cover **all** my family's living expenses except food, would come to **less than my rent!** And if I worked, they'd slash the check down.

But my caseworker insisted.

That's right, taxpayers. That guy was urging me to go get on welfare. You provide his paycheck, and he wanted us added to the dole.

I thanked him for his "service," and then I saw him out the door. From then on, I ignored all his phone calls.

I had always assumed that there were "programs" available for all the families like mine. Now I knew that they were out there, all right, but inadequate to a nearly useless degree. Now I was aware, more than ever, of just how dangerously alone we were.

I devoted myself to strategies for staying strong and sane. I managed to get to the gym. To this I devoted my lunch hours, or small windows of time between jobs and the kids. Like a nicotine addict pursuing her butt breaks, I grabbed every chance to work out. Exercise became my survival. It was prayers of sweat and machines and iron, deeply pooled strength around a killer knot of stress.

Working out and trying to eat right preserved my physical health. I believe it increased my emotional resilience. But no such lifeline would prevail for long before the tidal wave of circumstance engulfed me.

The wave relentlessly approached.

It was overwhelming to feed and clothe my kids. As growing boys, their appetites were huge. They outgrew all their shoes and clothes long before they were a quarter paid for.

My old little car, which got me from job to job, was suffering as much as my family from neglect. To find the time or the money for even oil changes took planning.

Ayden's rebellion got worse. He wouldn't get up to go to school. Consequently, my day might begin with a dubious challenge to my fine state of physical fitness. After sweet-talking him, then nagging him, then desperately badgering him, I would shoulder his mattress off its box spring. I would roll him right onto the floor. Or I might end up trying to pull him off Jeremy, who could inspire Ayden to violence, right from his deepest sleep.

In the late afternoons, I'd come home to a tiny apartment made crowded and stuffy by a pack of lounging teens. I could smell the beer and the weed, and I could see all the glassiness in matching pairs of eyes conspiring to try to look normal. I could never find their head toys, however. Kids got high, kids got drunk, but they ingeniously hid their means.

Before I would leave for my night job, I would attempt law and order by sending friends home. But I knew that in my absence, they'd probably come right back. I would fix supper, help with the homework, and pray that no beatings would happen that night, no partying or mischief while I was away.

The rent got raised. That was done in conjunction with the landlord's threat to oust us. He was mindful of the hazard of routinely unsupervised kids.

I had rented this place because it was an easy move-in, a cheap weekly rental that cost little to secure. I had discovered, in being a renter, that cheap can be synonymous with unsafe and unhealthy. There were Health and Fire Department violations all through the apartment and outer house. I dared not report them. As a result, we'd end up evicted by a retaliating a landlord who already wanted us gone. So we were stuck there. There was no way I could save the money for the first and last months' rent plus security required for a better place.

In other words, if the landlord threw us out, we'd be homeless.

So we languished there, in a dilapidated Victorian house with siding peeling from mildewed boards. There were rotting holes in the porches. There were three small musty apartments. Ours--a three-room hovel that I shared with my large male children—was complete with decaying flooring and noisy, inadequate heating.

An alleged cocaine dealer lived upstairs.

The neglected yard was strewn with years upon years of moldering litter.

On one rare day off, I got out there and cleared it all away. I was motivated not only by the pain of looking so shabby, but also by the fear of injury to my kids. All around the foundation of the house, there were half-buried glass smithereens. Some time before we moved here, a vandal must have smashed all the windows. The windows had been replaced, but the deadly pieces of broken glass had never been thoroughly removed. What a fine, safe play area for my youngest little boy!

I knew that it was useless to complain about it. My slumlord would do nothing about it. His contempt-hardened eyes would convey to me: *You don't like it? Move.*

So I picked it all up myself. I threw myself into the horrible chore with the attitude that this was a blessing. This was an outdoor activity. This was healthy. This was an escape from the poor ventilation at my jobs, and even my gym. And for once, I was being domestic. I was home.

As I worked in that dangerously glittering dirt, I occasionally looked up. I was enjoying the cool breeze and warm sunshine intermingling on my face. I breathed deeply of the fresh, sweet, autumnal New England air. I pulled off the cheap, tattered gloves I was using, and grimly inspected my fingers. They were bloody and filthy. Then I drew the gloves back over them, and resumed my collection of shards.

In our first springtime there, I purchased some two-holed cinderblocks. With the help of my big sons, I laboriously placed them in a solid row on the planks that topped the plywood that enclosed our ugly porch. That May, and each May that we lived there thereafter, I filled those cement holes with potting soil and grew pink and purple cascades of petunias. I watered them with a plastic pitcher that I filled at the kitchen sink.

Those cinderblocks were so heavy and strong. They were cheap but comforting symbols of the security my kids and I painfully lacked. Those burgeoning, bobbing, trumpet-shaped flowers defiantly asserted their beauty. They were bright and fragrant gushes of color against dingy tenement grays.

On one fine summer day, my drug-dealing neighbor walked out on his rickety balcony. It overlooked my first-floor porch. He gingerly leaned over his warped and sagging railing, and gaped down at my flourishing contrivance of a garden. He spied me obsessively tending it, and said:

"You know, when it comes to being fucked up, there's such a thing as bad fucked-up, and there's such a thing as good fucked-up. *You*, my friend, are definitely *good* fucked-up."

My sons found less constructive outlets. There was damage to both capillaries and sheet rock from Ayden's punches of rage. There were calls from neighborhood merchants. They were holding my resourceful Jeremy for his newest accomplishment: stealing. There were hangovers suffered by my eight-year old, Jesse, who considered it a big-boy privilege to be fed beer, in my absence, by his oldest brother and friends.

My two older sons were often hateful to me. As residents of a middle class, small New England town, they were profoundly embarrassed by our poverty. Before my last ousting of a partner—their stepfather—we had lived in better housing. Ayden in particular was upset by our material loss. It shamed him. He felt small in front of his friends. He punished me for it with surly attitudes, disrespectful language, and utter disregard for my rules.

My poverty and my absences were damaging my kids in ways that I'll never forgive myself for. And I wonder whether my eldest sons' father has ever learned any remorse. His total desertion, at that time in boys' lives when Dad's needed like the sun, was turning his sons into monsters.

In their heads their real father's rejection was coupled with the memory of stepfather cruelty.

Boys don't whine or cry. They rip out their pain and shape it into missiles.

I was a logical target. So were the walls Ayden pummeled. And the neighbors' properties, burgled by Jeremy.

And God help me, so were some animals.

Ayden and Jeremy's abusiveness to me was a behavior learned from their ex-stepfather, and also from their own father. They had seen it unloaded on me. When they were tots, their father would assault me. He'd verbally attack with the emotional brutality that seems to be the signature behavior of deeply insecure men. A couple of times, he got physical. He permanently damaged some nerves in my face. He punched rainbows into my skin there. He thoroughly reddened the whites of my eyes. Once, for a whole month, my face frightened children. Even my own babies were scared by my appearance. Adults who saw me were horrified.

That had been the death knell for that marriage.

I divorced him and met Jesse's father. Then that union fell apart. I cried a copious rivulet of tears, but doggedly kept on going. I embraced my new status as three boys' single mom. I had an upbeat, pioneering, feministic verve. I believed that I could handle it all. I believed that I could be fine, all alone. I believed I could nurture my sons by myself. I believed I'd prevail and succeed through it all with no burned-out holes in my solitary courage.

Sure.

I was slaving, around the clock, for children who seemed to loathe me. I remember becoming certain that the pain would never end. Things got so ugly that, on one grueling afternoon, while Jeremy was being particularly disrespectful, suddenly someone was knocking on our door. I pulled aside the curtain on the window in the door. The cocaine dealer from upstairs stood out there. I opened the door to him. He entered and immediately strode over to Jeremy and slapped him, hard, on the face. Then he turned to me and said:

"I'm sorry, but I just couldn't help that. You work so hard, and these little bastards treat you like shit. I can hear it going on, all the fucking time. I'm sorry. I just couldn't stop myself."

Then he sadly returned to his dump.

My preteen son was shocked. But he was angry, too. The audacity of that scumbag going moral on him! At the age of eleven, Jeremy knew that he could turn the guy in for hitting him.

But Jeremy never did, and he watched himself after that. He actually tried harder to be good. Until the guy moved away.

I also remember a guidance counselor who attempted to comfort me. She looked like a well-seasoned grandmother. She was one of just a few school officials who didn't make me feel harshly judged. She told me to picture my kids all grown up. She confided that once, she, too, had been stranded in my single-mom world, exhausted and alone, with hostile children.

"It's horrible, I know," she gently empathized. "It's a nightmare."

135

She continued: "But it does end. It really does. They grow up. They thank you. Things get better. Try to believe that."

I believed nothing. But somehow, I kept going.

From his sixth year to his twelfth, I had kept Ayden in Little League baseball. Now he spurned all sports. But Jeremy and Jesse were avidly athletic. They were both in Pop Warner football. They loved the game, and both were star players. Though I always feared injury to them, I appreciated the normalcy of their involvement with that sport, that disciplined outlet for masculine aggression. It sure beat the hell out of Jeremy's new habit of stealing.

I had neither the money for the fees nor the time to watch them play, but somehow I managed it, anyway.

I would crouch on the hard metal bleachers, alone amongst the other boys' cheering moms and dads. I cared little for football, and I didn't understand all the various rules and plays. Usually, it was cold out. The cold actually hurt me, and I knew that I should be elsewhere, accomplishing something, like laundry. But I shivered away and stayed put.

Both of my boys were always starters. The one I was there for would glance at the bleachers. He'd pick me out and wave, relieved that I'd made it; I could see his surge of elation right through his shoulder pads.

Then he'd play like hell.

The electronic revolution was taking over homes. The national indoor pastime for kids was a riveted crouch in front of luminous screens. Remotes were clutched in fiercely jabbing fingers. Social ineptitude threatened my sons, if they couldn't be hooked up to those games. They were already horribly parentally deprived. I couldn't deprive them electronically, as well.

I saw it as a strategy. Video games and MTV might help to subdue them, to keep them off the street. So I took on the expense of cable TV just as though it were essential, like the heat and the phone. I made sure that my sons had their *Play Stations*, or whatever they were called back then. Those games were important, like my stash of nutritional supplements. I made sure that we had those survival aids, even if I had to self-sacrifice to the point of holes on the bottoms of my shoes, or tampons made of toilet paper.

A computer for them was beyond my reach, and that always worried me.

Everything, all the time, worried me. Everything related to home. I learned to use work as an uplifting escape. I would arrive at my jobs with a smile on my face. It was a mask that I wore with a flourish.

At my waitress jobs, coworkers called me a riot. Whenever they needed good humor, it was me to whom they'd turn for a laugh. "When are you working again?" they'd implore me. "It's only fun when you're here!" At one of the restaurants I was called "Funny Girl." That I could pull off such a cheery-seeming image is a testament, I guess, to the success of my cover-up of where I really was.

The people who I cared for as a home health aid regarded me as their angel. It was soothing for me when I comforted them, and so I attended them well.

Whenever I worked at a health club, other trainers and the members made me feel supremely special. They called me "the workout queen." They thought I was otherworldly. They construed my physical fitness—and my signature good spirits—as the sign of a superior life. They had no idea that my disciplined workouts were a desperate attempt to survive.

My college education had prepared me to teach. I was certified to teach English to kids in grades six through twelve. I didn't last, however, as a substitute high school teacher; I had lost the desire to pursue a fulltime position; the work didn't pay well, and worst of all, it reminded me too much of home.

People who enjoyed me in the workplace had no inkling of my failures at home. The same was true of my friends. I should have been seeking out comfort from them, but I almost never did; I kept them unaware of my shameful situation with the excuse that I was too busy. *No, I'm sorry, you can't come over, because I'll be working, I won't be home.*

Occasionally, however, we'd gab on the phone. On the phone I'd convey to them that things had gotten rough, but I wasn't going to let them come *see;* though the distance I created from all of my friends increased my isolation, it also saved my pride.

I needed to conceal the truth. I was a triple disaster. At home, I was bombing every which way. As a homemaker, a parent and a provider, I was a miserable failure. Luckily, none of my friends lived close by, or surely, they would have **noticed.** It was bad enough already that other people saw. Teachers, school principals, the landlord, juvenile judges, the neighbors, the local police, ripped-off local shopkeepers, and other disgusted witnesses—they *knew*.

Only my kids saw my shame. They saw my head hanging, and my pain-stricken eyes, and the dampness on my cheeks from the brushed-away tears. My kids could see I was diminishing. I was caving in to the constant horror of being too alone, and soul-crushingly poor, and much too overextended. And regardless of all of my efforts, my sons were becoming punks.

I was close to falling apart.

That only made my kids worse.

THE CALL OF THE DANCE

I dressed up in my sexiest…to dance on amateur night.

"Why'd you wear those stupid pants?"

Ayden's indignant question shot down the stairs to me. I was perching on a low step between floors one and two. Ayden was crouching on a step high above me. We were waiting for Ayden's probation officer to come out of his pre-court meeting.

It was Juvenile Day at the courthouse.

Outside of the probie's office, long wooden benches were crammed with first-come, first-sit parents and their children. All of the minors present were lawbreaking offenders. Ayden and I had arrived too late to get anything better for sitting than these narrow slices of stair.

It was always like this. The waiting.

I was determined to get a whole act read from Shakespeare's ***Othello***, right here. But the step was so hard on my butt! And there were interruptions.

"Mom!"

"What."

He repeated his question, a bit louder this time.

"Why'd you wear those stupid pants?"

I couldn't say why right away. I never knew just what to say when Ayden bugged me for not dressing "cool." He wanted me to look like the girls at the high school. I knew it was a roundabout compliment, and I didn't want to discourage the few that I got. Ayden would never tell a washed-up old frump to stuff herself into Juniors fashions.

But I wasn't going to turn myself out like a teenager, and sometimes my garb fell so far from the mark that my son got a little annoyed.

I steered my mind just far enough from Act Five to retain what I'd just read, and thought of an answer to shut him up.

"All my jeans are dirty."

"Well, wash them."

I went back to *Othello* and tried to get completely immersed. It wouldn't happen, of course. But my will to attempt it had to hold on, or I'd get lost in the pain of having to be here. It would swallow me up and I'd die.

Motion suddenly gathered before me, and I shoved myself over to allow the ascent of a handcuffed kid and his cop. Ayden knew the kid; I could hear their hearty exchange. I forsook the dilemmas of *Othello* to turn around and sneak an upward glance at my son.

He was smirking.

Smirking!

Why didn't he find such things grim? What could be so goddam funny about a friend pushed upstairs in cuffs? I thought of the work hours I was missing to be here with my smirker, on this court day for wayward youths. My mind riffled through the rest of the week, trying to land on a spot of free time when one of my bosses might let me make up for the monetary loss of today. Then my thinking shattered into a randomly strewn collage. The fridge (what's in it?) the supermarket (which one can I hit the fastest?) how much gas is left how much time before they shut off the phone is there dog food did I pay Sears oh my God the *laundry*.

I forced my eyes back to *Othello* and couldn't remember a thing. Then a feeling bloomed, a wrenchingly sad one that felt good, and I recalled that Desdemona was about to get killed. Murdered by the man she adored!

Lately the world of great literature had been doggedly tugging on my brain. It was urgent, a pull as consuming as a birth. I'd responded by bonding with Shakespeare. His characters were so real, so perfectly flawed.

I'd encountered the bard while digging in a closet for a half-crushed box of old clothes. The clothing would do for my youngest son, Jesse, the child still too small to be obsessed with the latest in exactly what his peers would let him wear. I'd spotted the dilapidated carton full of castoffs, my savior from a plummet into Walmart's greedy maw, and then noticed, or perhaps I remembered, that directly behind it stood a sturdier container than the beat-up boxed hoardings of distressed single moms; it was an ancient box loaded with textbooks from my long-gone college days.

What a find!

And now I was caught up in rereading those treasures. They were proving to be precious old friends. How much more I could glean, at this older, more bleak and dire time of my life, from their abundance of strife, pain, and wisdom!

My plan, in bygone years, had been to spend my working life as a high school English teacher. For a while I had somewhat enjoyed that endeavor. But later, my troubles as a solitary parent made me need to lose the workplace full of what I faced at home, which was acting-out kids with big issues.

And besides, went my thinking, when you counted up the nights full of lesson preps, and those papers corrected after hours, and the time you were expected to sacrifice for extracurricular clubs—it was clear that teaching school shared way too much stress with the snaggings of parenthood. Teaching was noble and enriching, it was sometimes all those things, yes—but it was nerve-racking too, on a regular basis—and with no hope of monetary gain.

So now, as you know, I worked as a waitress, and I companioned the old and the sick, and I advised the members at a health club on how to melt off their fat.

My best income came from the waitressing, but I'd been doing that way too long. Though my restaurant skills had honed over time into a grace that was almost athletic, I always felt a little like a jerk out there, serving diners and drinkers with the hope of good leavings, for smidges of cash left along with the crumbs.

Waiting on tables felt like some sort of desperate. Working for tips felt like scavenging.

How many times had my coworkers said that they'd do this til they found a *real job?*

I'd once lived for the ideals of teaching.

Once upon a time, I'd felt that teaching could be like the lifting up of a heavy, priceless urn, and then trying to pour its gleaming contents into thousands of empty cups. But teaching often ended up as only the heavy and the trying.

Just like being a parent.

So now I enjoyed teaching *me*. Here in my old college literature books lay the beauty of constructive escape. In my readings, I self-connected. I got to explore every facet of myself that wasn't just a waitress and a young lawbreaker's mother.

Right here in the courthouse, I digested one beautiful page. I carefully, lovingly savored each Elizabethan phrase. Then the door to the office swung open, and out strode the juvenile probation officer.

It was time to follow his lead.

We rose from our perches and trudged behind the probie, up to the second floor. All of the other families followed. Once there, we scored ourselves a length of bench that was clamped to the wall before the big courtroom doors.

The doors were cryptically closed. Ayden's turn in there loomed before us like a dark, inscrutable cavern.

"This better not take too long," he warned. "I'll be so fucking pissed if it does."

"Ayden! Don't swear."

"Yeah, yeah, yeah."

Othello was stashed deep away now, down in my purse where it might have to stay until I found myself waiting again, like at the end of a shopping-cart line. I focused completely on my son. He was slouched against the back of the bench with his long legs splayed far apart, big shoes pointed straight up. He drummed some big fingers on his slim thighs, staring straight ahead at nothing. His eyes were like mine, but not his expression.

"Ayden," I began. "You're about to face the judge. Don't lay around here like you're at home! Sit up straight! Be *respectful*."

"Yeah, yeah, yeah." He pulled himself up, just a little. It always got me, how after all these years of trying to teach him the right way to behave, Ayden could be such a blueprint of his father.

How could that be? Ayden hardly knew the guy.

The guy didn't even have a clue that his eldest son was in trouble. He wasn't worth the telling.

This was Ayden's first criminal offense. I had yet to see him in handcuffs, and my mind wouldn't focus the picture. We'd wound up in here on other Juvenile Days, but always just for Ayden's truancy, or his craziness at home; in the past I'd had him before the judge for skipping school, for beating on his "tween" brother Jeremy, and for violently attacking my apartment. According to the Massachusetts juvenile laws, none of that was quite bad enough for cuffs or incarceration. But ever since the judge got involved, things had improved a bit; Ayden seemed to be learning, at least in front of Mom, to tune out his irksome brother, and he'd been getting himself to school. And it had also been a while since he'd punched a wall or a door.

Of course, the kitchen table would never again be the same. Any time an elbow leaned, its round top flipped like a coin. Ayden couldn't fix all the things he broke, and neither could I. And I was still paying Visa for that table! But lately, most likely because of the judge, he hadn't damaged anything new.

Maybe Ayden was learning to live with his rage. Maybe he was learning to live without the love of a man.

Maybe the judge's stern face had achieved that.

But now he'd gone and done this stupid breaking and entering thing, with his friends. They'd gotten into someone's house when no one was home, and they'd taken all the beer, food and cash they could find. Someone had called the police, and Ayden got caught on the crapper with a beer. All of the other guys had already scampered off, and he wouldn't give the cops their names.

And now he was paying for that.

One at a time, other kids were getting called into the courtroom. Ayden got up and stalked off for a smoke. I searched the lobby for a watch. These were the days, the late eighties, before cell phones and other things that always double as clocks. My own watch was home, down with a dead battery I'd forgotten to replace. I located a wrist with the time mooning from it, and winced. The day was getting away. The judge had to see Ayden soon, because Jesse, only eight years old, shouldn't be left alone for long after getting home from school, and Jeremy, my busy twelve-year old, would be needing a ride to practice, and again, the images started to riot. Shopping supper homework. Dirty dishes dirty carpet the ***bathroom***. And there was the bank, and there was my aching tooth, and there was that noise in the engine.

And there was the most anxious question. Would Jesse's grandparents take him for me while I worked tomorrow night? Or would I have to leave him at home, on a crazy Friday night, in the care of his crazy big brother?

But wait. *Tonight* I wouldn't have to deal with such worries. Tonight I had the night off! *Aaaahh.* Such a sweet thought in the midst of the jitters. I knew I should find out whether someone called in sick, so I could go in and earn tips; but screw it. Not tonight. Something about court with my kid made me tired. I impulsively reached for my purse, and fished **Othello** back out.

Shakespeare had keen competition. Parents and their adolescents were waiting all around me, and court-appointed lawyers were scurrying amongst them. I glanced at them all and noticed, as always, that most of the parents were mothers, and most of the offenders were boys.

The mothers had that exhausted, single-parent look. They were dressed as though they'd been uprooted from their jobs, and their eyes looked eternally tired. But they all sat straight-backed, manlessly tough. The tenderness of early motherhood was gone from every worn face. Every pair of eyes looked wary, and maybe a little bit grumpy, but way beyond any tears.

Their sons wore a different expression. They all seemed content, quite at home in this place. I thought of Ayden's smirk on the stairs, and found glimmers of it on every young face.

My own son returned, all smelly from his butt break. His lawyer came over, and the two of them sat down on either side of me, and we all discussed his case. Then the courtroom doors swung open, and someone stood there calling Ayden's name.

As we stepped over the threshold and into the hall of justice, the heavy doors whooshed shut behind us. The buzzing from the throng in the lobby was instantly cut off. A blaring silence hit us.

Ayden was a minor, so his case was being heard privately. But this hall was too big, much too spacious for the few people gathered; I suddenly felt very small. I felt extremely diminished by the long, long expanse between myself and the man way up front, that grim-looking man who had adorned himself in drapey, ominous black.

He was motionless, bored-and-disgusted-looking, yet somehow imposing, very powerfully imposing, like an eons-old towering boulder. He reigned from an elevated fortress of podium, tables and gates; he could certainly make anything happen.

He could certainly crush my boy.

Somebody told us to sit down.

Suddenly Ayden's crime seemed tremendous. We took our seats, and my son didn't slouch. He sat there as straight as I'd taught him to, with his hands and his elbows secured to the chair arms. Above his upper lip, I saw tiny beads of sweat sprout.

In about five minutes, it was over. Ayden wouldn't be cuffed and removed; this was only his first real offense. But he was on formal probation now, which meant having to obey some important new rules. And restitution would have to be made. And the next time he got himself in here, the judge warned—the next time Ayden got himself in here for any reason at all—he wouldn't be going home.

We walked outside, to a sun-struck winter afternoon. The cold and the brightness hit me like slaps, but Ayden wasn't affected. Joy in his freedom propelled him, and he strode fast but completely controlled; there were brakes on his exquisite elation; there was loyalty to his macho boy code.

Yet I could hear his inner cries of relief, and I openly smiled for us both.

We got into the car. He announced that he was starving. Ayden was an eating machine. I knew that his breakfast must feel like yesterday; the vended carbs in the courthouse were nothing but appetizers to him.

"Let's go for a sub," he said.

I thought of a small loaded pizza, and my stomach rippled with need. Then the images started to tumble. The worst of them was Jesse, who was home from school by now, and very much alone. I saw his shirtsleeve, flaming, as he turned from the stovetop, screaming. And his dead blue eyes staring doll-like at his bike wheels, with blood trickling onto the street. My foot put more pressure on the gas pedal.

"I'll drop you off at the sub shop," I said.

"*WHAT!* Screw that! I'm not walking home!"

"I didn't say you have to walk home!"

Now a bad headache attacked me. It was pain spears that started with a merciless jab at my already down-and-out tooth, and then darted like a splinter through my eyes that saw too much, and slammed into my temples like the grip of a tightening wire. It happened in a treacherous flash.

Suddenly my hunger turned queasy. The mindscape of everything I had to do started spinning like a camera on a tripod that's been broken. Panic crouched low, getting ready for the kill, and I ended my response to his rudeness with a meek sighing string of phrases.

"I'll...pick you up...after I get Jesse."

"MOM! YOU'RE GOING THE WRONG WAY!!"

It was true. I'd made a wrong turn.

"You are the *STUPIDEST DRIVER I'VE EVER SEEN!*" Ayden roared. "You *ALWAYS DO THIS!* You have *NO SENSE OF DIRECTION!*"

"I KNOW WHERE I'M GOING!" I snapped, through the pain. I reversed the car in a driveway. "It's just that I have so much on my mind, *I FORGET* to make the right turn."

"You're so *STUPID!*"

"SHUT UP!"

We finally got there. In my purse, I reached past *Othello* for my wallet. Cash meant for laundry detergent and gas went into Ayden's hand. "Get me a small pizza with everything."

"Yeah, yeah, yeah."

Moments later, I got into our apartment. Jesse was fooling around with his dog. No burns, no blood, just a happy third-grader cavorting with his pet. But dogs play so rough. The animal could have gouged out one of his perfect blue eyes. One never knew.

Jeremy trotted up in his uniform.

"There's a practice game today," he announced. "Can you go?"

Guilt put the squeeze on my headache. My shoulders slumped just like a very old woman's, and my chest deeply heaved with a sigh. "Jeremy, I've got so much to do. I don't see how I can. But I promise I'll get to your big game on Sunday. Even if it kills me, I'll be there."

Somehow I remembered to ask Jesse whether he'd already let the dog out to do his stuff; he had. Now we shut in the dog, left the apartment, and we all piled into the car. I informed my younger sons of their big brother's new probation. I dropped Jeremy off at his practice field. Then I circled back to get Ayden, with his smallest sibling strapped in; I threw my mind into eight-year old gear to hear about Jesse's day at school.

Ayden was waiting outside of the sub shop, looking almost full. He held what I hoped was my pizza.

It was. I dropped Ayden off at the house, knowing he was eager to call all his friends and announce: *Yeah, yeah, yeah, I'm still here.* Then I began the afternoon's errands, eating as I drove, sharing the food with Jesse, and almost making two more wrong turns.

I kept my little guy with me, safe from my horrible fears.

Later on, back at home, as I cooked my hungry sons' supper, I planned for a spot in the night—this rare and restful night off—for my enjoyment of the end of **Othello**. It would be after the inspection of homework, after everybody's brushed teeth.

And then, after finishing **Othello**, I would finally get some sleep.

And yet...

Sleep just didn't feel like enough for me, tonight. Sometimes, even as fatigued as I was, I needed an escape a little merrier than rest.

A guy I'd been seeing sprang into my mind, and right away I snuffed out his image. Lately he'd become stabbingly honest about his feelings regarding my "baggage." He wasn't the first guy to make that confession, and I knew it was time to forget him.

Then I thought of someone else, and I busted out gleefully smiling.

Of course! I'd call my new girlfriend, Andrea.

Andrea was a twenty-three year old fitness director. We'd met at one of my job sites, a health club.

"What's so funny, Mom?" one of my boys inquired. I was stirring at the stove with a grin that wouldn't quit.

They rarely saw me smiling.

"Oh, nothing."

On the infrequent evenings when I could get free, my friend and I had been haunting the bars that provided DJ music. Weekend rendezvous' were out of the question, because that was when I worked as a waitress, and that was when Andrea dated. But that was okay, that was actually better, because on weeknights the bar business was slower, so we tended to have the dance floors almost entirely to ourselves.

Young, fit, naturally high Andrea thoroughly understood dancing.

And so, for now and for always, did I.

We'd strut together into those places, always heading straight for the dance floor. We didn't need a table or a drink first; just the floor. We'd drop our purses right at our feet, and peel off our jackets and fling them down too, and our bodies and souls would instantly begin to make beautiful love to the music.

We danced apart yet always attuned, each in our own state of rapture. Every now and then our eyes would chance to meet, and we'd laugh to each other and holler and hoot, two pretty witches empowered by music, the happiest girls in the world.

The men at the bar would stand staring, with their drinks all suspended at their breastbones.

I was almost old enough to be Andrea's mother, but the two of us hardly ever thought about that. We'd never once talked about that. Andrea was a friend from *work*. Andrea was a person from my *work life*. Andrea had never seen my other life, my sad, chaotic, angry-teen household, and my damaged and fatherless, latchkey kids.

Andrea knew nothing of my pain and shame, my poor-single-mother dilemma. And I would **never** show her.

At about nine-thirty or so, when I should have been bedding down for the night with that incredible man named Shakespeare, I peered for a moment at my sleeping younger sons, and I informed a groggy-eyed Ayden that a buddy of mine would be staying with them while I went out for a bit.

A luscious hot bubble bath awaited me. *Othello* was laid by, just past the danger of getting wet. I soaked and read and soaked and read until my body felt stressless and my mind felt the wholeness of a masterpiece fully revisited.

There were tears on my face for Desdemona and Othello, and for everyone else in this whole wide world who's ever been viciously deceived and betrayed, and lost their good sense in the process.

I cast the concluded *Othello* to the door, and then I gave the master his due. One can't finish one of his tragedies, and then just get up and go. I lowered myself further in the bubbles and hot water, and let all the sorrow seep in. Then I sighed, very heavily, very reverently, and I slowly began to wash.

Ah, the glory of taking control! With the simple but powerful little routines! I scrubbed away germs and dead skin from my body. I razored my armpits smooth. I shaved my long legs until my flesh there felt silky. Then I turned on the faucet and turned myself around and dunked my head under the cascade. I washed my hair and massaged my scalp, and then I used handfuls of advertised gunk that might give my tresses a little more body.

I rose dripping and steaming and pink from the water. Bubbles slid down and fell in suds from my breasts. I stepped out of the tub, and reached past the rack full of son-rumpled towels for the shelf with just one folded fresh one. I opened it, draped it around myself, and tenderly blotted my skin. Then I grabbed for my hook-hanging, tattered old robe.

I savored every moment of this alone-time in the bathroom, with my kids down and quiet—even Ayden. Sounds of TV were barely audible through the door.

This space was too humid from my bath, but so what—for now it was totally mine.

I toweled off my hair, and blow-dried it. I moisturized my skin, and touched up my eyes and lips. I left the bathroom, went to my dingy closet, and threw on an outfit that Ayden would approve of.

On the dented coffee table that graced my main room, which was not much more than an entrance, I set out some popcorn for my buddy. I placed the remote in plain view. I tried to shoo Ayden off the couch, but he stubbornly stayed put. He preferred this cool spot to the room with kid brothers, proud in his role as the couch alpha wolf.

I went to call the sitter, but there was no need; he was already walking to my door.

This was a guy who came over a lot, for no apparent reason. He seemed to be attracted to my turmoil. Or maybe he was hoping to rekindle a long-gone, foolish romance we'd tried. Whatever; he was cheerfully handy. I could never get him here on the weekend, when I worked and needed him the most; at those times, he was busy. But on weeknights like this one, no problem. He'd come over and munch on my popcorn, and kick back and watch cable TV; he was there for the kids while they slept.

As he made himself room on the couch next to Ayden, I threw him a grateful smile. It was one thing to leave the kids alone while I worked; it was quite something different to leave them for a bar. This buddy was the buffer for the worst of my guilt.

He didn't ask me where I was off to; the gleam in my eyes said it all. It was going to be an Andrea evening.

My girlfriend and I would dance for a while, and then, after working up a bit of a sweat, we would stroll to the bar for refreshment. We'd immediately find ourselves warmly surrounded by a group of admiring men. We'd end up not paying for any of our drinks. My eyes would be shining and my face flushed from dance, and the guys would unanimously guess my age at somewhere in my twenties.

I'd respond with a subtle but extremely pleased smile, and Andrea would knowingly giggle, and then I'd admit to having a son who was almost sixteen years old.

The men's jaws would drop then, and my friend and I would howl, and life would feel exquisite for a moment.

THE MOTHER
MEETS THE WHORE

It's odd, how the most desperate circumstances can lead to one's
salvation.

It was that popcorn-munching, cable-watching "sitter", that
"buddy" the kids and I knew, who turned me into a whore.

Some years before our introduction, he had run an "escort
service." He told me nothing about that until very late in our
friendship. He withheld that personal fact from me until he knew I
was ready to hear it.

Long before he taught me to "escort", we shared what I
assumed was a lingering bond. He often came over, but I wasn't
sure why; he seemed to just want to hang out in my world. I didn't
mind. For the sake of my sons, I felt grateful for the presence of
almost any adult male.

He was young and bright, if unfocused, and like me, he liked
to write. He was even poorer than I was, however, and drifting
from job to job. Yet the kids seemed to like him, and we had no
one better; the only other man around was the cocaine dealer
upstairs.

Even my crazy children seemed to know enough to steer clear
of *that* guy.

This guy could see that my situation crushed me. A total self-implosion was threatening. My own wan ghost was in charge. A typical week involved long hours of low-paying work and at least one wrenching trip to the school, the courthouse or the police station to deal with the current offenses of at least one of my sons. Even my youngest, now aged nine, seemed to be finding trouble.

Jesse was creatively gifted. The earliest proof of his talent was when he hoarded my notepads, and drew in them. Those notepads were tiny, about three inches by five, provided by the restaurant I worked at. We servers used them at tables, where we jotted down diners' orders, and then "touched" their requests from the computers to the kitchen.

A lot of those little notepads came home in my waitress apron. Jesse would fish them out. They were minus just a few pages— still thick with the promise of something to *make*.

Alone and completely unguided, Jesse spent hours making moving cartoons. I'd flip through a notepad he was done with, and discover some real animations. There were cartoons of rising and setting suns, going up and down over horizons, and baseballs thrown straight to the viewer and back, getting bigger and bigger and smaller and smaller. There were racecars zooming over hills, sometimes dramatically crashing, and stick figure warriors fighting, often complete with heads rolling.

My response, of course, was joyful pride in his talent.

But lately he'd found other amusements. He'd learned that standing guard while the big boys stole lumber was another way to kill time, and to win the big boys' approval. He also looked on while they built themselves a tree house, to use it to party in.

Some neighbors blamed Jesse for the wood theft. Now I got summoned to juvenile court with my child who was just a fourth-grader.

Years later my sons would admit to me that he hadn't stolen a thing—but yes, he *had* taken the fall for his brothers. At the time, however, I didn't suspect that, and neither did the town. The locals made a spectacle of me. In the paper an article was printed about my terrible little boy crimester.

Such besmirching of my artist, my baby, and its awful reflection on me, was the fatal last blow to my dying morale. The domino effect had reached its conclusion. Every last bit of my courage fell down.

The popcorn-muncher stealthily watched me. He saw my stamina die. He witnessed me stumbling and faltering with the heft of too much on my shoulders, and the exhaustion of carrying it alone for too long. I was lost in a state of despair and fatigue that must have resembled shellshock.

Besides the felon upstairs, who had recently moved out, this guy was the sole adult witness of my downfall.

He could see I was cut off from the herd. He could see that my burdens were slowing me down. He had known all along that was coming.

It was time to close in on me.

He was the only man I knew at the time who wanted to be there—with me. With me, so hopeless and overwhelmed. With me, so stranded in that crappy apartment with my hostile, disturbed, thieving children. With me, the forlorn desperado, overworked and having to answer for my chronically law-breaking offspring. Most other men who had got a good look had eventually backed away, sickened.

And by now I had become so despondent that I was just sort of a blur. I did get myself to my jobs and my workouts, but at home, I just kind of sprawled out, dejected and barely moving.

This guy, who called himself my friend, seemed to like me like that.

One day he offered to teach me a business that he promised would end all my troubles. This veteran of a floundered romance with me, who always came by just to hang—platonic in his affections, yet mysteriously tenacious—held my hand and started talking about a certain "way out."

When he finally said the word "escort," I just sat there, numbly nodding. I heard, I comprehended, and yet I could barely respond.

What did I care, anymore?

He was gaining on me. He moved in for the kill.

At his place, he had a business phone line installed. He placed an "escort" ad. And then, slickly and smoothly and amazingly fast, he turned me into his product.

I worked for him for about a week and a half. He sent me on sexual missions for miles and miles around, and then made me drive to his town, in order to give him a third of my earnings at the end of each working day.

Suddenly curt and businesslike now, he snapped up the cash without a thank-you.

At first I was far too preoccupied to react to his demanding ingratitude. It would also be a while before I realized that most of the money I brought him was going right up his nose.

Because I was oblivious to him. All of my attention was fixed on my exploits. Something amazing was happening. I was stunned, I was enthralled, and I was even getting giddy, with an astonishing daily discovery.

Even after I gave him his cut, I made hundreds of dollars a day. For something I'd been giving away all my life!

And the most amazing thing of all was the warmth of the men who paid me. They were sweet, they were gentle, and they admired my looks. They praised my bedside manner. Many of them even acted selfless. They wanted *me* to have orgasms. *They worked hard to make me orgasm, and then they gave me lots of money!*

For years and years before this, I had watched my maternal dilemma cause all of my lovers to flee. In the wake of all that rejection, I'd been dragging myself along. I'd been isolated, broke, depressed and masturbating, for what felt like forever and ever.

And now *this*. This sudden turnabout in my relations with men was awing me, jolting me…soothing me.

These men gave me compliments and intimate pleasure, and shocking amounts of cash.

This was unbelievable!

Had I rubbed a magic lamp?

And then…

I calmed myself down and observed my situation with a keener and cooler focus. I saw that there was even *more* to get excited about. My buddy's role in this business was easy.

I saw that I didn't need him.

I didn't need to drive all that distance, every day, to deliver his big cut and put up with his new cold attitude. I realized that *I* should be doing the phone-screening—why the hell should *he*? He wasn't the one daring to face the unknown, that meeting behind those closed doors with male strangers.

I thought, *Shouldn't I, the person who's going in there alone, be the person who determines whether I should? Shouldn't I be the person who evaluates prospects? Talks to them first? Sizes them up? Decides who might be a threat?*

It was *I* who ought to be handling all that! And keeping all the money for myself!

By now I was growing disgusted by my manager's coke-induced surliness, and his increasingly desperate-sounding growls for more money. And then my kids, who usually concealed their shenanigans, indignantly reported that this adult, my peer, had treated *them* to cocaine.

He'd done that to my kids—my seventeen-year old and my fourteen-year old—with money that he'd made off of me!

With no remorse, I dumped the bastard, and embraced my autonomy.

To protect my sons from inevitable conflicts, I hid what I was doing from them. In the room that I slept in, I had the phone company install a separate line from the one my kids used.

That was just before voicemails and pagers. I relied on an "800" number.

I placed my own "escort" ad, and immediately found myself flourishing. Using what I'd learned from watching my ex-manager, I carefully qualified my prospects. I went to see whomever I chose from an endless volume of calls.

In just *two or three hours a day*, I earned even more than what had taken me *sixty hours a week* to earn before. *Overnight,* I had plenty of money and time. Time for the real job: my family.

In just a couple of weeks, I had enough money saved to move us to a decent new rented home!

Soon there was money to buy us whatever we needed, no matter what it cost: healthier food, new clothes, a reliable car, a computer, and enriching family excursions.

My children began to get better.

Before that my sons had been suffering from an emotional sickness I recognized. They'd been helplessly internalizing their nurturer's black despair. Hadn't I done that myself, long ago, when I was tragedy's child?

Being male had made my kids violent. Paternal abuse and desertion had honed their aggression, and so had my wretchedness. Just as it goes with an autoimmune disorder, they had viciously turned their pain homeward, attacking each other and attacking me, and finding ways to harm themselves.

But *their* mother wasn't going to die. And things were looking up.

Now I could afford to be at home for them—a lot. I could heal them just by being around, and not with a stressed or exhausted demeanor, but with my new self, a breezy lady. Now I could show them the positive outlook of middle-class, not under-class, America. Now I could give them what's due every child: lots of quality time with their mother.

My sons still desperately needed a man, but now they at least had a lot more of Mom.

And, speaking of me—well, my new job kept being amazing. I was learning so many new things!

During those first few months as an "escort," every time I knocked on a strange man's door, I was sick and shaky with fear. My heart pounded. Prostitution was supposed to be dangerous. Customers were supposed to be rude and crude. I was supposed to feel degraded. Men were supposed to be monsters.

And of course there was always the additional terror of getting set up and arrested.

Imagine how all those fears multiplied with kids waiting for me at home.

But when it came to my clients, none of what I feared ever happened. My paranoia decreased with every encounter, because every single guy behaved nicely.

Not long before this, my life had been the crush of an overwhelming burden. I had been losing my strength. I had been losing my way. A blinding darkness had gathered. While endlessly floundering in that murk, finally I began to fall down.

A predator found me and sank in his teeth. He dragged me into his lair. Once there, I shook myself free of him. Then I discovered some hidden truths that hardly anyone knows about. Few women veer far enough to see them. To discover them is prohibited, and yet their value is high.

Those truths are:

(1) Men of all ages will eagerly pay three digits an hour for our company.

(2) Most of those men are not the creeps and psychos we've all been taught to expect; for the most part they're normal and decent. Most of them are responsible types, and would be considered by many a "good catch."

(3) Most of them are gentle and respectful, and often even worshipful.

(4) Even the "weirdoes" are usually men who are expressing a fetish of adoring submission.

Those truths are denied to women.
SYSTEMATICALLY DENIED.

In my darkest, most desperate hour, when despair was so thick and heavy that I was almost paralyzed, my opportunistic buddy informed me that my troubles could be instantly over. Though he wasn't what you'd call honest, on that point he told the truth.

Then a bursting forth of much plenty—of adequate money and family time, and the sweetness of successful self-employment—immediately healed me from depression, and redefined my life. It was a pattern of positive, personal growth that rooted in me, quickly, when I became an "escort".

The only thing wrong was the lying I did. I was forced to be untruthful to my children.

I had become a sex worker. In our culture, one can't let that on to her children.

Whenever I considered their delinquencies—the violence of one, and the thieving of two—I knew it could be a disaster for them to be aware of my unlawful new identity. They might use it to justify their own illegal acts, which, unlike my "crimes," were true crimes.

And there was that other thing, that social conditioning, that huge patriarchal mindfuck. No one completely escapes it: the belief that a woman, and particularly one's mother, ought to be sexually "pure."

My sons were already emotionally disturbed. What would they do with the knowledge that their mother had turned into a whore? They were living in a world that teaches that a woman who whores is despicable.

So I began to live the paradox that's etched in the secretive life of the whore. My work was saving my family, but it couldn't be revealed. The savior and the liar were united in my heart.

I told the kids I cleaned houses by day, and that at night, I still worked as a home health aid. But they knew something was up, because I was nicely clad when I walked out the door, and I exuded an upbeat and happy frame of mind. What an amazing change in their mom! Gone was my grimness from the days when, dull-eyed, I would leave for low-paid multiple hours in uniforms or sweats.

The most telling thing of all was that I no longer worked a lot. Whenever I left for work now, I would only be gone a few hours, or less. What a drastic difference from when they hardly ever saw me! And I took a lot of free days now, whole strings of days when I never left the kids, and made homemaking and chauffeuring my round-the-clock devotions. Yet my financial situation had drastically improved. We had money now, and plenty of it, even though I only worked part-time, even though I'd moved us to a bigger, much more decent, much costlier dwelling.

My children were hardly naive. They had learned enough street smarts, and enough lawbreaking, to be anything but naive. Sometimes they called me a liar. I told them I got paid to vacuum and dust, and help sick people bathe, and they just looked me up and down, and smirked like knowing cynics.

Most of the time, however, they enjoyed our new prosperity. Even though they chafed against my new presence and dominion, as anyone's children would, for the most part they loved having their mother at home.

I enjoyed watching them heal.

Then they said my dumped buddy had called, and had spitefully informed them that their mother was a whore. I considered what admitting that might do to my sons, and I firmly denied what he'd said.

I kept thinking about a discussion I'd heard, when I was just fourteen, between a couple of girls more experienced than I was. It was all about how to survive as a female in the treacherous ninth grade jungle.

"If anything happens when you're alone with a guy, and he goes around talking about it, deny it! Deny it!"

"*Deny it!*"

Oh, the lying we girls have to do. All of us. All too often. All our lives.

So irony took over, as thick as my family's blood. I knew my sons needed to tell me they knew; at the same time, however, they needed my denial.

Jeremy is now in his twenties. He's working toward a Masters Degree in Marketing. These days he squarely faces the truth, and tells me he understands.

"Mom," he says, "what you did back then was, you basically became a *man*. When you became a whore, symbolically you were being a *man*. We didn't have a man, and we needed a man, and you knew you had to become what we needed, so you did what a man would do, you did what was **necessary**."

"You didn't whine, you didn't give up; you got down in the trenches and rescued your family, and you **won**, just like a **man**."

"And Mom," he finishes, and this is the part I need:

"I love you for that. I respect you for that. No one can tell me what you did was wrong."

FLOWERS THAT BLOOM
IN THE TRASH

Prostitution came to me at the intersection of my needs and proclivities.

Now that I was an "escort", I always felt well off. I felt beautiful, and free, and in control of my life. For the first time in a long time, I felt like a good mother.

It made sense to me, immediately, to defend the profession that was saving my family.

I had a driving need to share what I was feeling. It was instinctive to write about it. I wrote mounds of journal-style thoughts about it. I relentlessly sought books on prostitution. I read twenty books either by or about other prostitutes. I had a ravenous hunger to learn more about this secret, this forbidden way of life that had lifted my life out of hell.

When I delved into the published writings of American activist prostitutes, I got amazed and excited all over again. In most of the accounts that I read—those of Norma Jean Almodovar, Dolores French, Cosi Fabian, and others—each was reporting that as soon as she learned the callgirl lifestyle, elation was her dominant emotion. Each was expressing a sense of liberation. Each was describing her discovery of whoring in glowing, exultant terms. Each was insisting that once she'd gone down that prohibited, stigmatized path, her circumstances dramatically changed—for the better. And what's more, they changed *right away.*

The same thing had happened to me, with the same sense of lightning-bolt truth.

Money abruptly came into my life, but without the destructive emotional price that I'd been led to believe that a prostitute must pay. At first, of course, I had qualms about my acts; social conditioning is a vice grip on the mind. But social conditioning is only a spin, and a spin can be brought to a clattering stop on the ground of concrete truth. For me, that truth was threefold. It was the new look of peace on my well-attended sons. It was the health of my bank account and credit rating. And it was the major eye-opener, the thing that clinched it all: the sincere appreciation of my clients.

As I've mentioned before, all of my customers acted grateful and sweet. No one I saw when I started, and no one I've ever seen since, was abusive. It's been quite the contrary.

My customers all act respectful. They often act downright adoring. I enjoy an outpouring of gratitude. They're usually happy to pay my fee, and some tip me. Most make appointments to see me again.

Clients are always expressing their thanks. I think I've come around to a fairly good understanding of what they're all so pleased about. Each client sings at least one of these praises:

Thank you for being so friendly and sensual, without any hesitation. Thank you for being all mine, my dream come true for one perfect hour. Thank you for taking charge of my need. And thank you for the honor of allowing me to try to take charge of yours. Thank you for letting me have this fun. Thank you for helping me through this transition. Thank you for accepting my polygamous nature. Thank you for letting me relieve my stress, exactly the way I need to, through my cock. Thank you for committing me to only your fee. Thank you for providing these wonderful "sins" with respect and a sense of humor—with the attitude that what I badly need isn't wrong.

All of the "escorts" that I've read about describe that appreciation. And most of those women's conclusions are a perfect mirror of mine. We recognize the stupidity of making prostitution illegal. We consider all the meanings of "criminal," and we know that our happy transaction simply doesn't add up to a crime.

Dolores French is the president and founder of the Atlanta-based support group for prostitutes called HIRE (Hooking Is Real Employment). She remains a working prostitute and a dedicated activist for prostitutes' rights. In 1988 she published her book, **Working: My Life as a Prostitute.** Throughout it she expresses her sense of awareness that prostitution is inherently a helping profession. French quotes from her mentor, the woman who got her started, a courtesan who declared that whoring is a benevolent human service.

> ...even the weird clients are usually nice people. You're providing a valuable service to these people— all of them. You're helping someone with a crippled sense of self-esteem...Part of the art of prostitution is using sex to create a feeling of trust and intimacy...Men might not even understand why they keep coming back...They think it's for the sex. But they're coming back because we touch them emotionally...

French concludes the passage with her own convictions.

> The way [Elaine] described it, prostitution is a noble profession, right up there with nursing and teaching...As I started working, I found out that many of my clients were isolated and lonely...If I could make that client walk out the door feeling happy, feeling good about himself, feeling he might actually be interesting and fun to be with, I had performed a great service. To do that a person has to love men and enjoy being with them, which I did.[1]

In 1993, Norma Jean Almodovar published **Cop to Call Girl,** her account of how she came to prefer whoring over her career as a policewoman for the LAPD. Being a whore felt like honest work. Being on the LAPD force felt despicably corrupt.

Like French, Almodovar remains committed to the fight for prostitutes' rights. When asked why she doesn't think a callgirl's work is wrong, Almodovar echoes my feelings.

> It was not degrading to me because I think that sex is a positive, nurturing act...I cannot fathom how making another human being feel good for a fee could be

degrading or demeaning unless it is degrading to make other people feel good.[2]

Mayflower Madam was published in 1986. Its author is one of the world's best-known twentieth-century madams, New York City-based Sydney Biddle Barrows. Though I'm against third-party management, in Barrow's case I make a heartfelt exception. Her book is a treasure of avowal for the honor in the profession, and her nurturing respect for her girls.

Barrows states:

> Like their counterparts in the other helping professions, our girls brought tenderness and comfort into our clients' lives. We were *there* for them. We listened to them. We made them feel better. We gave to them emotionally, and we gave to them physically....Our society still needs to learn to tolerate the idea of women making a living by being intimate with men. Some people say that prostitution is degrading. Certainly it can be, but not in the agency I operated....

And from her girls:

> Melody: You can have millions of dollars...but if you don't have anyone to share it with, what's the point? Some men try to buy that companionship. I'm not saying it's as good as the real thing, but it beats the hell out of being alone. Besides, sometimes the real thing isn't that good, either.

> Sunny: For most of our clients, who were hard-driven, hard-working men, an evening with one of us was an extra-special treat they looked forward to every now and then, just as I sometimes reward myself for....strenuous dieting by going out for a hot-fudge sundae.

> Lisa: Although sex was certainly part of the package we were selling, I knew all along that we weren't really in the sex business. We were in the happiness business. The Constitution guarantees the right to life, liberty and the pursuit of happiness, and all we were doing was helping people pursue a little happiness.[3]

From my earliest days as an "escort", I for one have felt certain that I'm not harming or cheating anybody. I know the uneasy feeling of being pressed into the role of a quasi kind of cheat; in the past, in conventional sales work, sales managers have subtly urged me to scam people. I've despised myself for complying.

As a whore, I feel proud to be able to acknowledge that my service is all cards-on-the-table. Other than my fib about my chronological age, which feels okay because I state an age that people guess anyway, there's nothing dishonest or damaging about what I say or do. I'm not deceiving people. I'm not selling drugs, or weapons. I'm not stealing. I'm not polluting the environment. I'm not causing negative ripples in the universe.

I use condoms.

And I'm not a robber of quality, as in the cheating of a service of its advertised promise. Right from the start I devoted myself to a healing-priestess sort of model that I decided to call the *true whore*. That standard has driven me to always make sure that no one among my patrons feels dissatisfied, or uncomfortable, or ripped off.

I'm not a phony. I don't fake orgasms. I've always heard that whores are fakes, and I don't want to be like that. I aspire, instead, to be like Dolores French. She writes that she's used her sessions with clients to teach herself how to more easily come.[4]

I either have a real orgasm, or I don't, and I admit to either if asked. Whenever I'm in a relationship, I never come for the clients. That would feel like I'm cheating on my lover. And even when I don't have a lover, I don't come for clients all the time.

Who could!

So whenever I don't come, which is often, I tell the clients who need to know that they've made me feel really good, but no, I didn't come, but that's okay, they're good lovers, what they've done for me is great. And every time I say that, they tell me they like my honesty.

Back when I was a brand-new "escort", inexperienced and scared shitless, even then I knew that I was onto something good. I knew that I had it in me to make it the best it could be.

I considered what makes for a "moral crime," and I realized I was guiltless. I was sumptuously paid for bringing natural pleasure. My clients and I each walked away with equal satisfaction. I gave men what they wanted. They gave me lots of money. All was fair, a balanced equation.

Soon I learned a joyful way to respond to the outcome of casual sex. Newly absent, in that kind of sex, was the pain of getting discarded. The desolate black hole left by hit-and-run loving had become, overnight, a big wallet; it was stuffed with glorious cash. This was a whole new world! Now I knew that casual encounters could be lucrative employment. The money erased any sense of hurt. I never felt "used." I felt no more used than anyone else who receives great money for a sale. I never felt "slutty." Who can feel slutty, or anything ugly, when she's basking in compliments and cash?

People vary somewhat in their definitions of "slut." As a new whore I realized that for me, the term was inaccurate. Some might call me a slut, but I knew better. The image evoked by that slovenly word is a woman who lacks self-esteem. A slut is guilty of cheating her own worth. She sleeps around, and gets little from it. Even the self-respecting slut is construed as a woman who's wrongful; she's perceived as deceitful in relationships, and therefore unworthy of trust.

None of those negatives applied to how I felt. I felt honest. I felt trustworthy. I felt like a quality woman. And it was the very men I serviced who made me feel that way. They made me feel desirable and needed and respected. And they always put their money where their mouths were.

As a new sex worker, I knew I was still a good person. But now I felt powerful, too.

I had the world by the balls!

I do yet. I'm lavishly paid for what I give of myself. As I mentioned in Chapter Two, just what I give, and when, and to whom, and for how much, is entirely up to me. If that's what it is to be a slut, then go ahead and make me sew an "S" on my bodice. I'll embroider a vertical slash right through it, and smile all the way to the bank.

But when I began my new life as an "escort", the gratification of making great money was only a part of my sense of well-being. My debut in whoring was a merge with my healthy lifestyle. The result was a profound combination, in me, of professional eroticism and holistic-health awareness. I soon got past my first motive to whore, which was desperation for money. Prostitution became more, to me, than just the way to acquire great cash. I saw that the work is important.

I intuited, right from the onset, that whoring can be healthy because whoring can be spiritual. My patriarchal Christian upbringing had never impressed me much. I had always understood that my birthright, the American culture, the so-called Mecca of pluralism, is a place where "spiritual" can mean something other than Judeo-Christian persuasions. "Spiritual" is a catch-all expression. It applies to anything intensely benevolent that feels profoundly right—profoundly right with one's soul.

As a whore I felt sexually spiritual.

Every woman understands that to nurture is intrinsically spiritual. I had always been very maternal. I had always been a person who wants to help, comfort, and heal. As a whore, I was doing that. My proof was my clients' gratitude. My self as a prostitute was weaving into all that was nurturer—me. I was a mother, homemaker, gardener, exerciser, healer, writer, and whore. All were seamlessly, wholly, my path.

Holistic integrity mends dualism.

As a new whore, I realized something. With the obvious exceptions of rape and coercion, and the molestation of children, sex is *always* righteous. When professional sex is completely freed up from a conditioned sense of disgrace, its goodness is as clear as the daylight. It's as natural as the selling of the fruits from my backyard garden.

In the beginning, when being "professional" was an uneasy, clueless act, and I found myself in front of one man after another who wanted to pay me for *me*, I instinctively saw that the key to my well-being lay in giving myself *joyfully*. Deliberately controlling both my fear and my reservations, I tended to my clients with the same sense of *right* as those times when I mentored a child, or when I gave instruction in exercise, or when I labored to grow my garden, or when I worded a written story. Something simple, yet tremendous, occurred to me. In spite of the fleeting nature of certain modes of intimacy, and regardless of the power of societal infliction of shame, our genitals are a major gateway to joy. That is not an opinion. That is an absolute truth. Some may choose to ignore, despise or shrink from that truth. Regardless, that truth stands.

I decided that to be a *true whore* is to embrace that absolute. I decided to believe that a customer's need to have his genitals stimulated, and his need to try to stimulate mine, is no more disgraceful than a caregiver responding to a baby's cries for food, or a personal trainer pushing his client to feel the surge of his blood, or a gardener breaking up clods so that roots can feed from the soil, or an intellect pursuing more effective expression.

Right from the start I coached myself to maintain that sense of esteem. I had to go at myself. I was boldly taking a stand against everything I'd been taught, since my patriarchal girlhood, to view as the worst, the most reprehensible, sexual person a female can become.

To value prostitution is a huge revolt for a woman. It's the overthrow of her upbringing, and I did it. Few women share it with me. But as I've mentioned before, the reason is simply that *most women don't know the truth.* Not enough women are out there, working without exploiters, and learning, just as I did, that independent whoring is exalting.

And yet the worldwide number of autonomous whores is definitely on the rise. My proof is the promotional websites, like *IndependentEscort.com.*

It's been encouraging to find that my professional ideals are reflected in some recognized theisms. I thrilled to an article in a holistic-living publication, written by the late Zen Buddhist master, Philip Toshido Sudo. His piece is entitled *"The Zen of Lovemaking."*

> *Sex is sacred.* All of us began as a combination of sperm and egg, man and woman. At its best, sex takes us back to that beginning, transcending the mere fulfillment of our animal desires to reveal our inherent divinity as creators: it's a spiritual endeavor, as profound as any religious rite or ritual.
>
> Like sex, the study of Zen takes us back to our origins as well…Zen is simply an absorption in life— the *essence* of life.
>
> The way of Zen is to allow nature to express itself through all of our actions, whatever they are…
>
> Religious adherents sometimes renounce sex as an earthly desire to be transcended. Zen monks are no different…they take strict vows of asceticism as a means to self-purification. But "pure" Zen decries attachment to religious orthodoxy or any doctrinaire pursuit…Consider the revered 15th century Zen master,

Ikkyu Sojun. In poem after poem, he sang the praises of wine, physical love, and even brothels...

To Ikkyu, sex deepened the path toward enlightenment. No one can enter this world without being born of both a man and a woman, he said: we are connected to sex by the "red thread" of blood at birth...We're of sex. That fact should be embraced, not avoided, Ikkyu said. He wore his priest's robes to the pleasure quarters to signify the spiritual nature of his activity:

> Me, I am praised as a general of Zen
> Tasting life and enjoying sex to the fullest!

Zen sex can take place anywhere, anytime, with anyone, because Zen truth is available at all times, for any person willing to practice.[5]

I know.

As I've grown in my sex work identity, I've developed profound respect. Respect for myself, respect for my clients, and respect for the service I render.

At first, I was alone in that venture. No one mentored me, and at that point, no other "escorts" worked with me. My aloneness was a pained isolation, but I kept at my new life just the same. The books I read by activist whores were a tremendous validation. So were the websites of prostitutes' rights organizations. But most of all, it was my clients—my steadfast "partners in crime"—who kept me going strong. They bolstered me with money, protectiveness, and gratitude.

They do yet.

I eventually bumped into a formal definition for the liberating process I'd created for myself. In my continuous quest for holistic-health awareness, I happened upon the insights of the famous medical intuitive, Carolyn Myss. When I read her book, *Anatomy of the Spirit*, Myss helped me see that my whore identity is transcendence from counter-productivity.

Myss justifies such defiance as a means to self-empowerment. When a person's "tribe" is prohibiting her from her own kind of spiritual growth, and destroying her unique self-invention, her continued compliance with the rules of that tribe is wrong for her and for anyone she might have otherwise helped. In that case, to rebel against her tribal restrictions is the virtuous thing to do.

Given the power of unified beliefs--right or wrong--it is difficult to be at variance with one's tribe. We are taught to make choices that meet with tribal approval....

From an energy perspective, becoming conscious....is extremely challenging, and often very painful....to evaluate our own personal beliefs and separate ourselves from those that no longer support our growth. Change is the nature of life, and external and internal change is constant. When we change inwardly, we outgrow certain belief patterns....

Evaluating our beliefs is a spiritual and biological necessity. Our physical bodies, minds, and spirits all require new ideas in order to thrive....

Seen symbolically, our life crises tell us that we need to break free of beliefs that no longer serve our personal development...

Myss goes on to add that, *no matter what the situation, the honor of oneself and others is crucial.*

From a spiritual perspective every relationship we develop, from the most casual to the most intimate, serves the purpose of helping us become more conscious....

We can more easily see the symbolic value of our relationships when we release our compulsion to judge what and who has value and instead focus on honoring the person and task with which we are involved.[6]

As I strengthened my professional identity, I gleaned what I needed from mentors like Sudo and Myss. As I built on my respect and compassion for my clients, my conscience knew nothing but peace. For the first time, my children had an available mother. My bills were now paid—some were even paid *off.* I enjoyed self-employment with appreciative customers who mirrored my self-esteem. This was all because I had crossed a line that women are ordered to never approach, with a moral certitude that I, myself, had created.

At first, I didn't know I was exceptional. I thought that all "escorts" have scruples. I had immersed myself in the published writings of virtuous prostitutes. Like me, they tended to ennoble their work with standards and ideals. I had made myself a callgirl with some conscientious ethics, and so had most of the peers on my bookshelf. I had cloistered myself, as might any thinker, from the mercenary mentality.

I knew about streetwalkers, of course. A lot of them, of course, are drug addicts. Given the "ambience" of curbsides, alleyways and the backseats of customers' cars, I felt safe to assume that they don't deliver much in the way of the sexually spiritual. Substandard behaviors are expected from addicts, and so is a self-degradation, and so is a lack of compassion. But I wasn't aware that corruption is a typical trait of my peers. Those are the women in my venue, the "indoor" prostitutes, always referred to as callgirls or "escorts".

My discovery of their flaws was distressing. It was my clients who made me aware of them.

Clients repeatedly told me that there was something different about me, that I was "better than the others." They didn't mean my looks or my sexual skills. Most had spent time with "escorts" who might be better looking or younger than I was. But my clients had learned to dislike them. Those girls failed to win repeat-patronage. Those girls would promise the clients an hour, and take off in twenty minutes. Some of them used "bait and switch" tactics. They or their managers would quote a flat rate to a prospect on the phone, and later on the client would find that that rate was just the beginning, just the fee to get the girl through his door. He'd have to cough up a lot more money for what he actually wanted.

But most of all, it was the hurried, cold, "all-business" attitude that put clients off, shut clients down, and made them want to never call those girls again. Those negligent girls were the ugly antithesis of the sought-after Girl Friend Experience. They were the actual reason that the GFE was distinguished.

Men told me I was more "sincere" and "human," and that I took much more time with them. They said that I never made them feel ripped off. They said that I made them feel comfortable. They seldom expressed it in so many words, but I sensed that they were trying to say that I made them feel uplifted.

Occasionally, I would be asked:

"What's a nice girl like you doing in a business like this?"

"Making it nice."

I was serious.

Their relentless grumbles about other "escorts" made me realize, with mounting dismay, that my pride in the work, and my *true whore* intentions, were the exception to a rather dismal rule. I eventually came to the conclusion that a customer's chances of feeling glad that he paid are about one out of three or four. The reports I was hearing about the lousy attitudes and wrongful business practices of many of my peers became a troubling but powerful cornerstone of my own growth in the work.

As time went on, and I heard more and more clients' complaints, it became obvious to me that in many sex workers, a con artist mindset prevails. I thought of a book I'd skimmed through, entitled *Ladies of the Night.* Some of those callgirls have great things to say. They report that they experience the work as self-empowering. They express much compassion for clients. But others sound harsh, all business. One of them actually boasts that she's "conning." That word left me ice cold.[7]

Unfortunately, the coldhearted girls are an accurate portrayal. I was coming to realize that girls who con are more typical than girls who care. They're like carnival cheats whose loftiest goal is to *hit 'em up for all you can, then take down the tents and run.*

For me, the natural next step was to agonize over why.

I knew that for many prostitutes, a bad self-image must be part of it. How can someone feel respect for her work when the world keeps telling her it's a bad thing to do? But then again, why not? I'd gotten over that stumbling block; why couldn't other women? I sensed some hostility in them. It drove me to demand: *What the hell are man-haters doing in this business?* People uncomfortable with animals don't work in veterinary clinics. Democrats don't work for Republican candidates. Those who know they're allergic to poison ivy don't romp, bare-skinned, through the woods. But some people will do anything if the money's right. That was it. That was just it, and that was where the unscrupulous and I had a parting of the ways. Financial desperation was our common denominator, the point at which most of us got started. We all remained in the business because of the awesome money. The personal consequences were the place where we differed. I, through whoring, was spiritually growing. Many other whores were not.

I knew early on that I wanted to change that. I wanted to make other "escorts" understand that whoring can be made honorable. And to those who didn't care enough to join my objective, I wanted to holler: *Get out!*

I honed in on the causes of their negligence.

I realized that in some cases, the cause could be the simple matter of a girl being just that—a girl. She's too young. To that whore I wanted to say, *Get out, and come back when you've been around longer. At this early point in your life, the work is harming you. And you are harming the work. This is an extremely responsible job, really demanding psychologically. It's meant for strong and compassionate practitioners, not kids who feel like the "victim."*

In 1986, hundreds of activist whores from around the world got together in Belgium for a history-making conference. They called it the Second World Whores' Congress. (The First was somewhat smaller, held in 1985.) Many critical issues were discussed. Among them was the subject of age. At what age should a woman start whoring? It was decided that before age twenty-five, psychologically most women aren't ready.

I recently read a new novel that seems to support that point. The title of the book is **Whore**. It's about a young girl in a brothel. The narrative is so finely detailed and raw that I assume that the author, Nelly Arcan, has been a whore in real life. The whore in her story is twenty years old. She repeatedly complains about the likeness of older clients to her father. That seems to deeply disturb her. She feels as though she's having sex, every working day, with her father.[8]

Her book made me understand how paternally molested a very young prostitute might feel. That feeling could make the work hell.

I also realized that if a woman of *any age* feels herself to be a sexual victim, then her erotic service to men is going to lack warmth. She's going to infuse it with the chill of her own self-loathing. She might use sex work as a vengeance, a way to get back at the gender that's abused her. She'll cheat every man every way that she can. Such women are emotionally unfit for whoring, yet the business seems to be full of them.

Get out! I wanted to tell them. *Get help! And don't come back til you're well!*

I knew that another cause of dishonor is the escort agencies. Many of them are nothing more than pimps who have learned a few phone skills. Think of my "buddy" who got me started.

They push a perfunctory work force of "bodies."

I know what it's like to feel worthless, like nothing more than a "body." It happened to me when I waitressed. Once I worked for a big restaurant chain with "stores" (eateries) all over the country. Up-and-coming managers were assigned to different "stores." These guys weren't local, they came from all over, and they didn't give a rat's ass about any of their staffs, because soon, they'd be moving on.

My "store" was just another rung in their ladder to the top.

On one particular night, a lot of the wait staff had quit, and not enough new people had replaced them. This was a busy restaurant—a "very high-volume store"—and we knew we were in for a tough time. I'll never forget the inhuman comment that one of the managers made.

"I need bodies," he said. "I need more *bodies*."

That guy made me realize how heartless the corporate mentality can be. There we were, second only to the food and drinks in importance, we were the staff who made patrons feel comfortable and happy. Yet to management, we could have been robots. We were miniscule cogs in its huge rutting wheel.

On another night, a waitress ran into the restroom. She couldn't stop throwing up. She'd been stricken by a terrible flu. The manager on duty was unsympathetic. He gruffly told her to leave. She felt almost fired because she was sick. And once, I fell down with a big tray of food. The bastard just stood there, assessing the loss. He never offered to help me get up. He never asked me if I was okay. I was one of the best of his workers. I was reliable, friendly, and fast. That was the one and only time that I caused him any loss. But all he did was scowl.

Motherfucker.

A lot of the owners of escort agencies view their sex workers that way. They compel their "bodies" to be businesslike, and most of all, to rush. They're unapologetically mercenary. They teach their "bodies" to grab the money, hurry through, and dash off to the next guy.

To those "bodies" I wanted to say: *Why are you working for them? If you think they're protecting you, please wake up. Why are you giving huge portions of your fees to pushers determined to make you machines, getting from you and your clients as much buck for the bang as they can?*

Get free! Get real! Get out there on your own!

Toward the addict-prostitutes, I was nullifying.

You are not prostitutes. You have nothing to do with erotic professionalism. You could care less about being an honorable whore. All that concerns you is the copping of your drugs. You are addicts; addiction defines you; you usurp and steal our profession just to get the fast money you need for your fixes.

Because you tend to be walking the streets, and you're the most visible among us, you hurt the potential for the public to perceive what a true whore really is. If you manage to leave the streets, and infiltrate the "escort" profession, you hurt the potential for our clients to perceive what a true whore is.

Get clean or get out!

I define the true whore as an independent agent, someone completely self-employed. She's also emotionally healthy. She's addiction-free, content with herself, and professionally caring and responsible.

In other helping professions, like social work, counseling and nursing, empathy for clients or patients is required, a qualifier, a given. In the service performed by the "escort", the need for compassion intensifies. But judging from what I've been told by its patrons, only a glimmer of compassion prevails.

Amongst clergy, psychotherapists, social workers and the like, their exploitation of those they help is unforgivable. When their wrongfulness is made public, they're defrocked or shorn of credentials. In prostitution, however, the cruel exploitation of clients is often the horrible norm.

I got morally outraged about that. I considered how nice my clients were. I came to suspect that the surliness reported by some "escorts" about some clients might in most cases be the clients' bitter response to the callgirls' shitty behavior toward them.

They dole out so much money…and for what? To be treated like just a "blow job?" To be bothered by an "agent" who calls to say "Time's up!" in the middle of something intense? To be told, after paying a lot just to *see* her, "That will cost you a hundred dollars more"? To be deserted, minus hundreds of dollars, the second an orgasm happens—which could be in the first five minutes?

I'd be resentful and difficult, too.

My concern about dishonest "escorts" grew as fast as my fledgling expertise. It drove me to formally characterize the way I think whores should be. Carol Leigh, a famous whore activist, had coined the professional term, *sex work*.[9] I would follow that up with *true whore*. I would designate high prostitute standards. Actually, I would *re*designate them. According to my readings in feminism, I had a **herstorical** precedent. I had a grand template for my mission. It was Goddess and her sexual priestesses.

The **true whore** is loving, the clergy of Goddess. She knows that her sexual service is holy. She's known it forever and ever.

A true whore performs a sort of magic on men. She creates an immediate intimacy. So whenever an encounter meant to be stress relieving gets somehow tainted with hate, I call that professional failure. That isn't the work of the true whore.

The true whore can render a tiger a baby. If she encounters an absolute asshole, more often than not, she can get him to purr.

I don't want to blaringly toot my own horn, but just the same, I should be truthful. Alienation has never once chilled the exchange between clients and me. Not even with those who act distant at first. I put them all at ease. Even the obnoxious ones melt, and get sweet. Maybe it's because I'm a mother, and my nurturing ways runneth over. Maybe it's because I'm a "Daddy's Girl," and men sense I harbor a deep love of maleness. Or maybe it's because I'm mature. Or maybe it's because in a previous life, I was a temple priestess. Whatever the reasons, I cut right through men's defenses. I sense the right words to say. I sense the right ways to touch. Even the brusque ones start to relax. Soon, they all show me respect.

I realize that a serial killer of women would be undeterred by my charm. But how many psychopaths are there? I feel there aren't nearly as many as people seem to think. And aren't most of them preying on streetwalkers? And isolated housewives and joggers? The psychos tend to leave "escorts" alone. They feel that we're highly protected.

And if we're smart, we really are. I'll explain that in Book Two.

I leave all my clients contentedly drained, gratefully smiling, and feeling really good about the money they've just spent. I want every callgirl in America to be able to make that claim. Not one "escort" on the face of this world should be disliked or bitterly remembered.

Yet many are.

One day, while I was channel-surfing, I stopped to check out a madam on the **Jerry Springer Show**. Before millions of viewers, she was boasting:

"Men are stupid. I take their money."[10]

I wanted to hurl something hard through the screen.

Imagine a mental health therapist proclaiming on TV: "I don't care about my patients. They're stupid. I'm just out there taking their money."

She'd lose not only her clientele, but probably also her license to practice.

Well, prostitutes and their managers get away with that attitude, every day of the week. Illegality feeds the prevalence of such offensive profiteers. Legitimacy would get them all ousted. Just as it goes in any licensed helping profession, an enforceable code of ethics would remove, from prostitution, the jerks out there screwed up enough to show disrespect for their own clientele.

I recently learned that the clients themselves have found a way to fight back. Just as it goes for a zillion other issues and interests and collectives, the Internet unites them. There's a website out there just for clients. It's called *TheEroticReview.com*. I haven't visited the site myself, but clients who have gone there inform me that sex workers in diverse locations and venues are getting critiqued by them, there.

Way to go, guys.

When I entered the business of whoring, I enjoyed the windfall of money just as much as would any mercenary. And there *were* a few situations when *only* the *money* made it *bearable.* Like when I found myself trying not to breathe through my nose while I washed off the crotch of a man so obese that he couldn't clean himself down there. Or when a guy kept an insanely territorial pouch, barking its head off in the next room, jangling my nerves the whole hour. Or those moments when I'd finished what a "submissive" had me do to him, and it was time to pull out the dildo. Or when a pubic hair got stubbornly stuck, way down in my throat. Or when a guy just couldn't come, no matter what I tried.

Those are some physical realities that do *not* contribute to a feeling of spiritual exaltation. At times like those, there's no way in hell that I'd be there if I weren't so terrifically paid!

I soon understood, however, that the money wasn't the only thing that would maintain my sense of worth. I could see that unless I developed a very high standard of caring, I would lose respect for myself. If I didn't live up to that standard, I would cheat the goals of nurture that had always shaped my self-esteem.

I knew it could be easy to simply stop caring. To cease being human about sex work. To grab the money, do something robot-like, and run. It could be easy on the surface, but also a way to self-harm. To cease being caring in sex work would be a path to internal decay—a path to the loss of my nurturer identity, the core of my life's deepest meaning.

As I raked in that thrilling and head-swelling money, I immediately saw the importance, for me, of sustaining compassion for the people who paid me. Even for the obese men who stank to high heaven, and had to be made presentable! As with any other work that reaps profit from human need, I saw that it was my sense of caring which would make my work *more* than exploitation of that need, and much *more* than a hollowed-out version of me.

Then I realized how badly most "escorts" need a model. In the absence of an example, a major percentage of prostitutes just bleakly muddle through. Painfully aware of the brutality of whore stigma, all "escorts" struggle to maintain self-esteem under the staggering burden of public contempt. Loathed, criminalized, and forced underground, we're left on our own to figure things out. Some of us flounder in self-understanding, and are severely at risk for self-hate. Clients are given the dubious honor of paying for all that ambivalence.

Few people know—far too few callgirls even seem to know— that *true* prostitutes are spiritually evolved. Those whores are paragons. Those are the women who have written about themselves, and a growing number can be accessed online for their valuable advice. But even the "outed" tend to lay extremely low. Their terror of arrest keeps their outreach minimized. Because of the misdemeanor status of whoring, and worse, the *felony* status of pandering—the leading of others in—those mentors have to be cagey. So a lot of their faltering peers don't know anything about them, and are deprived of their beautiful guidance.

It's just as whore activists say it is. We're systematically held back from uniting, and bettering ourselves, and each other, and the work.

In the end I came to understand that the model that I envision for "escorts" reflects the ideal for *myself* that I picture, the strong, magnanimous, liberated woman I've spent my life hoping that I could become. The true whore *markets* that positive selfness, straight from within, to the world.

And her product helps out the world.

The ideal whore—the true whore—perceives that she inspires. She understands that she's vital. She thoughtfully shapes each professional encounter with a customized serving of sex and soul. She sets a high feminine standard. She responds, at least subconsciously, to an inkling of feminine deity.

A true whore is lit. A true whore is magnetic. A true whore virtually glows. She's freer, than most females, from female paranoia. Her smile is a lot less guarded. Indeed, she smiles at the drop of a hat. When she's out in public, and strangers' eyes meet hers, even on a bad day, her own eyes remember to twinkle. She's the one who stands out in the crowd.

If she's short, she seems tall. People pass by her, and they feel something. It's not her clothes that draw the eye; she could be turned out in drab sweats. It's not her body; her curves could be average. It's not her parts; it's the confident sum.

The true whore understands the uniqueness of her purpose. She recognizes her worth. She knows that it's not shameful to be fondled by the world. There's a proper way to do it. What makes her *true* is her awareness that there *is* such a thing as *proper* in whoring—in a world that never showed her.

To be proper, as a true whore, is to graciously alleviate and naturally rejuvenate in an atmosphere of beauty and warmth. It's the professional provision of a beneficial process. It's the work of a woman who's "exploited" by no one but herself.

To be "proper" is to comprehend that payment for sex can be appropriate. Sexual service is not "stupid" or degrading. It's the enabling of natural pleasure and healthy relief of stress, for a living.

In our culture, a host of different therapies for stress is readily available. These days, almost every common pastime, and sometimes even some chores, are informally dubbed "therapeutic." The therapy of the true whore should not be confused with informal. It's professional and closely kindred to the licensed, legitimate helps. Yet whore therapy is unique. It's immediate, thrilling, and incessantly sought, because unlike any other sort of therapy, true whoring is the beautiful fusion of spiritual balm and naked abandon.

As it goes with any professional achiever, the true whore thoroughly understands that self-discipline is crucial. To succeed with other people is to first succeed with herself. To help other people relieve their stress is to effectively deal with her own stress, first. She works hard to maintain a fit, healthy body and a positive, loving attitude.

In America, the true whore prevails with a joyful rebellion against her depressive surroundings. She knows that a key to her professionalism is to resist the American obsession with self-indulgent excess. Like anyone in our country who tries, in this stuffed-face culture of glut, to "stay straight," "dry out" or "eat right," she knows that the toughest of her battles lie within. She must grapple with the threat of unhealthy addictions brought about by the temptations of our world of gross consumption. She must work at remaining well toned in both her body and her mind.

In our high-fat, sugared and drugged, lethally sedentary culture, such physical and spiritual feats are supreme. As a victor over the toxic way of life that makes Americans fat, pharmaceutically dependent, barroom-fixated, seeking drugs, sucking on smoke, and chronically morose, she understands that the point of her work is to reunite people with their natural joy.

Of equal importance, and in consideration of the constant strife that goes on between the sexes, she also understands that her arbitrary affection for men is exemplary, refreshing, and even unusual.

She might brood over words like "blowjob." That's shoptalk from the cynical street. The term should be replaced by an expression more apt, a word for what actually happens.

What happens is a natural ecstasy, immediately followed by a natural state of peace.

How about "mouthpeace"? Or "joyjob"? I've thought of those terms as replacements for "blow," which is a comically insulting descriptive. And yet "mouthpeace" and "joyjob" sound asinine, too. They sound stupid because we've been taught to believe that fellatio is degrading and worthless.

But almost any man will tell you it's one of the most wonderful things you could do.

Even the prostitutes with questionable self-esteem have had some moments of glory. They've witnessed lots of joy. One of my favorite examples of that joy is from a recently written memoir by a former Boston callgirl.

When I first heard about her book, I rushed right out to buy it, because she lives in my area. I was also compelled because she's touted as a community educator with a doctoral degree.

On account of our shared locale, I felt an immediate bond. And even more importantly, I assumed that her book would be a positive read. I've usually found that the educated whores write with upbeat, enlightened insights. They tend to be living the true whore paradigm.

I was bitterly disappointed. I found that her book smacks of cynicism. In her account entitled **Callgirl**, Jeannette Angell reveals, far more often than a fondness, a smoldering resentment for the men who see "escorts". She seems to scorn most men, period. A downhearted tone permeates her recollections: toward herself, toward the profession, and toward life in general. She clearly relates as a victim.

Angell describes the conditions that helped to create her dark outlook. She admits to a Catholic upbringing and a mother-inflicted guilt. And then there's much terribly more: the thievery of an ex, the rotten response to her whoring by her best and most trusted male friend, the usury and slyness of her madam, a couple of criminally abusive clients she never should have been sent to, her own abuse of drugs, and her lack of autonomy.

If I were in Angell's shoes, those horrors would have rendered me groping for the shards of my shattered idealism. But here I want to make the point that during her trials in the work, even this coke-addled, misused, victimized-feeling woman was able to acknowledge the joy that "escorts" bring.

> I have to say that some people are so delighted with you and what you do for them, it's hard not to get caught up in their happiness. This guy was like a kid at Christmas, exclaiming happily over my breasts, transported by joy when I touched him…His orgasms were the closest thing to complete delight that I think I've ever observed. Does it matter that it was a callgirl who got him there? Hell, no; joy is rare enough in our world, you've got to grab it and feel it and love it whenever you can. A woman had done that for him. It didn't matter who she was, only that he felt it.[11]

The service of Eros is a therapy that attracts the true whore just like blossoms to the sun. The pull she feels is strengthened by impressive financial rewards, and by the persistent intuition that what she's doing isn't wrong.

I hear this praise so often that it starts to sound like a mantra:

"Thank you so much, ****. I feel so much better. I'm going to sleep like a baby tonight."

THE PRIESTESS
BECOMES HERSELF

I tried to find my righteous niche…

Whoring has taught me a religion.

That's right. *A religion*.

Okay, before I continue, I'll back that statement up. I'll recommend some reading. That way I'll provide some ironclad proof that when I claim whoring and religion might have anything in common, I'm not taking leave of my senses. Not on my own, that is.

The following books that support my claim are the fruitful collections of arduous research. Its authors and editors dug deep into archives that have apparently been deliberately obscured. See *When God Was a Woman,* by Merlin Stone. See *The Women's Encyclopedia of Myths and Secrets,* edited by Barbara W. Walker. Read *Laughter of Aphrodite,* by Carol P. Christ, and *The Yoni: Sacred Symbol of Female Creative Power*, by Rufus C. Camphausen.

And while you're at it, do a little thumbing through the Pentateuch—that's the first five books of the Old Testament. You'll soon get a sense of sheer hatred. That section of the Bible notes the early Hebrews' role in the vicious, global, genocidal attack on the religion the other books talk about.

According to the Old Testament, the deity behind that popular faith was the "Whore of Babylon." Her worshippers were contemptible "fornicators." Unless they converted to the brand-new, patriarchal God, they didn't deserve to live.

Well, for the past thirty years or so, an erudite faction of feminists has been clarifying and modifying that biblical claim. They've been casting out terms of hatred. They've been calling that deity Goddess. They've been discerning Her cultures as matriarchies. They point to the evidence of how peaceful, how sensual and creative, how downright unfamiliar with warring Her people apparently were. And they've coined a new word: ***herstory***.

My own perceptions of Goddess, and of course Her ancient whore priestesses, are inklings I've come into on my own. But it's been wonderful to find that I'm not alone. My awareness of Goddess has been greatly enhanced by the books I've just cited here, and by other, similar writings. The scholars behind them have honed their impressions not only from karmic intuition, as I have, but also from a global cache of archival revelations.

As you read my following reverie—which may actually be my recollection—please bear that in mind.

I am an ancient whore-priestess. I'm living in a beautiful temple, built just for Goddess and me. My body, and especially my vulva, is adored by parishioners. The worshippers bring me their ritual caresses and what passes, in my culture, for money.

My female forebears invented agriculture. I and the other priestesses communally own the land.

My female forebears can also take credit for the momentous invention of writing. My legacy is to spend countless meaningful hours expressing myself in cuneiform.

Priestesses invented pottery; it was priestesses who first sculpted and drew. As one of the members of that revered group of women, I embrace life as a daily opportunity full of freedom to create.

As a holy woman, I also know the secrets of healing the sick. And I and my peers are tribal midwives.

We priestesses invented music and dancing. I and my peers in the temple are the community musicians. We are the origin of *choirs. We sing at all rites and celebrations, play on the instruments we've fashioned, and dance the inspirational **horas**.*

*We perform the circular dances that all future cultures will copy. So will the shapes of clocks. Our female forebears made the concept of time. I'm one of the many whores, also known as the **houri**, who are creatresses of the **hour**.*

In tandem with the spherical concept of time, our forebears have also created the zodiac.

I inspire love. I am the holy medium for Goddess, and as such, I am adored. My "bastard" children are royalty.

I, as a priestess who lives in Goddess' temple, am admired and exalted, a leader. My vulva itself is holy. I am a sacred whore.

Consider the verbal alliance between the words *hora* and *whore*. And consider the Spanish word for *hour*, which is *hora*.

Consider the word *horoscope*.

The temple priestess lived thousands of years before male-god religions defiled her. She and all worshippers understood that the female gender, the life-giving gender, was the obvious sex of power. Therefore divinity was feminine. The divine was the Goddess, the Great Mother, the first-ever deity acknowledged. She was the worldwide precursor to God.

Goddess is a joyfully sexual deity. In primordial religion, lust and women and worship were one. Ritual sex was a sacred ceremony, the holy means to adore Her. Lust was a spiritual gateway, and priestesses were facilitators. Whenever I read about ancient Goddess worship, I become sexually excited. It's as if some long-gone incarnation is drawing me into remembrance. I find myself swelling with sexual joy. I usually need to set the book down and masturbate to the feeling. And when I do....wow. The visions! I'll share with you a favorite vision of mine. It's anywhere from 4,000 to 25,000 B.C.E. The location is somewhere in the Near East, the Middle East, the Far East, ancient Europe, or the Americas.

The season of planting and reaping is here. This is the time of the creatures, the herded and the hunted, to mate and swell and burst with their young.

This is the arduous but glorious time, when life flows in abundance.

This is the season to honor Astarte. Or Inanna, or Isis, or Venus, or the sexual Goddess by many other names.

Always, in all seasons, the parishioners worship Astarte. But in this, their time of much ploughing and sowing, they greatly increase their adulation. They praise their Fertility Giver, their Goddess of Life and Loving, with greater and greater passion. They adore Her with every expression of worship their minds and bodies can bear.

They believe that in return, She will bless them with bountiful harvests.

Their temple is constructed of hand-hewn stone. It's a striking addition to the natural vista of blue mountains, deep rivers, lush forests and wide plains. Spreading in all directions from that structure are acres of orderly human design meticulously dug in the earth. There are gardens and groves and vineyards, and designated lands fenced for pasture.

Around the tilled land are the commoners' dwellings. Men are in motion, intent on their work. Men drive their beasts to break ever more earth. Men roam the woods with arced bows and sharp arrows. Men fish from boats on the tributary waters. Men tend their livestock, gut their caught fish, and skillfully skin their mammalian kills. They dig wells, repair roofs, build wagons, and carve spears.

Men live in peace with the women and themselves. They live as their genes have intended. They're hunters, builders, protectors, and team players. They're completely sexually free. But rape and pedophilia, the modern man's horrible manias for power, aren't craved by these men, and don't happen.

Women work hard in the gardens and vineyards. Some of them fish and hunt with the men. Some of them smoke meats, some of them tan hides, and some weave grasses into baskets and mats. A few are attempting an art they've seen practiced by the sacred women of the temple. They light ovens built for the baking of clay. On wheels that they spin, they form bowls, urns and pitchers. With sticks and brushes and dyes, they paint on them pictures and symbols.

Small children and babies are tended by their mothers. It's likely that their fathers aren't known. It's likely that fatherhood itself isn't known.

The temple imposes on everyone's vision, an immense peripheral presence. All of the adults look forward to the evening they're going to spend there, in a glorious ritual called Rite of Spring.

Everyone pauses in their labor now and then, and gazes at the temple, and blissfully smiles.

When evening arrives, the adults are clean. They've purified their bodies for Astarte. They're draped in light robes very easy to doff.

The road to the temple is lit by soft sunset, and rippling with the eager progression of the crowd.

The shrine they approach is so high that it's almost like a mountain. This isn't the overdone outcome of some architect's pride in his creation. The edifice was built with the ardent belief that the farther upward its stone blocks aspire into the sky, the closer its worshippers are to Great Mother.

One hundred steeply graded steps lead up to the enormous entrance. The doors are more than twenty feet tall. They've been pushed wide open, and held back by stones, in a welcoming gesture of summons.

The steps before the temple are flanked by stone sculptures. Most are mounds with slits sculpted in them. Their cavitied centers are so deeply carved that animals often seek refuge in them.

The worshippers begin their ascent. They're burdened by cornucopious gifts. Much of their tithe is varieties of food: smoked or freshly-killed meat, fowl or fish, and cumbersome armfuls of the produce of spring, all that can be pulled from the gardens this early. Some labor to proceed under big sacks of grain. Others drag huge skeins of cotton. Barrels of wine are being rolled up the steps, the product of the grapes of the vineyards. Some trudge with clay urns of precious thick fluid that's pressed from the fruit of the olive tree groves. Others bring plants and roots that are healing.

The mothers in attendance turn left at the steps and lead with their children to a ground-level entrance. There, they hand over their little ones. The caretakers are priestesses in all stages of motherhood. Some of them are pregnant. Some of them have infants swaddled on their backs. Others are busy with older children. Still others are affectionate grandmothers, crones who have wizened to that mystical time when an all-purpose love consumes them.

All of them welcome the worshippers' children.

The worshipper-mothers return to the great stone steps, and hurry to join the others. They rush to aid their neighbors in the tiring task of bearing their gifts so far upward.

The gifts are for the priestesses of Goddess.

No one has brought live animals to sacrifice to Astarte. The time for such slaughter is when trouble arrives, when drought or pestilence weakens the crops. Then Goddess is implored with donations of throats which spout Her red fluid of life. Tonight, hopes are high, for the season is young. Tonight the patrons have no thoughts of killing. They need only to offer their own hot, unspilled blood, their living and personal passion of worship.

As they reach the last steps, a few yards from the entrance, the out-of-breath worshippers can hear a commingling of beautiful feminine voices. Somewhat a keening and somewhat a song, the intoning is a lilting, ululating sound, an expression of pure invocation. Strings are being plucked on woman-shaped instruments. Drumbeats are throbbing like the visitors' pulses. Rhythm and melody enter their ears and flow through their bellies in sync with their excitement. Incense pleasures their noses.

But the vision before them, the reward for their eyes, is the worthiest reason for their arduous climb.

Sweet naked priestesses are swaying inside. All of them are smiling, all of them are welcoming. They beckon to the commoners with outstretched arms, and also with their undulating pelvises. Their breasts gently loll with the movement, arousing the spectators' urge to caress.

It is now. It is now we pay homage to Astarte.

The priestesses help the worshippers in. Gifts are accepted and bodies are disrobed. Very little is spoken. As with garments, words are dropped and forgotten.

The throng of naked people now sways to the music. Every body gently collides with multiple other bodies. All feel the piercing of sexual passion as a lightning bolt coursing all through them. All feel its power. All become one.

The music and song is by priestesses arranged on a tremendous, pillowed altar, the forerunner of a stage. Unlike their naked peers in the crowd, those women are half-clothed. From just beneath their bare, rounded bellies, a gossamer skirting flows. Under those transparent sheathings, thick shrouds of cotton are molded to their groins.

It's the time of the sacred blood for those women.

A holy pyre is blazing behind them. The smoke from it rises to a portal in the roof. The fire has been kindled by discarded, reddened cotton.

O see the thick smoke from our blood, kind Astarte! We beseech you with the blood of our wombs! Your sweet Gift of Life, we give back to the heavens, that you may look upon us with mercy and love!

The priestesses who sway with the commoners are holding little carafes of oil. Each thrusts a finger of her free hand deep into her vagina. Then each one removes her finger, holds it high and glistening for everyone to see, then plunges the honeyed digit into her carafe, and vigorously stirs. Then each of them locates the penises present, and drips her potion on them, and rubs them.

*Now all of the men are **christos**—-anointed with sacred oil.*

The altar of the menstruating singers is flanked by two smaller platforms. The one on the left holds a priestess in labor. She's rhythmically breathing and wailing. A large shroud is heavily draping beneath her, sodden with water that has burst from her womb. This fluid of birthing has made the cloth sacred; it, too, will eventually be thrown on the pyre. The great hiss and smoke will cause shivers and prayers.

Two priestesses attend her with care. Her face is tensed up with the hard work of birth. Her spontaneous moans are a moving refrain to the song of the women close by.

But the influx of commoners, and the christening of phalluses, has somewhat eased her stressed features. Though she's overcome by pain, her eyes tear with joy. Her child will be born at the Holy Rite of Spring, and nowhere on earth could there ever transpire a more wonderful omen for a mother.

On the altar to the right of the singers, a dying old man is attended. He too wears a smile on his suffering features. To die on this night, this holiest of nights, in the midst of this sanctified, lovemaking gathering, is the sweetest last joy one could hope for.

The floor of the temple is soft everywhere, with mats and divans and large pillows. The music continues, and bodies go downward, engrossed in the acts enjoyed off of one's feet.

But eight of the worshippers walk off.

These are four couples, and their role here is special. Each walks to one of four sanctuary corners. Once there, they ascend up stone stairways to balconies. Each balcony faces the parishioners below. These twosomes, now hovering, remain on their feet. The women are all priestesses. The men are their choices.

Each of the four priestesses arranges herself so she's leaning far forward, with her elbows and hands on a railing of stone. Their faces and breasts now loom over the crowd. From behind, the men push in their penises.

In front of these holy women, just at groin level, is foliage on branches that sprout from large urns. The vulvas of the women are nestling in there. The motion of fucking causes rubbing in the leaves. The leaves are all soft and yielding, yet just a little spiky, just right for a frontal caress.

The balcony priestesses are losing themselves.

Penis pounding deeply and leaves gently touching, O Goddess, your essence fills me! My womb tightens, my vagina constricts! My clitoris, the peak of your power, is commanding the fire in my blood! O Beautiful Penis, O Organ of Passion, don't stop! Don't stop! Don't stop!

The eyes of the balcony priestesses roll upward. Their mouths are wide open, forming four perfect O's.

Below them the patrons and priestesses are a roiling sea of bodies in thrall. Their sounds and the sounds of the women on the altars are a fanfare of wailings and drumbeats and strummings that are heard in the sky by the birds. Orgasm bursts in a balcony priestess, and she bucks and piercingly screams. Her release instantaneously heightens the lightning, and this time, the bolt comes with thunder. The other three hovering respond to her screams with swelling wombs and exploding vulvas that cause them to shriek all together. One of them is lactating. While she orgasms, her milk sweetly sprinkles the crowd.

The men behind them are fucking them hard and starting to come and to bellow. In unison, all four of their penises spurt.

Every single worshipper on the temple floor below responds with a ululating cry.

The baby in its mother is crowning. The dying man expires in ecstasy, with his aged manhood erect. The menstruating women feel a unifying gush.

Hear us, O Goddess! Hear our worship! See how we glorify you! Remember us, Astarte, we who adore you, all of us, woman, man, body and soul!

My vision of that holy orgy is as clear as a memory, as vivid as recall.

In her book, **Laughter of Aphrodite**, the feminist scholar Carol P. Christ refers to a journey she made to Greece. Her ultimate goal was communion with the ancient sexual Goddess. She visited the ruins of one of Her temples, which was built before the Golden Age, in prepatriarchal times.

> Our excitement builds as we scramble over a barbed-wire fence and find ourselves standing amidst thorns and thistles in what must have been the temple's forecourt....
>
> We step into the temple. She is everywhere. We find womblike spirals and vaginal roses carved in stone. We start to make an altar on one of the broken columns, but I feel myself drawn to the space between two trees, at the center of the temple. I go to the spot, remove my shoes and my dress. I sit between the trees, opening my body to the midday sun, my golden shawl reflecting rays of golden light. I annoint my body with milk and honey....I pour milk and honey into the rose-colored shells, which open and close like my own. The sun warms and transforms my body. Though [my

girlfriend] is standing nearby, I am alone with the Goddess in her sacred place. I feel myself opening. I become Aphrodite.[1]

As I took in her account of excitement, it seemed to me that she had to be erotically aroused. I myself was on fire. I needed to touch myself. It took me only moments to come. What could be more perfectly sexual, more intensely aroused and orgasmic, than to *open* and *become Aphrodite*?

But this writer, who actually knelt in Her temple, doesn't say as much. She expresses herself only in terms of the symbols, the emblems outside of herself. She speaks of the golden shawl she's put on, which represents the Goddess' sunny joy. She emphasizes the liquids she's poured: milk for the life-sustaining seepage of breasts, and honey for the life-creating lust of vaginas. She refers to her seashells, which are shaped just like vulvas. She writes of an opening, an atoning, but what does she mean, exactly? Did she have a sitting-up orgasm, as I most certainly would have? Or not?

Is her reticence about it that "good-girl" reserve?

I thought to myself, *if I ever enjoy the privilege of visiting that very same place, that primordial, genuine ruin, then the real love-syrup, not honey, will be my reverent tithe. My womb will swell up and my juices will gush. I'll shake, my pelvis will rhythmically thrust, and my wailing will bounce off the boulders. **That,** not shells and the products of cows and bees, will be my communion with Goddess.*

A couple of pages later, I saw that this feminist refers to herself as an Aphrodite priestess.

A titter of doubt escaped me.

And then I read a statement by Dr. Christ that indicates sexuality is *puzzling*. She feels that she's a priestess not because she comprehends, but rather, because she does *not.*

Huh??? That struck me as absurd. A priestess would be a woman who *supremely understands*.

It seemed that I could sense a hint of evasion.

I decided that this woman is conveying that she's simply not a whore. And that she doesn't want to be. She'd rather hold off and be mystified, not altered by a whore's carnal knowledge. That's it. Of course. She can't give up being a "good girl." But she needs, just the same, to immerse in the sexual Goddess. She passionately needs to. Without going all the way. Without putting her pussy where her shells are. It's a typical feminine quandary. A debilitating wound by the patriarchy. A problem true whores have surpassed.

Then she becomes expansive. Dr. Christ turns away from the symbols of sex. She avows something wonderful that anyone, whore or not, orgasmic or not, can extract from the sexual Goddess. After her temple experience, she advises a pubescent, virginal girl that *every* brief moment of joy is Her gift, *every* kind of joy.

I found myself agreeing with her credit to Goddess for all the varieties of happy. All people, including the virgins and celibates, should be able to know Her, and exult in Her, in some delicious way. *But whoa there, sister*, I wanted to say. *Don't try to dodge the lust.*

Lust, after all, is the core of this deity.

I could sense that this feminist is afraid to embrace what her peers judgmentally label as "profane." But in spite of her fear of disapproval, in spite of her distinctive *un*whoreness, she manages to reveal that she's aware, just the same, of the Goddess' sensual joy.

Because she's heard Her beautiful laughter! She's heard it in her head! And she's made it the title of her book!

Women in sex work who love what they do are full of that sunshine, that Aphrodite mirth. Have you ever watched *Pornucopia*, the late-night *HBO* series that documents the making of porn films? If you've watched their personal interviews, have you noticed that the actresses giggle and glow, just like carefree girls on a cruise? And also, on *HBO*, have you ever watched *Cat House*? The documentary about prostitutes at that "ranch" in Nevada? Their radiance is so palpable that you can almost slice a piece off.

I've heard that laughter emitting from me, whenever I'm with a client. It's a pretty little bubbling from deep inside my mind. I can feel it infusing into me from somewhere far beyond me, and it helps the client relax. Even though he's just met me, it makes him instinctively glad that he's with me.

MEN, THE GODDESS, AND ME

Other women walk around in fetish gear for free, sexualizing themselves at every opportunity, and I'm not supposed to get paid for this role. It's all whoring just the same.

Hi ****! This is BOB! Call me back as soon as you CAN!

I listen to that message from that very expectant client, and my brow begins to scrunch up.

I don't know who he is.

Obviously he's someone who knows me, but I can't recall his voice or his number, and if I had a dollar for every "Bob" I've met...

When I call him back, I tell myself, *I'll pretend I remember him.* What he says when we talk might help me recall him. But there's a very good chance that it won't.

I dial his number. He answers, hears it's me, and goes bonkers. I'm still clueless, but I return his enthusiasm. *Why not*, I think. *Why should I break his bubble? It's better to float in it with him.*

Then I do my breezy little flirt that's really an act of detection. And he reveals to me, with no inkling that I'm digging, that he saw me one time, two years back.

Only ***once***? ***That*** long ago? How am I supposed to remember ***that*** Bob?

But I was a memorable experience for him, so of course he's got me stashed in his brain, and he thinks I remember because he does, and whenever I phone-chat with someone like this, I can't bear to let him realize that I don't recall a thing.

Sometimes when that happens, and I actually go *see* the guy, I still can't dredge up who he is. That's especially likely to happen if the first time, I met him at a motel, and here he is perching at a motel again. There's never been a property I've driven to, no location to arrive at once more, no personal space, no revisit, no house or yard or car or dog to help me bring it all back.

Because the truth of the matter is, a lot of guys are very much alike. No woman knows that as well as a whore. But I always want to try to live up to my ideal of being a true whore, which amounts to sensitivity to my clients' emotional needs. A guy who isn't memorable needs to know he's made an impression, somewhere, somehow, on someone, and that someone might be me. *Oh, boy.* The need for so much tact gets exhausting. No wonder I need my naps! As a born "people person," using that trait in this work, I'm on endless patrol for men's feelings.

But prostitution is generally defined as an act without any feelings. It's called paid, anonymous sex. *Anonymous.* That word sounds so desolate. A true whore wants to do better. A true whore makes every man she's with feel special, not like a nothing.

Sheer volume, however, makes it impossible for her to remember every one.

I think about the pastors of huge congregations, who counsel their multitudes of church-surfers each year. I think of the behavioral therapists, who tend to the legions of the seekers of quick-fix. And I think of inspiring college professors, who blow off the lids of the minds of so many. Sometimes, just as it goes with me, they must fail to identify someone. Surely they must get assailed by people, people who've splashed up against them like sea froth breaking on rocks, grateful souls who will never forget them for that thrill, that lit light, that catharsis, but those mentors can't recall *every*one, they don't know who some of them are!

The many. The over-and-over. The threat of impersonalization. I guess that's a pitfall of professional success.

And some "escorts" in some situations let it really get out of hand. Some have exploiters who slam them together with far too many men. And some make their own greed the culprit. They push themselves to death for the money. Those women's attitudes plummet to hell.

Anonymity, coercion and too much recurrence, when mixed with the most intimate act in the world, must rot someone's soul like an unending rape.

But it doesn't have to be that way. The trick is to be full of self-knowledge and love. To behold to only that radiance. You've got to be the person in charge of your work. I can't repeat that enough. No one but you should be dictating things: how many, and when, and with whom, and how much; it's *your* soul and body, after all.

And to hell with your own stupid greed! You've got to know when to back off, and rest.

But no matter how much you control things, no matter how many days off, no matter how well you prepare yourself for each and every tryst, you're not going to remember all your clients. You're not going to remember *every* guy who lost his mind in your mouth, or bared his soul on your breast, or took some much-needed encouragement from the gleaming rays of your smile.

And that's okay. That's not wrong. You're a priestess. You're in sexually spiritual service to the world.

But I think that the thing that's *not* okay is to turn completely callous, to do nothing to prevent a client from knowing that you can't recall him at all. He's suffering enough from insignificance, in other parts of his life.

Indeed, lots of guys are distinctly aware that I just might forget them. Many of them try to avert that. They get consumed by that driving masculine need to compete, to excel, and stand out. In attempts to impress me, they do lots of sweet things. They give me roses, fine wines, jewelry and massages. They tip me. They ask me to dinner. And as I've mentioned before, they expend a lot of effort in trying to please me in bed—even though they're the ones paying.

That's why, when the feminists who want to end whoring insist that I'm being mistreated, all I can do is laugh.

You're the ones mistreating me, ladies! Trying to take that away!

Can you imagine the pleasantness, the bliss, the feeling of feminine power, in a lucrative occupation where men try to be your best? Come on now, ladies. Most men aren't monsters. They're as needing of approval as we are, but with dicks.

"I want to be the one who makes you happy," so many clients say. And I smile and nod and never reveal that I hear that all the

197

time. Let them all believe they're the best boy! Who's it going to hurt!

And then there's all their sheer gratitude. That sweetens the scene even more. When I arrive, some clients are tensed-up and miserable, and when I leave, they're profoundly content. They're more than happy to pay me my fee, and as I ready myself to depart, they're aglow just like warm dying embers. They thank me over and over. They appreciate more than the sex. I've been the time-out they've needed in order to resolve something big.

When men get completely naked, have cataclysmic sex, and then bare their hearts and their troubles to a naked and listening stranger, they seem to be more able to self-connect and find some solutions for their problems. It seems to me that that may be a specifically *male* way to cope.

As a woman, I know that when I have a problem, the last thing I want is to bed with a stranger. If I need a dramatically physical release, I implode and have a wrenching and soul-soothing cry. That's what works for me. But as a whore I'm aware that men seem to know that a cathartic hour of sex and talk, especially with someone detached yet understanding, can be just what's required for the clearing of their heads.

Could that be the *male* recollection of Goddess, temple rite, and priestess?

I feel that the musician, Trent Reznor, the talent behind *Nine Inch Nails*, expresses that truth in his famous song, "*Closer*." All through the song, he refers to a "you", and this "you" is a person who allows him to rapaciously possess her. In "you" Reznor finds his "help", his way to be "somebody else", his solace that he pointedly and passionately aligns with the holy and the sacred. When he fucks "you" just "like an animal", "you" bring him "closer to God." That unrestrained slaking of sexual thirst is the sure way to a redemption. His words aren't sentimental, not evocative of romance, but they convey an atonement, a sharing of release, that eases "isolation" and "the hate that it brings," and renders something "perfect" out of "flawed."[1]

Nowhere in modern poetry or lyrics has there ever been such an ardent commingling of the two words "fuck" and "God." There's also an interwoven ribbon of verse, hard to make out unless you have a superior system, murmuring about "the honey" that "keeps me alive." The song is unforgettable, a riveting homage to sex, a mid-nineties hit that will be taken to the grave by everyone who's even just casually listened.

A client of mine philosophizes: "For men, sex and survival are the same thing."

That client is fifty-five. He's married. His wife no longer cares about sex. He tells me: "If the woman a man lives with doesn't want to have sex, he's got to get it somewhere, or he's truly in danger of dying."

He continues, "It starts as just a frustration. An emotional kind of death. But in the end it starves his spirit. I believe a man without sex is a man in the process of dying."

My client may be right.

Men understand a whore's purpose. I think all of them do, on some primordial level, even those men who are very severely morally conditioned against it. No matter what they've been taught to believe in their patriarchal religions, men know that *true* whoring is the beautiful fusion of spiritual and sexual nurture.

Men dream of it, obsess over it, remember it.

Men are the people who chafe the most against bars to erotic freedom. Men have this pesky instinctive need to always be "spreading their seed." In a previous chapter I've said this to wives, and I believe that it's worth repeating: no amount of erotic attention from one woman, no matter how much she's adored, can entirely erase that male need. In our culture, where men are expected to ignore that need, and can't—women respond to their strayings with fury, even if they're only to porn sites.

"Men are dogs," women hatefully fume.

Every once in a while, however, a woman with a different outlook emerges from the throng. It's usually a compassionate sex worker. But I found one female philosopher, one who's *not* in the business, who seems to give men a break. Camille Paglia, the well-known lesbian feminist author, published a book that makes a strong case for *men* as the victimized gender. Into vindictive feminist laps she dropped her large tome of contrary views. The year was 1990.

I read her book after becoming an "escort". I ingested *Sexual Personae* with a sex worker's unique perspective. At times, the author enthralled me. At other times, she let me down. Sometimes, she struck me with a glaring correctness. It reminded me of the erotic truth that every whore learns to service.

Sex is a subset to nature. Sex is the natural in man...
[the] grandeur of culture, the consolation of religion...
win his faith. But let nature shrug, and all is in ruin...
[sex] is the point of contact between man and nature.[2]

Paglia talks about maleness with a view that approaches sympathy. She portrays men as casualties of nature. According to Paglia, heterosexual sex is a trap. For the human male, she reasons, sex with woman is a skate to the edge of the all-consuming procreative suck hole. She likens the uterus to a dungeon. She likens women to its wardens. Because of their maternal plumbing, she insists that women are fixtures of nature, and that nature rules all, and takes all. It's the ravaging force that seeks species replication, and cares for nothing else.

According to Paglia, the human male has been historically determined to flee that megalomaniacal mire. The result has been our grandest civilizations. Paglia starts history where most people do, after the demise of Goddess. She doesn't accept the feminist belief that loving matriarchies once ruled the world. She admits that they existed, but not as commendable cultures. She admits that the sexual Goddess, the Great Mother, probably was the first deity, but She wasn't anyone's model for the highest of feminine gifts. Paglia describes Goddess as monstrous, just an ugly and brutal symbol of the procreative force. She refuses to credit primordial woman with a dignified place in artistic evolution. She cites men as the only humans who have created spiritualities that worship the gods in the sky. Men have constructed the gorgeous spires, both symbolic and actual, to honor the masculine "God in heaven" theisms that escape women's earthbound, nature-driven power.

But the human male is stuck. He's suspended between the demands of the earth and the liberating sky. His identity is a tug of war between the carnal stallion below, that passionately needs sex, and the heavenward spirit above, that reaches for something supposedly better. When he turns to woman, his "other half," for a loving break from that conflict, he encounters more clashes than comfort. He's terrified of her earthy, entrapping, baby-productive leanings.

Where shall he turn for relief?

Paglia implies homosexuality. She reminds us that gays don't procreate. So gays are the most elevated humans, she reasons, because they're free from the tyranny of nature.

Such thoughts exemplify Paglia's gift, her ability to bare the unheard-of. At times, she'll insist upon something that's shocking, but at the same time, inarguably truthful. Another example: "The fetus is a vampire."

I took in some of Paglia's thinking with a rebel's admiration. I concluded that her astounding opinions are in part a conscious taunting, an attempt to rile people up. She wants to get people thinking. She sure got a rise out of me!

Okay, so maybe the gays have it all together; maybe they've got nature beat; but what about all the other folks, the ninety percent who aren't gay? Where will straight men find comfort? Where shall *they* turn for relief?

In *Sexual Personae*, Paglia doesn't address that question. Not enough to satisfy me. She doesn't seem to realize she should seriously ask it; she's got bigger fish to fry. I, on the other hand, immediately think to ask it, because I've thrived as the answer. Men find the comfort they need in true whores. Those are principled women, aware of their mission, who soothe both the stallion and the heavenward spirit, but never try to pull either into the procreative goo.

In her provocative and widely-read tome, Paglia rarely mentions prostitution. She presents whores, conspicuously briefly, as nothing but a shadowy, condom-clad outlet for men's part in brutal nature. Back in the nineteen-eighties, as Paglia worked on her book, she apparently viewed whores as not much more than recipients of seed-spreading frenzies. In that book she implies that no whore deserves dignity, and that even the famous whores of literature are doomed defilers of the womb. Of course, when I gleaned that I felt disappointed. As it goes with most academics, those who have never been prostitutes, Paglia seemed ignorant of meaningful whoring.

But then I discovered an interview that took place in 1995. The person Paglia spoke with was Tracy Quan, an activist prostitute. It seems that at that point, Paglia gave whoring a deeper consideration. She asserted that prostitutes are the only women who are completely in control of sex and men. She repeatedly expressed admiration for whores as the women who are truly in charge, because, to use her word, they are pagans.[3]

Now she was speaking my language!

When appealing to women for sex, men are notorious for trying to get all their pleasure without a commitment. Commitment would be a submission to the Paglian dictatorship of nature. Some men shrink from that harness as though it were a deadly strangulation; others are strapped in it—married—and need to escape for a moment. I'm not disparaging marriage, here. I admire good marital unions. In fact, I perpetually long for one. And with regard to Paglia's radical view of natural women as quagmires, I have trouble understanding how this woman, this lesbian, can ferociously spin such a nightmarish image of the origin of her gender, and then obsess over it, expound on it, and doubt female beauty that hasn't been artistically contrived. Is she serious? How can a thinker so completely adhere to that truthful yet horrific and inadequate view, which is that women have all of us coming to life from that hole between shit and piss?

Yet Paglia's viewpoint is useful to me for flushing out truths about men, sex and whores.

No matter how emotionally satisfying they may be, monogamous love and marriage are just a long-term distraction from the nature of the stallion. The stallion is ruled by nature; he lives to mount many mares. He'll take one, and gallop away to the next, leaving each mare to deal by herself with the pain and gore and duty of birthing and caring for young. In the human male, of course, far more is going on under the dome than maniacal seed-spreading urges. In men, the ways of the stallion can be repressed, resisted, and effectively surpassed by much more compelling intentions. Contemporary men spend more and more time in happily unisex hookups with pregnancy and child-raising settings. Some men are changing diapers. Some men are family cooks. Men tend to be more sympathetic, these days, toward the pain of menstruation and the crazy bodily changes a woman endures when with child.

Some men are like monogamous penguins.

But the stallion in men never totally dies, and his need can be disruptive. At different times in their lives, men crave sex without so much as a hair of female ensnarement. As the outlet, we whores have plenty of business, and no movement, no religion, no foolishness of feminism, is ever going to change that.

Paglia concedes that with a wink and a nod.

Society is wasteful in its futile attempts to destroy our role as that vent. A *successful* objective would be societal support for the Paglian pagan, evolved. A *successful* objective would be societal support for the magnanimous, priestessly whore.

Whether she's a multiple-degreed courtesan, or a working class woman with only a GED, the quality whore, or true whore, is a woman of quality in her depth of understanding that she bears a responsibility. There's more to the true whore than mere orifices for seed. That whore is conscientious. She understands her worth. She's sexy, earthy, professionally promiscuous and never seeks commitment from a client, and yet she's principled. As I stated in the chapter expressly written to wives, that whore is never an enemy of marriage—she always uses condoms for intercourse, and she always sends clients home.

She accommodates the stallion without offending the spirit. Unlike the Paglian mother, who entraps men in uterine mire, or else the Paglian whore, who is only a vessel for wanderlust sperm, the true whore communes with the spirit, supporting the needs of the soul, even as she tends to the beast.

Back when I was a beginner in whoring, and my thirst to learn more about it was a driving, relentless urge, I made myself seek out some well-written books that have the word "Sex" in their titles. That's how I bumped into *Sexual Personae*. Another of the wonderfully relevant tomes that I found myself standing in front of, and thumbing through and then keeping, is the work of a contemporary author who was apparently named after Sir Thomas Moore. The title I believe he's best known for is *Care of the Soul*. The Moore book I bought was *The Soul of Sex.*

A distinguishing aspect of Thomas Moore is his deep theological background. A stint in the Catholic monastic life is a significant part of his past. But oh, what a wonderful rogue he's become! As I ambled along through his chapters, I could sense his sweet liberation, his palpable personal release, from the sexually guilt-inflicting doctrines of his church. Deep in those prohibitive canons, Moore detects an improbable connection with the joys of pagan sex. He expresses a heartfelt blasphemy, a love for the sacred eroticism that prevailed in the temples long before Christian faith.

I, of course, love his sacrilege.

Throughout *The Soul of Sex*, Moore points out that sex, when freed of moralistic anxiety, is a time-honored means to spirituality.

Regardless of the depth of the relationship between partners, he feels that such transcendence can always apply.

Sex is a kind of gnosis or holy knowing.[4]

Drawing upon the earthbound carnality of the primordial worship of Goddess, Moore discusses the "religious base of sex," and the "erotic nature of religion."

It was Moore who coined my favorite expression, *sexually spiritual*.

According to Paglia, sex for man is a downfall. Sex is the drive, and women are the bait, that bind him to the tyranny of nature. Art and patriarchal religion are his noble attempts to escape it. But Moore's view is radically different. In *The Soul of Sex*, Moore explores the access, through sex, to an upward-spiraling fulfillment of the soul. According to Moore, one can find the means to a divine soul connection in *any* type of consensual sex, be it fantastical or actual, be it fixed in monogamy or not. Unlike Paglia, who sees in heterosexual sex an interminable conflict between female/earth and male/sky, Moore perceives a harmony, *through heterosexual sex,* between the male, the female and the divine. He refers to pagan deities, echoing Paglia's use of those symbols to reveal the pagan pull on us all. But for Moore, paganism is never a plummet into bloody and filthy, maniacal nature. On the contrary, paganism is holistic and beautiful. He refers to the spiritual power of sex—often even "sinful" sex.

> Sex takes us into a world of intense passions, sensual touch…many levels of meaning…It makes the imagination come alive with…reverie, and memory. Even if the sex is loveless…still it has strong repercussions in the soul….
>
> In sex an inner life of strong emotions and vivid fantasies meets with a real person to create a moment of exceptional intensity when life is full and reason is dim…The soul craves such excursions from literal reality, and so it is no mystery that sex is so compelling and so enticing. But it is the soul, and not some inanimate body, that feels the hunger and can't resist the appetite. An altered state like sexual trance is not empty. Much goes on during this excursion away from daily living, though this special activity accomplishes things in the soul that may be quite different from what

we aim for in ordinary life. In sex we may subliminally discover many truths...[5]

A perceptive and sensitive prostitute intuits all that on her own.

I always encounter, in clients, a uniquely male erotic complexity. They entrust it to my care. I see the roving stallion that responds to the primal urge, throws himself into mating, and then bolts away just before Paglian nature can snag him. With me, the stallion slows down and relaxes. He trusts me. He knows that I'm the only woman who doesn't embody the Paglian threat.

But the steed and I aren't alone. In my clients I also see the Moorian soul, freed from inhibition by Eros. It floats above rigors of worries and cares. In bed, my clients release it.

Whenever they introduce themselves to me, new clients are outwardly pleasant. But they're also detectably shaken. Their nervousness betrays to me that this is no casual meeting. Their fear that I'm a cop notwithstanding, there's a whole other reason for their jitters. They're like people on some kind of pilgrimage. They've reached a holy or haunted place. They're clearly intimidated. They're often quite palpably trembling. They seem awestruck by the presence of something from *beyond*. They seldom refer to the act that comes next with a disrespectful air.

In the beginning, I came to understand that their shakiness is a submission. I was there to take them away. I was their medium of transport to a world they approached with passion. They craved that encounter with body and soul. It mattered not that they'd been taught this is sin; their need knifed to pieces a lifetime of moral conditioning.

I learned to admire men for having the guts to listen to the wisdom of their bodies and the longings of their nature. Men have the courage to *risk all*. Regardless of censure, they hunt down what they need. Men sometimes need no-strings pleasure and comfort. It's a category of worship. They need to worship the naked female body, and they need to possess it completely, and then they need to leave. They need to pay homage to Goddess, and then they need to go. They relentlessly seek ways to do this, in spite of a culture that screams: *Don't you dare!*

Thomas Moore dares to exalt the whore. He knows that in prepatriarchal times, when the godhead was fully female, prostitution was a benevolent ritual, a rite of religion that he's come to understand. Though he doesn't say much about modern-day whoring, Moore does make the point that, *Venus, Aphrodite* and *Astarte* notwithstanding, another name for Goddess is *Porne*. He adds a seldom-taught fact of our past. He informs us that in ancient Greece, before the total takeover of patriarchs, Porne was the patron goddess of the temple priestess-whores.

His reference to prostitutes ends there, on that meager but positive note. Apparently he's communicating something like this: *Okay, I'm a Catholic ex-priest. But I'm telling you that whoring was once a sacred act. Do what you will with it!*

Throughout *The Soul of Sex*, Moore tamps down his approval for pagan sexual freedom with his often-repeated opinion that it's not necessarily actual sex, but erotic awareness alone that transports us. Perhaps that's enough, he implies. I can sense in Moore a refusal to bluntly condone promiscuity. His restraint most likely arises from the restrictive drills of the Church. Yet he constantly slips away from his grounding at the Christian alter. Moore tiptoes up to my kind, and he peers at the alter *we* grace. His gaze is warm with homage.

I know this. I can sense it. There's awe behind his fond wording. It's just like the glow in the eyes of my clients.

In concluding things for himself, Moore appears to have achieved a comfortably balanced view. He speaks of restraint and indulgence as though they're righteous yin and yang, two natural halves of the human sexuality whole. He hints of a mutual place in the world for both whores and celibates.

I would add one point to Moore's thoughts. I would assert that the true whore provides the same solace as churchy, buttoned-up clerics. Her erotic-based mode is unique, but not wrong, and *men inherently know it.*

As an erotic professional, my greatest insight into men has been this:

The encounter that women find offensive, the "hit-and-run" loving or "one-night stand," is a tryst where men want to *worship.* Nothing, in a one-night stand, is cheap or sleazy for a man. It's *woman's* perception that makes it so.

An "escort" is a woman who's rewarded for that worship.

The true whore knows something that most other women seem not to: that when men shake off their conditioned contempt for the women in prostitution, and respond to their inborn male nature, *they want to respect the one-night stand, and they want to respect the woman who provides it.*

And when men encounter a true whore, they experience a provider who understands that they're trying to pay homage. She knows that they're attempting to instinctively worship the primordial Great Mother Goddess. *She knows she facilitates that homage.*

Generous "tithes" are given the whore for her provision of that *rite.* And then, like parishioners after a mass, men need to feel free to take off.

A classic hit by *The Doors*, called *"Hello, I Love You"* portrays their need to pay homage. The song is a tribute to the one-night stand. It expresses the hope that it will happen. You can argue that I'm crediting animal lust with more spiritual depth than its due; you can say that Jim Morrison is only expressing the horny obsession of the male. If that's the case, then why does he exalt his verses with images of feminine deity? Woman is never referred to here as just a delicious morsel, just something great to fuck. She's the "queen of the angels," she's the "statue in the sky." Man "begs" for her. The world "crouches at her feet." With regard to her form and function, there's no Paglian fear or revulsion. "Her arms are wicked and her legs are long, when she moves my brain screams out this song...."[6]

Man instantly adores her.

This is not the lasting, marry-me commitment, and yet this is a love, an all-consuming emotional moment. "Hello, *I love you,* won't you tell me your name?" He loves her without even knowing her name!

Thomas Moore apparently agrees.

> Sexual attraction is not at all a purely physical event. The soul is always in search of whatever will complete its desire, and our physical eyes are never separate from the eyes of the soul.[7]

Women fail to understand that getting hit on, right on the street, is a glorification of those of them who inspire a vision of Goddess. It's an honoring by men of the sexual deity, immediate, intense, and needing its own hymn. It's the visual turn-on ascribed to the male; at any time, around any corner, the Goddess in woman overwhelms him.

As a novice "escort", I soon became aware of my Goddess-inspired mission. It was to leave each client feeling more than only bodily drained. It was to make him feel better in general. I strove to leave each client in an improved emotional state. Right from the beginning I could see that a lot of them needed that from me.

Then and now, I try to give every worshipper a fulfilling encounter with Eros and grace. I try to make an hour momentous. I never leave a troubled man without a sense of hope. I leave the undesired man with the sense that he's worthwhile. I make sure that the lonely man reconnects. I see to it that the man bogged down by cares can rediscover his buoyancy. The youngest need to know that they're manly, and I show them how they are.

My distinction from others in the helping professions is that I go straight for the penis.

Naked as babies and sexually fulfilled, when relaxing with me men can bask in their element. They can bask without fear of entrapment. They can briefly detach from their jobs or their families, and look to their own renewal. That, as much as the sex, is what they pay me for.

Clients all praise their favorite whore for the fact that she knows all their secrets. They tell her the things that they can't tell their wives, or their mothers, or even their friends, or even their licensed counselors. She's their proverbial confessional, but not the one at the church; she's listening, accommodating, and exactly what he wants: sensual, compassionate, nonjudgmental, and **naked**.

In that short but memorable hour, in that tiny leak of time in which a man permits his escape, I subtly learn what pains him. I learn what drove him to call me forth. Then I try to intuit the just-right response—the sensual skills and the powerful words—that will leave him not only sexually sated, but also cheered up and rejuvenated, and ready to face the major people in his life.

When it comes to either sexual or spiritual comfort, I've learned to erase any difference.

Perhaps some people might scoff at my assertion that priestess-identified whoring provides a spiritual solace. Such people might never be able to integrate religious experience with "anonymous" sex. To those I would offer another justification. I would offer the down-to-earth outlook of a delegate at the Second World Whores' Congress. When she expressed her opinion, she enshrined whore validation in totally practical terms. She reasoned, "All men want the same thing: they all want to sleep with women on the first night. So...why not get paid for it? That is the most sensible procedure."[8]

I'm a priestess-identified prostitute. If I weren't, I'd derive less fulfillment. But just the same I have to admit that the pragmatism conveyed above is logical and sufficient. It stands on its own as a perfect rationale for a woman to profit from what men desire.

I'm reminded of a scene from the film, *American Psycho*. The main character has a night of sex with two young women, together. One of them he's just met. The other girl he knows on a casual basis.

Later on, as they're leaving, he hands the one he just met a sumptuous fistful of cash; the other he just pats on the back.

No matter how the viewer may feel about prostitution, I defy her or him to tell me that when they take in that scene, they don't get an inkling that the unpaid girl is slighted somehow, or a fool.

Hey ****, this is Dave, goes another guy on my voicemail. *I'm calling just to say hi.*

This guy is one of my regulars. I remember, no problem, who he is. He's called to give me an update.

I think I'll have some time next week, I hear him eagerly say. And then:

I can't wait! See you soon! Have a wonderful day!

I LOVE YOU JESUS,
BUT...BUT...

Ideologies writhe in contortions.

For most of my life—my life as a spiritual seeker who was raised to be a Christian—I've occasionally found myself talking to Jesus in a state of angry frustration. What I say to Him tends to go something like this:

I love you Jesus, but I hate religion. And Jesus, I've got a very strong feeling that you don't care for it, either. I don't see how you can love those beliefs that make you more autocrat than angel.

*For instance, in that book that people composed about you and the God who supposedly sent you, it's written that you insisted, back then, that the **only** way to redemption is **you**.*

It must shatter your heart to see all the hatred that egomaniacal allegation has caused!

Jesus, sweet Jesus! You, the walking embodiment of pure unselfish love! How it must hurt you to see all those people who think you're so full of yourself! How it must hurt you to see all those "faithful" who give you such low human limits! "There's no other way but by me." Incredible! They've made you out like a pompous professor, or even a schoolyard bully!

Jesus, sweet vessel of pure love incarnate, how unbearably sad that must make you.

*Their scriptures also have you saying the most beautiful sentence on earth: "Love thy enemy." Now, I believe **that** command may have **really** come from you, because the wisdom behind those three words sounds so perfect.*

So, how would you rate your most zealous "followers"? Do they honor your request?

*Once I got into a religious discussion with one of your "followers." I told him where I stand, which is **not** on the "straight and narrow." He responded:*

"You're going to Hell."

How do you deal with the pain, sweet Jesus, of knowing that people who make judgments like his are the ones who insist that they're closest to you?

I guess he forgot something else you're supposed to have said: "Judge not, lest ye be judged."

*So if that guy suddenly found himself recalling your admonition, he probably regretted his slip-up with the fear that **he** might get sent to the fire.*

As if Love would create a Hell!

How do you stand the pain, sweet Jesus, of seeing that the people who vow that they love you are walking around with this Bible, this tome full of manmade fear, and are calling it your literal Word? Their hatred for anyone who doesn't obey it must hurt you even more than when they nailed you to the cross.

I've known a lot of people who try to be like you. They're lovely, and loving, and forgiving, and gentle, and many of them aren't Christians. Many of them don't care for a church or the Bible.

But your "followers" call them "heathens."

It seems that a lot of your "followers" are a lot like the Pharisees. They couldn't see Love when it stood right before them!

On the news I keep seeing your "followers" with signs that say God "hates" this or that. They actually put the word "hate" next to "God"!

Jesus, how do you bear it? How do you bear all that malice in His name?

The only kind of hate I recall you displaying—if biblical stories have some kind of merit—is your wrath at the tax collectors working in God's temple. And while I'm on the subject of taxes—didn't you supposedly say that we can't worship both God and money?

If you did, then how can it be that your "followers" tend to pray for more wealth and power?

*Those people get crazy over abortion. But they'll send kids to die in defense of Christian values! They think that it's perfectly righteous to kill, not just for our country's security, but also in **YOUR** name.*

I read a description of the mindset of our zealously Christian President, George W. Bush. He's on a warrior mission for you and for oil, over there in Iraq. A former defense official said of him:

> "Bush is a believer in the adage 'People may suffer and die, but the Church advances.'"[1]

Jesus, I think that the suffering and killing is what you'd want him to stop. I think that you'd want him to wake up and see that his war is just terror in YOUR name!

*And what of the women, Jesus? The gender the most like you? How do you bear it that so many of your "followers" want to keep women down, with no voices? Even the women amongst them go along! And how do you bear it that some women who defy it tend to become so **unloving**?*

It was a man who wrote that you stated that women should always submit to their husbands. And on the next line he wrote that you said that slaves should submit to their masters.

As if Love would justify slavery, or the subjugation of the motherly!

Sometimes I get so angry, I have to fight myself to remember the things that Jesus would want me to. I'm sure love and forgiveness are all that He'd want me to practice.

I recently read a *Time* interview with the eminent Deepak Chopra. He's one of our nation's spiritual leaders. He's written no less than forty books on how to live in peace. But Chopra isn't a Christian. In fact, Chopra considers the patriarchal God an obsolete idea.

He imagines a world where peace is put first, where people approach their adversaries with compassion. Now, doesn't that sound like someone attempting to *love thy enemy*? He doesn't live by the Bible, and yet he emulates Jesus.

Chopra disdains religion. He refers to religion as "discordant." He uses the word "idiotic."[2]

Chopra feels that if God does exist, then God must be a woman. He senses that God is female because women tend to be nurturing and caring, and men are "the most predatory beings on the planet." So here is a brilliantly spiritual man who's come all the way full circle. He's taken it all back to Goddess. From his famous West Coast center, where thousands attend his seminars, he advises us all to encompass the feminine face of divinity.

A conservative Christian would tell you, of course, that Chopra's going to Hell.

Then there's Bono, the lead singer and songwriter for *U2*, the greatest rock band on earth. Bono and Bill and Melinda Gates have made the front cover of *Time*. The three of them are *Time's* 2005 selection as "People of the Year." Their humanitarianism is why. The Gates are known for sharing their billions with legions of worldwide poor. Bono lives to see human rights realized for the starving, beleaguered Third World. In the midst of the rigors of musical achievement that won *U2* the 2005 Grammy award, he prevails as a tireless campaigner. Bono visits powerful leaders, and prevails upon them for money. His earnestness and benevolent love for the poorest people on earth compel the wealthy Americans in high political office. They know they'd better comply with his wishes, or they're going to look like Scrooge. Little by little, this eminent rock star is doggedly changing the world.[3]

But Bono isn't particularly religious. So the fundamentalists insist, no doubt, that he and his band are Hell-bound.

And what about that guy, Neale Donald Walsch, who's published several books about his amazing rap sessions with God? He claims that his pen started writing by itself, and has kept it up for years. He claims that this phenomenon is word from Heaven Itself.

Apparently God uses Walsch's pen to reveal divine reasons and thoughts. This Lord is neither male nor female. You could also say It's both. It expresses unconditional love for every human on earth, and is appalled that Its "faithful" always make It a judge.[4]

Well, I'll bet that the people It's talking about are absolutely sure that Walsch is a "false prophet" who will only burn in Hell.

Back when you attended your Sunday School or Catechism or Hebrew class, you were taught that "pagan" is heinous. Do you remember the biblical story of that notorious fertility symbol, worshipped by those awful "idolaters," the terrible "Golden Calf"? How about Sodom and Gomorrah, those infamous cities of deadly heathen sin? Do you recall those hate-filled referrals to the "Whore of Babylon"?

The Bible makes them sound like the scourge of the earth.

Those evidently peaceful cultures, evidently ruled by women for many thousands of years, were gradually overtaken by marauding, raping males. Men had decided that they and their deities could run the world a lot better.

Well, there's an awful lot of discussion, these days, about whether or not they were right.

I for one feel that in our time, humanity is struggling with a first-ever merging of feminine and masculine powers. We've all seen what patriarchy can do; some of us are aware of how matriarchies were; I feel that now, in this terrifying epoch of anxiety and confusion, no matter how torturous the process, the world is moving toward a beautiful resurgence of the cooperative pagan wisdom of Goddess. She will temper and balance the warrior cultures of Yahweh, Christ and Allah.

I feel that most difficult conflicts—whether they're personal or societal, religious or political—may be offshoots of the ongoing striving for the earthy, nurturing Great Mother mindset to powerfully reemerge. Lifestyles considered all wrong by conservatives are manifestations of that Goddess-based revival.

I feel that Her renewal is a giant step forward in the ever-evolving psyche of humans. *Change is ordeal*, someone noted once said. Yea, but positive change is good.

Right now, in the midst of unparalleled social changes, the collective human family is emotionally heaving and thrashing. Religious conservatives are ferociously clinging to old patriarchal ways. They're trying to make them the law of the land. And the multitudes that defy them, however justifiably, are making a lot of mistakes. The destabilizing effects of their confusion bring on, to name just a few of the problems, substance abuse, relationship troubles, and broken homes.

The progressives among us are thinking their usual, wonderful, visionary thoughts, but a lot of them flipflop and flounder. The ultra-conservatives are sure of themselves, but their way, to the mainstream majority, is offensive, inadequate, passé, and delusional. It seems that all people, everywhere, are either absolutely sure of their religious beliefs, which glorify their lifestyle and vilify everyone else's, or they're absolutely uncertain about everything. Not one charismatic person or group is making enough sense, or inspiring enough minds, to bring people, or nations, decisively together.

I love you Jesus, but, but...

For several millennia now, we women have subsisted as a worldwide-conquered empire. Each of us stores just a ghost of the knowledge of our prepatriarchal power. We, the inventors of agriculture, who were also most likely the creators of the very first written words, whose life-giving image was worshipped as divine for thousands of years before Goddess became God, have been psychically crushed by patriarchal dominion. Whether we piously accept that condition of defeat, or defy it with bared teeth, many of us spend our lives wrestling with a sense of mysterious loss. Many of us feel, quite often, overtaken by that loss. We become depressed, self-loathing, maladjusted or angry, and often for no obvious cause. The obscured ancestral reason is only revealed when feminist scholars unearth its buried archives, and then, so few people care.

What all people need, male or female, is something to believe in that's bigger than they are. In America, the Old and New Testaments are the most often served-up platters for that always-sought-after solace. They're fed to us from babyhood on.

Well, the holes in those dishes are so big and gaping that I keep losing my food.

I love you Jesus, but, but...

I'm a sexual professional, loathed and feared, especially by the religious. At times I need to ponder those people. I feel compelled to look in their direction, and venture an uneasy smile, just as I would for the strangers beside me in an elevator stuck between floors.

With regard to those loyal to patriarchal religions, I realize that they're the most hostile when it comes to the world of sex work. Irregardless, I'm not offended. Just as it would be pointless to try to win them over, it would also be silly to get all upset because of the reality that I never will. Oh, I'm sure to point out, with a *"Gotcha!"* sense of justice, the gratitude of my many regular clients from that camp! But I won't waste my time in a useless appeal to the huge, rigid group as a whole. I can only hope that none of them decide to persecute me. To hunt me down, find out where I live, and, with rape as a probable prior distraction, shoot me right to pieces.

Or burn me at a stake. They burned down the house of Dolores French, hoping that she was in it, soon after French made it known in Atlanta that she was an activist for prostitutes' rights.[5]

No, there's no appealing to the religious. Their Bible has the story of a famous whore, yes—that one on the verge of getting murdered for her lifestyle. Do you think that Christians will ever enshrine what Jesus is supposed to have said to her attackers? Do you think that they'll ever drop their stones?

You won't find beloved whores in their Good Book, even though in Jesus' world, some still prevailed in pagan temples. What you will find amongst Bible theorists is a current conjecture that the woman who was almost clobbered to death was no whore, after all.[6]

But of course she was a whore. There's no escaping it, folks. The original meaning of "Mary" is "whore priestess," and "Magdalene" means "from Magdala"—a vicinity that was known for its paganism.[7]

But I'd never implore the God-fearing to accept me as a whore-priestess. I would never reveal myself to them. I'd probably get killed. I do have some questions to ask them, however, from the safety of this tome. Or maybe my questions are all just for Jesus. It's hard for me to say.

My biggest question concerns zealousness. Religious zeal is a phenomenon that I totally fail to fathom. I've always been astounded by the staunchness of it all. Such an impassioned commitment occurs, and in the absolute absence of justifying proof. How can people stop questioning things, and live by one unverified creed? How can they ignore all the holes that I see? They must be aware of them!

I have to confess that I'm embarrassed by my triteness. I'm aware that my agnosticism is humdrum, the thinker's predictable doubt; maybe my misgivings are too common to mention. If they are, please forgive me. I can't help it. The religious mentality just flabbergasts me. I don't get it.

I don't get it that their dogma is *legion*. I don't get it that it's *their way or no way*.

I recently saw a write-up in *Time* about yoga classes in churches. Some Christians are worried about it. Original yoga is a practice of Hinduism, so they feel it's a blasphemy. Some are concluding that yoga—even a Christianized yoga—should never be taught in "God's house." Conservative Hindus are a bit uneasy, too, because some of the yogic mantras have been turned into Christian prayers.[8]

I almost lost my lunch when I read that. Why can't people just sit themselves down and lose themselves in the peace? Why should yoga and Jesus be divided, in anybody's mind? What does it matter what mantra or prayer? What makes people so terribly scared to melt and stir and enjoy altogether all the beautiful pathways to God?

It's as clear as the day to me, Jesus. Religion separates people.

In another issue of *Time,* I read about a large, West Coast, Christian university. It boasts of a swollen enrollment. The comparative statistics are impressive. During the past decade or so, this parochial center of higher education has enjoyed a proportionately greater enrollment than the nation's private secular schools.[9]

Most of the students that *Time* interviewed said they'd chosen this school because they'd gotten the impression that its focus on them is more caring. But most of them also indicated that something deeply disturbs them: the refusal of instructors to allow free debate.

Isn't academia the place where *everything* is supposed to be freely debated?

Time reported that all of the professors who teach at that school must certify, when appointed, that they absolutely believe that the Bible is the true and literal word of God.

How can enrollment be so heavy in a school where the students admit that they're troubled by that dogmatism?

You can tell me that it's all about people attempting to feel more secure. You can tell me that it's all about people attempting to overcome weakness. You can say it's about the reassurance of some omnipotent Big Daddy. He makes all the terror of the unknown go away. He renders the addicts and predators among us more able to rein in their manias. He provides an acceptable way to be maniacal, and with rules for behaviors allowed, or not.

But a lot of uncomfortable students and I see Big Brother's face on Big Daddy.

Then I discovered a *New Yorker* article about a Christian college in Virginia. This extremely fundamentalist school grooms its students for positions in government. Almost all of them were home-schooled as children. Their everyday educations, from preschool through the present, make me think of American wilderness tutoring, about two centuries gone, where no schoolhouses had yet been built, no teachers were to be found, and parents were teaching their children the Bible, and very little else.

Almost all of those students are Government majors who plan to infiltrate D.C.[10]

Whoa.

Again, I felt a bit queasy. It's very unsettling to face it: such radical religion is here in my country, the place that's supposed to be the "land of the free." Yes I know, that same mindset *started* my country. But you see, I'm a born progressive. I'd like to believe we've evolved to a place way *past* that rigidity.

I guess not.

But nothing I've been saying about Christians is meant to devalue Jesus. I'm awed when I imagine divinity incarnate, when I picture Christ walking among us. I actually break out in chills. I've been moved to tears by every single "Jesus" movie I've seen. I recently watched *Ben Hur.* I wept in response to the scenes of Christ with emotions no less piercing than when I first saw the epic as a child.

My feelings for Jesus are a worship of his love. He embodied love as unbeatable power. Everything he supposedly did, whether it literally happened or not, is a stunning illustration of the power of love. He advised us to always forgive.

Love thy enemy. I've always been astounded by that maxim's implications. If the entire world were to simultaneously obey that simple instruction, life on earth would be ideal in a minute.

Jesus' love conquered everything we fear: evil, heartbreak, pain and death. But I'll never believe that we have a Creator who sent His most beloved to be punished for our defects. That concept seems twisted to me. What father would do such a thing? And why would any divinity be inclined to suffer so harshly for us? Even if that Creator made us much like Himself, and loves us? So what if we've failed Him? His purest creation should be martyred for this, should be flayed and destroyed like some sacrificial beast? The idea of His begotten Son, arriving here and living to be slaughtered for us, and by us, feels awful to me. It feels gut-level wrong.

My sense of wrong is reflected in *The Da Vinci Code*, the novel that's made the patriarchs who want us to believe in their dogmas gnash their teeth with pure poison rage. Its author, Dan Brown, based his story on esoteric truths. The novel's main character, the scholarly Robert Langdon, is a man who has devoted his professional life to the study of ancient pagan symbols. He informs us that the pre-Christian cross was square-shaped. It represented the perfect intersection of male and female natures. It predated Christianity by about fifteen hundred years. He compares it to the Christian cross.

> ...this kind of cross carried none of the Christian connotations of crucifixion associated with the longer-stemmed Latin Cross, originated by Romans as a torture device. Langdon was always surprised by how few Christians who gazed upon "the crucifix" realized their symbol's violent history was reflected in its very name: "cross" and "crucifix" came from the Latin verb *cruciare*—to torture.[11]

For that very reason, I refuse to see *The Passion of the Christ.* I suppose the viewers who are sated by that nightmare are the people who believe that the real event "saved" them. Well, I'm certain that the reenactment of the last twelve hours of the life of Christ, which, by all accounts I've read, is a horror of overkill, would only profoundly upset me. And for what? My heart goes running for cover behind the complaint of David Denby. "Gibson's timing couldn't be more unfortunate," the film critic wrote in his review. "Another dose of death-haunted religious fanaticism is the last thing we need."[12]

The success of that film has made Denby incorrect. Millions are obviously hungry for scenes where Jesus gets ripped asunder on a par with the jumpers from the towers.

But I stand by Denby's opinion.

Another critic dubbed the film "Bloodheart" and "Gandhi as Rocky." Not entirely in jest, Richard Corliss coined a new genre, "religious splatter art."[13]

I'll pass. I can't get into the mindset of torture and murder mixed up with perfect love. No matter how well you slice it, no matter what beautiful concepts loom behind it, I just can't stand the idea.

The comic Bill Maher puts it well. He jokes with the painful demeanor of a bitter survivor of Catholicism. With what I feel is just a tad hyperbolic, he assures us that right until the day he drops dead, he'll always have some church-inflicted psychic wounds to lick.

"Religion is something they terrorize you with when you're little," he grimaces. "And when you grow up, it becomes a neurological disorder. Then you spend the rest of your life trying to deal with that."[14]

Maher's talk of such damage begs the question: how far is any Christian leader from adopting the ruthless infliction of jihad? Especially when his brand of jihad evolves to emotional assault?

If one person, even one, feels forced to ponder such things, then I suspect that zealous religion must be deeply repugnant to God.

And Jesus, that always brings me around to more agitated questions for you.

The Resurrection was supposed to be proof of the mission of Jesus as God's holy Son, but all I get from it is that Christ, who was a soul of phenomenal dimensions, could literally traverse death. That's a mind-rocking, glorious thought to consider, but it doesn't help me to justify the brutality of his murder, his sickeningly slow and vertical death, his nailed-up expiration in the searing desert sun, and all to atone for *us*.

Christians believe our salvation is the point, and that's supposed to make it all great. Well, that's a useless point for me to ponder, because I don't believe we need to be "saved." Even though there are those among us who have raped or murdered the innocent, I'll never believe that as a whole, we humans are wretches, unworthy.

I think theologians might call me a Gnostic.

No, I don't believe that we require a Savior, and I don't believe in Original Sin. I do believe that to teach that to children amounts to a form of abuse. To impress upon children, or on people of any age, that they're basically cursed from birth, and that they can lift that curse only by believing what they're told, is certainly abusive and coercive to me.

And when I consider the source of that curse, *whoa!* It began in a mythical garden. A big booming voice without a body told a man and a woman what to do. Then a talking snake—a *talking snake!*—got the woman to break the big rule. And then she, of course, got the man to. We're all cursed because of that fairy tale?

Yes, I know that the snake was supposed to be Satan. But I don't believe in Satan. I don't believe in an otherworldly source of all our evil. What do we need a Satan for? We screw things up just fine without him. And when I'm informed of the thousands of years of Goddess worshipping matriarchies, that prevailed in the world before the Hebrews invented their story of Eden, then the snake takes on a terrible significance, and not because it was evil. If anything there was demonic, it boded in the hearts of the murderous males who created that woman-damning Paradise myth.

Any feminist who's done her homework will tell you that in prepatriarchal, Goddess-ruled times, the serpent was beloved. The snake represented Her wisdom and counsel. The snake was the mascot of Goddess. Some artifacts unearthed all over the world are sculptures or carvings of the deity with her hands holding regal-headed serpents, suggestive of animated wands.[15]

So the guys taking over made the sanctified snake into Satan. Oh, the power of spinning and mindfucking!!!!

How much has *your* mind been fucked with???

I've never been afraid of snakes, and I used to wonder why. Now I don't wonder so much.

Yes, the ancient marauding patriarchs took pains to demonize those reptiles. As their part in the drive of many different tribes to annihilate the worship of Goddess, the Hebrew leaders designated, in their myth of the world's creation, both serpent and woman as the defilers of man. For verification of all that, remember the *herstory* books. I've just paraphrased from several, above. If you go to *Amazon.com*, and do a search on, say, **When God Was a Woman**, a title by Merlin Stone, the website will pull it right up for you, and present you with an additional list of titles of related revelations.

Go ahead. Indulge yourself. If you haven't already done so, acquaint yourself with *herstory.*

You'll never be the same again.

And remember, the vile record of the ruin of Goddess worship is right in the drawer of any motel room, in the beginning of the Old Testament. The language is straightforward and simple. A savage and relentless persecution is described.

Not a lot is made of that horror. Jews and Christians are raised to believe that the biblical Hebrews killed entire tribes of "Whore of Babylon" patrons because they were peoples who were far too depraved to be allowed to live. I've learned to be amazed at their unquestioning acceptance of that founding genocide, that murderous launch of the Judeo-Christian dogma that's valued by religious Americans.

Secular probes of biblical times reveal the political motives. Though a "holy war" against pagans is the accepted rationale—the campaign of a "righteous" ethnicity cleanse commanded by a "righteous" new Lord—the secular scrutiny shows reasons of a far more political nature. According to feminist scholars, and others not swayed by patriarchal religion, it was about the destruction of matriarchies, those long-established civilizations empowered and governed by women. Power for men, and not power for God, was the true motivation for the atrocities of patriarchs so thoroughly described in the beginning of the Bible.

In the Old Testament, Joshua was the famed Hebrew warrior who led the pogrom against thousands of pagans who worshipped the popular Whore. Well, check this out. In today's world, the founder of that fundamentalist college in Virginia—the leader of that college full of home-schooled Christian kids, located next to D.C.—refers to his students as the "Joshua Generation."

Whoa.

So we've got people who want to be Joshua, who would purge the national consciousness of every idea except one. According to the article regarding those students, they adhere to the Bible, just the Bible, and even avoid *U2* music.

Does that make your blood run cold?

After I found out about ***herstory,*** my agnosticism no longer straddled the fence. It fell off in a stunned state of shock. I was no longer bemused, just peering around, no longer just a skeptical seeker. What a big difference a spin makes! Especially when it hits me like a blast of perfect truth! *No wonder*, thought I, *that I've never seen patriarchal religion as unassailably upright. No wonder I've never seen patriarchal religion as the one and only true way.*

Some deep instinctive part of me has always warned that I shouldn't.

For people raised and programmed on the patriarchal religions of today, religions that affect us in even the most secular aspects of our society, perhaps there remains a lingering, almost innate memory of sacred shrines and temples tended by priestesses who served in the religion of the original supreme deity. In the beginning, people prayed to the Creatress of Life, the Mistress of Heaven. At the very dawn of religion, God was a woman. Do you remember? [16]

I do.

Not long ago I came across an article by a Harvard instructor in the sciences, the late paleontologist, Stephen Jay Gould. In it, the scholar was discussing his agnosticism. As I casually scanned his piece, his friendly-armchair philosophizing graciously pulled me in. In his gently delivered, yet powerful points, I could sense a born mediator.

Gould saw improbable harmony between those age-old rivaling mindsets, religious belief and scientific inquiry. In his article he was expressing his puzzlement over the power of religion to cause hateful acts, and to also inspire great love.

> I am not, personally, a believer or a religious man in any sense of institutional commitment or practice. But I have enormous respect for religion, and the subject has always fascinated me....Much of this fascination lies in the historical paradox that throughout Western history organized religion has fostered both the most unspeakable horrors and the most heartrending examples of human goodness....[17]

Gould proposed a "respectful, even loving concordat" between the empiricism of science and the mysticism of the soul. He conceded that religion is far too important to far too many people for dismissal of the comfort it provides. Then he calmed the storm between religion and science. He weaved together theology and the theory of evolution in one smoothly insightful integration.

> I also know that souls represent a subject outside...science. My [scientific] world cannot prove or disprove such a notion, and the concept of souls cannot threaten or impact my domain...I surely honor the metaphorical value of such a concept both for grounding moral discussion and for discussing what we

most value about human potentiality; our decency, care, and all the ethical and intellectual struggles that the evolution of consciousness has imposed on us.

I wish for another sort of harmony. I wish for accord between the patriarchs and the pagans. I wish for the nurture of Goddess to eclipse the imperial God. I hope that it's not just a pipe dream, because it just might save the world.

Meanwhile, I sadly observe peoples' struggle. It's ironic to suffer any conflict on the path to the solace of faith, and it seems that most people do. It seems to me that any religion that creates misgivings is useless. I've always suspected that the millions who attend Bible study classes are seeking not only the comfort of Big Daddy, but are also attempting to rationalize all the biblical murder and mayhem and sexism.

I've always known that I can't.

A long time ago, when I was quite young, I learned that whenever I *stop* all my thoughts about religious conditionings and teachings, and then I just sit there and *open*, then, and only then, is when I "see the light." When I simply relax and open my mind and *let go* all the doctrines and dogmas, *then* I enjoy a sweet inkling of divine, all-powerful love.

But I'll never believe in a paternalistic, sternly judgmental creator. I don't see divine love being judgmental. How can true love be judgmental?

Whenever I read articles about current Christian writers, I'm assured that they're inspiring a loving way of life, and focusing more on the Golden Rule than the fire-and-brimstone threat. When I leaf through some best-selling, new Christian books, I get a sense of a strong directive for people to always put other people first. I can appreciate instruction like that. That's an endeavor that I hold dear, too. But on page after page I see nothing but quotes from the Bible. For me, that's dissatisfying. I'm filled with instinctive distrust for advice that draws from only one source.

According to some of those authors, Satan tries to make you do this, and Satan tries to make you do that, every day of your life. And of course, if you don't obey God, you're going to end up in Hell. The authors seem to be taking care to convey that warning gently. But it's there, and it's still ugly, and it doesn't strike me as true. That's when I lose interest and return their tomes to their book-promotion shelves.

I'm far too agnostic to accept the contention that every selfish temptation we feel is from an evil being outside of us who's trying to take us from God. What do the Christians think we all are, just a globe full of dim cosmic puppets? I guess they'd say no, they believe in "free will." But it seems to me that in their perceived world, "free will" is only just barely.

I think that the failure of patriarchal religion to ever win me over is not only because it offends me with its torture of prodigies, its desecration of Goddess, and its murderous history, but also because its most compelling attraction, that of questions firmly answered and uncertainty relieved, is something that I simply don't need. I'm okay with not knowing exactly what's true, and I understand that uncertainty is the only provable certainty. Though the pain of not feeling safe and secure has reduced me to awful temptations to binge too much with food, I don't need to hide in some concocted mental shelter from existential terror. The truth is, I'm used to that terror. Uncertainty has been my most constant companion since I was a vulnerable tot.

Christianity did attempt to claim me as a child. By the time I was six years old, I was attending Sunday school regularly, and learning both Testaments. But my ability to childishly believe had been destroyed. Mommy had gotten crippled, Daddy had totally left her, and then Mommy had completely ceased to be. My own parents, my own source of life and protection, had thoroughly taught their baby that security doesn't exist. That there are no certainties, ever, except human shortcomings and death, and the never-ending struggle to discern a meaning for them. That's mighty weighty stuff to unload on a small child's head, and it crushed me until I became a child that no pious doctrine could comfort.

I should add that my father was a Holocaust survivor. A decade before I was born, the Nazis occupied Holland, his homeland. He miraculously escaped them, and found his way to New York.

His parents weren't so lucky. Both of them died in the camps.

So I was born in the wake of the unspeakable, an evil that stole close family from me long before I was even conceived. As a child I was never informed of that horror. My father was a practical man. He had no use for a religion that had caused him to lose so much. He didn't want me to go through that. He didn't want it touching me at all. He figured his children would be safer and happier if they were raised in their mother's Presbyterian church. It would be years before I knew myself as the daughter of a Hitler-traumatized Jew.

And yet, I must have sensed something. I must have intuited my father, and others, attempting to recover from Hell. I'm sure that it added to my little-girl sense of something terribly broken. It rounded out my sense of the truth of uncertainty.

After my mother died, and my father was perpetually traveling on business, my brother and I were sent, for a while, to live with our magnanimous aunt.

This sister of our mother's was intensely religious. It was she who saw to it that I got Sunday schooled. The indoctrination never took. My family had been so violated, so cataclysmically wrecked, that it was almost as if I had died. On some mysterious level, I had left this world for a moment. Desperately clutching for my death-departed mother, I fell through some sort of void. Something then hurled me back into this life with a shattered but expanded perception. I was only in the first grade, but I saw through Big Daddy fixations. I was only a small child, but already I knew that such "truth" and "security" must be mythical and contrived.

That may sound dark and terribly tragic, but in the end it made me strong. To believe in nothing can be a beautiful paradox. It can bring someone even closer than believers to a blazing awareness of God.

That started to gel for me in my teens. I entered adolescence in the late nineteen-sixties, when counterculture thinking permeated my world. I was reunited with my father by then, in that breathtaking sea of diversity, New York City. And as if that intensive atmosphere weren't enough, a thrilling sort of coast-spanning communion prevailed. Spurred on by psychedelics and the truths behind Asian wisdom, Californians were gracing Manhattan bookshelves with their Far Eastern-inspired ideas. It was there, in the midst of Central Park "Be-Ins", Fifth Avenue peace marches, stoned reveries, and George Harrison's sitar, that I discovered the gentle and liberating words of the sixties philosopher, the noted Alan Watts.

Alan Watts taught me to carefully distinguish between *belief* and *faith*. In a book with a title that riveted me—*The Wisdom of Insecurity*—he told me that belief is a *clinging-to*, and that faith is about *letting go*. I read those words at the age of sixteen, when guidance consumes the young mind like a fire. I embraced that pivotal teaching with the deeply rooting internalization that only happens in youth.

I acknowledged the terrible dangers of belief. When their belief systems are threatened by anything at all, people become defensive, and often even hateful. They bristle at even the most reasonable questioning of their system's claim to the truth. So anxious, are believers, in their need to have their doctrines be true, that they ironically imbue their "forgiving" God with a jealous vindictiveness. They equip Him with a Hell for nonbelievers. Belief is the desperate dependence on the self-delusion of certainty. Threatened belief is the bedrock of intolerance and hate.

But faith is another matter. Faith is about pure love. Faith is about the absence of belief. It's the opening and emptying and freeing of one's mind until divine love flows in *on its own*, free of doctrines. Faith is Zen Buddhism's state of *samadhi,* attained in meditations that purge judgmental thought.

In his nineteen sixties song, *"Love Minus Zero/No Limit"*, Bob Dylan describes the perfect lover. Or maybe he's picturing Goddess. "She doesn't have to say she's faithful, yet she's true like ice, like fire." She possesses a loving serenity. "She knows too much to argue or to judge." I used to listen to lyrics like that and thrill to their glimmerings of what felt like the truth. Few biblical words could raise goose bumps on me, but poets with glimpses of Wattsian faith could cause me to lose sleep at night as I listened to their insights on my stereo.

I also rejoiced in the writings of an author much read in the sixties, Hermann Hesse. There's an unforgettable line from *Siddhartha*, his novel on the founder of Buddhism. For me it became an empowering mantra that I still intone, today: "I can think, I can wait, I can fast."

How quickly God flows into me when I think, and wait, and fast!

And, as an American, how hard it is for me to remember to think, and wait, and fast!

Though I'm obviously short on devotion to the biblical "Word of God", I do realize, nevertheless, that Judeo-Christian rituals and prayers can be, for some people, a way to attain real faith. When Christians advise me to "Give it to God," I feel they're expressing true faith. They're telling me to completely trust God to resolve my problems and heal me. Nothing is more faithful than that trust.

Nothing could be more of a *letting go.* And I do feel much better when I do that. And things do work out for the best.

My aunt is profoundly full of that faith. She's a devout Christian Scientist.

From the Church of Christ, Scientist, that innovative and exceptional of Jesus-based devotions, the belief in Satan and Original Sin gets tossed right out with the trash. The patriarchy also gets totally trounced. In this beautifully deviant Christian sect, one prays to the "Father-Mother God."

Christian Scientists are extreme idealists who emphatically reject any doctrines of damnation. Their position is so loving that it seems to have been beamed from the brightest portal of Heaven. They claim that *God is love, and God created us; therefore we too are love. There can't be any real evil in the world, because God created the world, and there's no evil in Him. Even illness can't hold sway. How can illness have power in a world that was made by perfect Love?*

There is a certain logic to their thinking, and they dare to apply it in deadly situations. Since Christian Scientists don't believe that sickness can be *true,* they don't see a need for medicine. When they or their loved ones become *full of error*, or better known as sick, then they refer to their distinctive text, *Science and Health with Key to the Scriptures*. Then they do some deep praying. Often, they do get well.

A short time ago, I called my aunt about something I'd found in my left breast. I had told no one else about this. I knew that if I confided this worry to others, they'd be burdened by concern for me, and they'd incessantly nag me to get it checked out.

On the day that I spoke to my aunt about this, she meditated for me. Then she wrote me this note:

> [****] DEAR:
>
> You have nothing to fear when you realize the infinite *allness* of God, *Good*, and the *Love* of our *Father-Mother God*, our only Cause and Creator.
> Let Love and its manifestations be all that is going on. Watch your thinking. Think only good thoughts, *loving* thoughts, and *true*. (Only good is *real*.) If Jesus had indulged in hating his enemies, he never could have survived the Cross and experienced resurrection. To love your enemies is to see the *real* man whom God

sees! Jesus separated evil from his enemies: "Father, forgive them, for they know not what they do." Love, love, love—"For every hate, love more."
Love heals.

Love and joy to you,
Aunt Sarah

I got my boobs checked, and they're okay. My aunt said, "Of course they are!"

Aunt Sarah has always been astoundingly optimistic. When I was little and my mother had died and left me to try to be her daughter without her, her radiant sister nurtured and shaped me. My aunt was not the only person who took me in and had an affect, and she wouldn't succeed in conforming me to her generation or church, but she did tuck a piece of unbreakable love in the deepest part of me. She instilled a permanent sunbeam. I disdain patriarchal religion, and yet I do love God. I reject many Christian laws and limits, yet I worship the Golden Rule. I've been hurt all my life, yet I still love life. I've always been a feminist, and yet I love men. And I became the kind of whore who knows that true whoring is healing.

To let go of fear—even doctors!—is certainly a huge act of faith. If Alan Watts is responsible for alerting me to true faith, then Aunt Sarah is my magnificent, in-the-flesh example. She demonstrates faith every day.

But she can pontificate, too. It's hard for her not to when her leaning, though enlightened, has its basis in the dogma of medieval religion. Though she spurns the threat of Hell and damnation, and her God is never punitive and therefore, neither is she, she *does* succumb to the weakness of the rigidity of belief. She proclaims, right along with billions of others, that *only this way is right, only these doctrines are right, and only our God is true.*

That's where she and I end our discussions.

Christian Scientists are faithful to the point of getting called crazy. They've even been criminally charged for their faith—for their refusal to send their sick children to doctors. And yet, such faith is on track. Even though a few of their children have died, this may be the most earnest attempt at atonement with the love of God and Christ. It's certainly the bravest endeavor to live by it.

But I'd never join up with them, or any other church. I'd rather hook up with diversity. For me, Christianity is only one aspect of a precious collection of conductors for my faith. There are other ways to know the divine, wonderful ways from wonderful cultures far too numerous to list here. Yea, all conventional Christians, I'm on that proverbial *wide* path to Hell, and it feels really right. The Hell and Original Sin that most of you believe in, and the supposed claim of your deity that "there's no other way but by me" feel way too much like a contrivance—a spin—and I'm talking about human, not divine.

I'd rather hang out with the Unitarians. I'd rather atone with a few perfect moments, like the ecstasy of cleansing, nonjudgmental Zen.

And for that matter, I'd rather work in my garden. Or care for a needy child. Or help someone explode in a glorious orgasm. That's when faith overtakes me. That's when I feel closest to God.

I think of the sweet little Sunday school song sung by Protestant children everywhere.

> Jesus loves me, yes I know.
> For the Bible tells me so....

No. It's not because the Bible says so. The Bible is a strange mishmash. It's chockfull of love and hate and war, and imperfect human concoctions, the reflections and passions and persuasions and contradictions of the many flawed people who wrote it.

Jesus loves me because I just *know*.

And isn't that the main thing you want of me, Jesus? To simply, faithfully know? To know that you love me, and to spread that love around? Whenever I'm being loving and forgiving, no matter what "sin" I'm committing, I feel right with you, Jesus, and I feel right with the world.

OUTLAW

It's hard to protect yourself from rapists while you're busy protecting yourself from the police.

I've never been raped. Not as a prostitute, and not in any other circumstance. But you know that I've been arrested, and this much I can say: getting busted for being an "escort" feels just like an assault.

Though I'm sure that arrest can't be nearly as shocking as the heinous violation of rape, I think the two horrors are similar. To "sting" is copspeak for the duping of a callgirl, and there's a terrible likeness of purpose in the images of stinging and raping. To be slyly wooed and deceived, then shoved and locked in a squad car, fingerprinted like a creep and then shut with your sooty digits in a cage of cement and iron—and all the while knowing you're a priestess, you're a lady, you're a comforter who's extremely well compensated to be what men, including cops, all want—can't be experienced as anything less than a devastating injustice.

The same can be said of the way you feel when the multitude turns to stare, bizarrely eager to damn you, on the day of your court appearance. The judge's assistant, acerbically scowling, clearly announces your *OFFENSE* of *PROSTITUTION*.

Knowing men as well as you do, you stand there wondering whether the judge, or any of his minions, has ever spent time with an "escort". There's an excellent chance that they have.

Well, one good thing I can say is that the cops who nabbed me didn't cuff me. They remarked that I didn't need handcuffs, because I behaved myself well. But I don't think they did that for me. Their lenience was probably a favor to the lovely hotel they set me up in. Their departure with a manacled woman might have hurt the establishment's image.

Another good thing is that my name never got in the paper. That was a big relief. But again, I don't think that they did that for me. It was either just plain damn good luck, or the cops had a strategic reason for keeping their nab of me mum.

For all of us "escorts" in America, where we're banned almost everywhere, our fear of arrest is unrelenting. We have to learn to live with that terror, just like victims of mental conditions. The terror is incessantly waiting to pounce, just like spells of dementia or seizures. If we manage, somehow, to love life in spite of it, our enjoyment is a yardstick for how well we've adapted to the chronic illness of fear.

But fear of arrest is just one of the pressures in this life overwhelmed by suspicion. My nightmarish bust notwithstanding, there's much more to being a paranoid whore than trying to avoid the detectives.

"Escorts" have to watch out for so many things. We have to watch out for people in general. If people find out what we're doing, a particularly damaging stress starts to hurt us. It's the kind that keeps us constantly poisoned by blasts of adrenaline.

If the people who find out are people who love us, we'll never hear the end of it. Maybe they'll even go so far as to not love us anymore. Maybe we'll lose a close friend. Or get disowned by our family.

Not long ago I was sadly afraid that an old friend had found out about me, and had decided she wants nothing to do with me. I hadn't heard from her in some time.

That friend lives in the same locale where I once got arrested. Her brothers are well-acquainted with some of the police. When she didn't respond to my reach-out at Christmas, I feared that the cops had informed her all about me.

I had never let her in on my life as a callgirl. I was sure that she'd handle it badly. I do have a few friends who "know about me," and the fact that I've told them is a credit to them. But I have many friends that I wouldn't inform, and she's very high on that list.

When I was pubescent, she was my best friend. She was actually my *first* best friend beyond childhood. We met when we were thirteen, and our young-girl bond was intense. At fifteen I got bounced from her area to go live with my father.

We stayed in touch, as young friends do, but we grew to be very different people. She married young, stayed married, and developed a narrow outlook. I'm fond of this woman, but she's very judgmental. The only right way is her way.

So when I got worried that she had rejected me, I sent her a sweet little card. It was one of those "friends forever" types with a photo of little girls hugging. Then I went about my everyday business, trying my best not to think too much about the pain of a friendship funeral pyre, burning to ashes in my heart.

Well, soon she got back to me, all happy about my card, and apologizing for falling out of touch. She wanted to get together.

Her contact made my day. And it made me reflect on how paranoid I am. If a friend doesn't call me or e-mail me, all I can think is that my secret's gotten out, and she's shunning me, now she hates me.

That's the price I have to pay for making five times more money than she ever has, and for having more time than she's ever had for being an available mother, or grandmother.

And now I'll tell the story of another old friend, a tale with an ending not nearly so nice.

We met as very young women, while pregnant with our first sons. We'd married into the same family. Our baby's fathers were cousins.

As young matrons, she and I became rather close, mostly because of a shared recognition that we'd blended our genes with the wrong clan of people. There was also some considerable mutual respect. We highly approved of each other as mothers.

Several years later, after the births of our second sons, I escaped my bad marriage. She stayed in hers—in misery.

For a long time, our friendship survived that difference. Through the years we remained in touch, sometimes with phone talks that lasted for hours, especially when our sons hit their puberties, when things got really crazy. We didn't see much of each other, but those meaningful gabs on the phone—God. I think we may have kept each other from going right over the edge.

Some shocking truths were emerging. She had been sexually abused as a toddler. It was all coming out in counseling. Though her mind wouldn't focus the culprit, she knew in her heart it was her schizophrenic mother. And she told me some horrifying details of her marriage. Her husband habitually raped her. He especially raped her *mouth*. She would vomit when he fucked her there, and he just didn't care.

She herself hated sex. She pretty much always had.

I let her know that I loved sex, and that I even loved fellatio. I told her all of that gently. I was painfully aware of how impossible that must sound to someone in her position.

So now we both knew we were dissimilar, in a very crucial way. Yet our friendship continued to flourish. We nonetheless shared a lot. We shared being mothers of sons the same ages. We shared deep anxieties over their troubles. We shared an intense love of animals. And we told each other all about our fits of compulsive eating.

Do you have any idea how fulfilling it is to divulge your private gobble fests to someone else who does it? We'd go into wild laughing spasms over details we'd exchange, face-stuffing that took on hilarious aspects when we put it into words.

Like, she would wolf a whole cake down, but not until after she'd wiped off the frosting, because she didn't like it. Once, she'd managed to do that at a great big family gathering! Without anyone noticing!

And I, the occasional purger, liked everything soft and gooey, mixed just right with liquids to ensure that it all came back up.

We constantly compared our twisted eating habits and rituals.

It was just so amazing and comforting, to be able to tell that sick stuff, and to infuse it with such silly humor! I was gladly aware that sometimes, such sharing can kick-start a healing, a possible freeing from the compulsion.

Then one year she told me that she'd threatened to cut her husband's dick off. If he ever came near her again, she would. She was still living with the man, letting him financially support her, and yet she hated him so much that it was natural to make such a terrible promise.

I guess she'd gotten encouraged by that cock-hacker in the news. What was her name...was it Bobbit? My girlfriend was deadly serious, and her spouse seemed to know it, for sure. He was leaving her alone.

Meanwhile, I had become a callgirl. I hadn't told my companion, but she knew. At that point I was free to visit her often. She saw that I always had a pager, a pager that was constantly beeping. She saw me making clandestine phone calls. She saw me take off on little "errands," and come back in a very short time. I wasn't holding down a regular job, and yet it was plain I had money.

I began to feel that I insulted her intelligence if I kept on evading the truth. It was like I belittled our closeness. And for sure I didn't want her to think that I was selling crack, or something.

And so, one day, I 'fessed up.

Well, for a couple of years she seemed to enjoy hearing all about my big secret. I guess it was like being in on my eating binges. We'd take long walks with our dogs in the woods, and I'd tell her all about my sex work. And I'd hear all about how her fiercely warned hubby was continuing to keep his distance. We realized he might call my service, in sexual desperation. She could care less if he did.

She'd tell me about his crumpled tee shirts, the ones she had to wash, the ones he jerked himself off in. I'd tell her about my most memorable clients.

She declared that she couldn't begin to imagine how I could enjoy what I did. She also didn't see how I could relate to clients as decent human beings. And most of all she could not understand when I told her that since I'd become a sex worker, my bulimic episodes had stopped.

Her astonishment didn't surprise me, of course; by now I was aware that here was a person whom a shrink might call *sexually arrested.* As a baby she'd been genitally traumatized, and she had never once enjoyed sex, and she had married a sexual abuser. How could she believe a prostitute who said she liked men and her work, and it helped her?

But our friendship held on, just the same.

I figured we came from such bizarrely opposite mindsets that our differences were too big to matter. What mattered was that we were freaks of a sort, both us way far off-center. Even though the gap between us was as deep as the contrast between day and night, we could bond over both of us being unique.

Yeah, that's me: the eternal optimist. Sometimes it makes me a fool.

I kept focusing on ways we were similar. Both of us were veterans of hell. We'd both had bad childhoods, bad marriages, and crazy relations with food. We'd each found a way, no matter how different, to assert ourselves over adversity. I figured the whore and the no-longer raped wife would dog-walk together, laugh together, and help each other along. We'd be sister-friends forever and ever.

But then, one day, she was gone.

She never told me to fuck off, she never read me the riot act, she never lectured me or stared down her nose at me or said one goddam word.

She simply dropped out of my life.

Nine Eleven happened. I called her house desperately needing to talk. She answered the phone, and pretended she couldn't hear me. I heard her say to someone, "There's no one on the line."

She was lying. She could hear me.

She hung up.

At first I was in sheer denial. I left messages on her phone, wrote her emails and notes, and sent her gifts. That went on for more than a year. I didn't get a response.

Then I sent her a letter, threatening to come banging on her door. I warned that I would do that if she wouldn't talk to me.

Well, she didn't respond at all. And I never drove up to her house because she lived an hour away. I figured: *Why should I go all that distance? She probably won't answer the door.*

In the end, I got indignant. I wanted to tell her how disgusted I was that she remained with a man whose dick she'd cut off if he ever touched her again. Her kids were grown up, so she was an empty-nester; there were no more excuses to stay there. What a coward, to never have left him! How sick of her to remain, and harbor such violent hatred, and make that her normal existence! I thought her life was morally heinous, just as heinous as she must have thought mine was.

But this is the thing that hurt me: *I never would have ended our friendship over it.* Even though I felt disapproval, I was more than willing to accept her.

And she had decided that she wouldn't do that for me.

Fuck her.

If she ever comes back, I'll be there for her. I love her.

But for now, fuck her. *Fuck her.*

Well, there's only one way around it. In order to prevent such heartbreak, an "escort" has to hide who she is. And indoor, autonomous "escorting" is the loneliest whore's life of all. If it's illegal, that is. There's nothing, no lifestyle more isolating, not even the poor single motherhood that used to make me feel trapped and buried.

If you're a freelance, self-directed callgirl, refusing to ever let third parties exploit you, then you're also refusing camaraderie. Your choice to work on your own, to stand as the proof of unmanipulated whoring, evolves with that desolating price. There are very few people available with whom to share the fears that consume you.

You have to fake out people, pretending all the time that you're not what you are. Only your clients know the truth, and maybe a couple of coworkers, "escorts" you meet through a client. And maybe a couple of liberal, understanding friends.

The lying you do to everyone else is exactly like the fear—it feels like a chronic disorder. It makes you feel knifed up. It fills you with a deep sense of wrongness.

It's not the work itself that feels wrong. It's the life of untruthfulness.

I have two close girlfriends who aren't in prostitution, and they know the truth about me, and they deal with it beautifully. One of them recently asked me whether I've joined a writers' group. Such people would support me in my writing of this book, and would helpfully critique it.

I told her no, I'd love to be in such a group, they're certainly easy to find where I live, but I have to think of the *content.* The subject of my book might make things uneasy.

So my friend and I reflect upon how isolated I am, not only as a sex worker, but even as a writer.

Everyone who knows me knows I'm working on a book set, but most of them don't know what it's really about. I tell them it's on "millennium feminism." That's not exactly a lie, but it sure is a generalization! It's the truth hiding under a blanket.

Everyone says they'll want copies of my books, after the two of them go to press. So all the time I'm asking myself, who will I be able to hand these books to, and not have to worry that they'll freak out?

The sad answer is, almost no one. And the truth is, that's all wrong. I shouldn't be feeling such punishment.

Women in my spot are called "marginalized," but I prefer the word "outlaw." Like it or not, that's exactly what we are. Because of that circumstance, our lives can be full of breakups, and also what I call break*aways*.

If the people who "find out" are people I don't know, I don't have to fear that they'll reject me, and therefore break my heart. But I'm going to feel the panic of the persecuted. I'm going to be struck by the terror of knowing that someone will probably call the cops. So no matter how settled and comfortable I am, no matter how much I *love* where I am, now I'm going to have to get going, now I'm going to have to *move on*.

I'll never forget the worst time I went through that, that crushing despair of the fugitive. I'd been working as an "escort" for a couple of years. I was no stranger to the aloneness. I'd been dealing, for all that time, with the relentless discomfort of lying to others about my choice of work. And I was no stranger to the terror. I'd already been through the ordeal of my arrest.

But whenever I remember the first, searing moment when I deeply internalized the anguish of the outlaw, I immediately picture a little motel in a lovely New England village.

What put me there was my frequent visitation to Jesse, my youngest son. As I've mentioned earlier in this book, his father took turns with me raising him. At one point I left Massachusetts for a while, and I lived about five hundred miles from Jesse's father. So whenever this son was in his dad's care, it wasn't a situation of having him near me, just down the road apiece; it was a sleep-losing, gut-wrenching circumstance: my baby was too far away.

Before I became an outlaw, I was tethered to multiple employers. So when Jesse wasn't living with me, I could rarely get free to see him. Then prostitution saved the day. Along with the myriad other good things, it proved an invaluable employment for me when my boy had to live at a distance. Now I could see him a lot!

As a totally self-employed "escort", completely in charge of my time, now I was free to travel. I could make great money wherever I went, as long as an ad paved my way. I could visit Jesse often, and for just as long as I wanted, making money on the way there, making money while I was there, and making money on the way back.

I made thousands of dollars in conjunction with each visit, all in just a handful of hours! So I brought home plenty of money, and that was a benefit for my other two sons, who were now old enough to be left, watched over by Aunt Sarah, while I went to see their little brother.

It felt as though my bases were loaded. The distances between those bases were huge, but this mom scored runs, anyway; I had found a great batter, the whore.

Whenever I went on that trip out to Jesse, one of the clients I saw there would always rent a room for our tryst. It was always at the same place. I liked the motel, and I loved the pretty town, and I decided to start keeping a room there, myself.

My son lived a few small towns over.

I ended up renting a room there three times, and each time, for a week.

A friendly young couple owned the place.

I had never done "incall" trysts before—that is, having the clients come to me. I preferred to do outcalls; that is, driving to the clients. Common sense told me that incalls would put me too at risk for arrest.

To have different men in and out of a place, each for a short duration, all day, most of the days in a week, is obvious prostitution. Any woman who does that is a raid that's waiting to happen. She's a fool if she thinks it won't happen. I was determined to play it smart. I knew that visiting men in their homes was the best way to avoid arrest. So my work was all about driving around, to calls away from my digs. It was all about being elusive.

In that particular situation, however, it began to make sense to do incalls sometimes. Every now and then, when I stayed at that motel, if a client who answered my ad had trouble providing a private place to meet, I figured, what the hell, why not let him come to my room? Jesse was never there; I saw him at his father's. I hung out with Jesse in his own town, which was half an hour away. So I wouldn't be mixing my place of work with my place of motherhood.

And I was so terribly tired of driving all over creation to work.

And besides, I reasoned, I was a transient at that motel. I didn't think I was there often enough to call attention to what I did.

So on each of the three occasions that I lodged there, I also did a few incalls. About one every other day.

And by my third stay there, uh-oh. I could see that the owners were getting suspicious.

I always requested a room in the back, and that, I knew, made them wonder. The reason I gave was my dog. I always took him with me when I traveled. The owners allowed him, and liked him a lot; they played with him whenever they saw him. They agreed with me that the rooms in the back were the safest and happiest place for him. That part of the motel was the furthest from the road, and near a big rabbit-filled field.

But motel owners know to observe things more closely than other people do.

I watched that couple watch me. I saw their heads turn when my pager went off. They noticed when I called clients on their pay phone (this was just before cells). The pay phone was located a distance from their office, and I always kept my voice low, but still, I was afraid they "could tell."

They started to eyeball my comings and goings with an interest so keen that they would stop what they were doing.

One day, right after a client left, the two of them came knocking at my door. They saw me in a bathrobe in the middle of the afternoon, and I knew that was why they were there—they wanted to catch me undressed. It wasn't *really* to tell me my cable wires needed fixing—that was just their excuse. Why would they *both* show up just to tell me that?

I knew it was time to get out of there. And to never return again.

And that's when I felt the hurt.

I loved staying there! I was happy there! I'd been reposing with my dog in that sweet little nook, maintained by that sweet little couple, located in that sweet little town!

Yeah, right. See ya.

Ostracized. Shunned. Rejected. Fearing real danger if you stay. Knowing that the world wants to get you. Knowing you're alone, and you're hated. When I look at my life, and I know that's been in it, I know I've been marked, pierced and singled. I know that the karma of the outlaw has grazed me.

It's made me a little bit different.

But I don't want anyone thinking I'm resentful. Not toward that couple, that is. No matter how much pain those situations may cause me, and no matter how desolate I feel when I leave, I'm wrong if I'm blaming the people who oust me for the status of *us* against *them.*

The owners weren't at fault for opposing what I was doing. They had every right to prohibit the use of their place for my work, or else to demand a percentage of my profits.

The trouble is, I had no idea which of those rights they embraced, or which of them they felt I had violated. And I wasn't about to ask. What I do is so taboo that an open discussion is out of the question.

All I could do was run.

That couple most likely concluded that I was a shady character, posing as someone up to nothing, a criminal using her pet as a front.

And if that's what they thought, they were right. Over the course of my three stays there, aside from my outcall excursions, on their premises I made about two thousand dollars. I made it illicitly and furtively, and they got nothing for it. To them I must have seemed a despicable rodent, using their place as a feeding ground, and then sneaking away to avoid getting trapped.

I wasn't just afraid to return to their motel; I was afraid to even return to their town. As a previously arrested prostitute, I had educated myself. I had thoroughly learned the drill. I knew that I should err on the *extreme* side of caution. No matter how over-reactive it seemed, I had to assume that those people had called the local police, had reported their suspicions, and had given them my license plate number.

So I wouldn't be responding to any pages from their town, no, not anytime soon; not even if I got fifty of them. *Especially* if I got fifty of them. No, no way would I, ever.

It amazes me that I've learned, so unbelievably skillfully, to think like a paranoid crook. What gets me is the incongruity. I don't have the heart of a criminal. Isn't the typical offender a sociopath? Someone incredibly selfish, who steals from people, hurts people, and cheats them with no remorse? I've always identified as a nurturer. I've always been a giver and a mediator. I love people. I want to help people. I want to be fair to people. How can I be a criminal?

I liked that nice young couple. I got no kick from trying to fool them, from sneakily using their place to make money. But I won't deny that I liked making the money, and I liked not having to drive for it, I liked not having to blunder my way through unfamiliar terrain, seeking out multiple far-flung towns, locating clients' houses down convoluted roads, in every kind of weather. Often, it was all in the dark. And always, of course, with the exception of my dog, I endured all those searches for addresses all alone.

It's so much easier to wait for a client in a comfy accommodation, and simply open the door.

But I hated having to hide what I was from the people who owned the door. I hated not being able to talk about it with them. I hated not being able to negotiate with them. I couldn't broach the subject at all.

And most of all, I hated having to leave them behind. I was the mourner of a good thing gone bad. I was the burner of a beautiful bridge.

And so I learned all about the pain.

For the outlaw, there's an absence of comfort. There's no such thing as relaxing forever in a precious, well-loved place. Not if you're working out of there. The minute things start to feel good, you're taking the gravest risk. That's when you're being a fool. There's no such thing as being able to *stay*. There's no such thing as maintaining relations with people who aren't in your game. As soon as they see what you're doing, they're going to turn on you.

You have to be on the run.

In retrospect, I see that *every stupid thing I've done as a whore* has been because of that pain. That alienation was breaking me. It was starting to crack my good judgment.

Being that isolated, that paranoid, *alone*, is something we humans aren't wired for. We absolutely can't take it. We have to seek relief from that aloneness. The relief might turn out to be worse than the aloneness, but we hurt too much to care. It's the reason why "escorts" might slip into drugs, or become alcoholics, or fall in with other kinds of lawbreakers, or accept the disempowerment of working for exploiters, or get involved with a very bad man.

Or all of the above, looped insanely together.

At first those things feel better than being out there all alone.

Any escape will do; anything to stave off the agony of hiding the secret *alone,* of fearing exposure *alone,* of feeling the shunning when we do get exposed, unbearably *alone.*

My strength, or my weakness, depending on whom I turn to, has always been to reach out to others. I warmly commingle with clients; the camaraderie I've shared with them has been my greatest refuge. But the trouble with that is, time spent with clients is just for an hour; what about all of the time in between? Clients, after all, are only my patrons; what I need is a constant companion.

All my life I've wanted a soul mate. To take another woman as a mate wouldn't do; I'm just plain too totally straight. Whether I like it or not, and even if it kills me, it's a man I need to adore. I want big bones, a hairy chest, and facial hair or stubble. I want hard-angled flesh, and muscles. I want to adore a penis. I even love the smell of his (freshly showered) balls.

I even love his ways that are different from me. No matter how challenging they might be. No matter how frustrating.

Sometimes, however, I wish I were gay. It would sure make my working life easier. I don't think a lesbian would give a rat's ass that I bed-hop, for a living, with men. I would go home to her, and she'd give me her love; most likely, her affection would never be ruined by turmoil over the clients.

But it's useless to wish for the impossible. I worship the human male. I want to lose myself, and find myself, in one good, loving man. Getting older hasn't changed that. Neither has the abuse of men, or divorce, or becoming a sex worker. Nothing. I'm so straight that it's almost pitiful. I'm also an incurable romantic.

Right from the start I could plainly see that the man for me could only be one who had met me in my role as a sex worker. It would have to be a man who knew my big secret, a man who I wouldn't have to lie to about my source of income. And this man would of course have to be one who could live, every day, with my work; as long as my kids were still young enough to need my financial backing, I would still need to "escort".

Well, I did find such a man. I found him sometime after my stint at that motel. And he did ease my loneliness…sort of. For a terrible, terrible price. Remember how I mentioned my good judgment was cracking?

That's all over now. He's been gone for quite a while. I'll save that sad story for later.

The only good thing about being an outlaw is that it forces the imperative for change. I'm inspired by pain to imagine a world that's far less hypocritical. I imagine a world a lot more realistic, a world that accepts my existence. And I refuse to just passively dream of it. That would be utterly useless.

So I advocate it. Right here.

In the world that I envision, a world in which "escorting" is decriminalized and there are *legal designations for our work*, "escorts" will be utterly "out" to motel owners, and accordingly, such owners will deal with them head-on.

In the world that I envision, a proprietor will be able to legally opt for either having an establishment that works with prostitution, or having one that does not.

If the proprietor does opt for it, then regulations, guidelines and paperwork will be firmly in place to protect the rights of all the parties involved. Those parties will be: himself as the maintainer of the lodgings, the self-employed callgirl, the customer, and Uncle Sam.

The owner will be provided with a system that enables him to document, without violating anyone's privacy, how many of his lodgers an "escort" sees each day. He'll receive a rightful percentage—something like twenty percent—of the daily take of each girl.

Now let's all get that straight. The motel owner won't be a pimp. He won't ever *manage* the "escorts". *He'll just be the landlord, that's all*. As it goes with any other business, any other business that needs to rent a roof, he'll be able to lease commercial space, and he'll be able to charge a commercial rent, legally and openly to sex workers.

Maybe he'll sport a little sign out front that's worded something like this:

This establishment welcomes adult services.

And if he doesn't want to offer that feature, he'll have the recourse to report a callgirl for the offense of using his premises in violation of his choice.

Now I ask you, America, does that sound so hard?

Okay, so maybe *only certain motels, only in certain districts*, would be allowed to offer our service. That would placate the people, the religionists and such, who might have a problem with knowing that professional Eros is flourishing in the place where they're trying to sleep. Fine, I can work with that. As long as the districts that sex workers are confined to are *decent, with decent lodgings.*

Such visions of the future help me cope with my dilemma. They ease the isolation, just a little. They help me to live with the fear. I think, what a wonderful world it would be! A world where I don't have to run. A world where I don't fear arrest.

The biggest threat in my world is the cops. They're predators too, you know. They're not very different from rapists and killers. I think of them as the bad guys, simply because I'm their quarry. Cops cunningly, stealthily hunt me. They strategize how to get me.

My dread of their "sting" consumes me.

I keep thinking of a song by Crosby, Stills and Nash. "Paranoia strikes deep...into your life it will creep."[1] They're talking about "the man"—the cops—who back in the day, and also right now, will arrest you for some things that they shouldn't.

That sixties song was written to remind us that a baggie of weed is not only fun; it's also a ticket to jail. We can't enjoy a magnificent high without being worried about getting busted.

It also means that our protest of things, like the sanctioned murder of war, can get us summarily clubbed and cuffed, and hauled off to sit behind bars.

The gist of that song remains sharpened for me. As an "escort" I "step outta line." The difference is, this is years later. I'm no longer roaming and grooving and communing with hoards of ecstatic and rebellious companions.

Now I'm out there all alone.

PART THREE

HER AFFAIRS OF THE HEART

THE WORKING GIRL FALLS IN LOVE

A man will be there to guide me. I'll make my world his home.

I'm sharing this account of my love life—my love life as a whore—because it occurred to me that some readers might wonder about that part of me. A good friend warned me to not get too personal, to not bare too much of myself—but that didn't feel right to me. That didn't feel honest, or *finished*, to me.

Indeed, if I were in the readers' shoes, I'm sure I'd be curious about what, exactly, the author has experienced as a sex worker in love, or even *if* she's been a sex worker in love.

Standing as I am in my own shoes, it seems to me that after writing on the relationships between "escorts" and their clients, and on man/woman relationships in general, I'd have to be pretty remiss if I left out my own affairs of the heart—particularly my affairs as a sex worker.

So here goes.

Those relationships—there have been two of them—have been a rough ride for me. The reader's going to discover what an understatement that is. My love life has severely impacted my work life, and considering what my work life has been, that should come as no surprise.

And yet, I sense that my love trials have been karmic. I mean karmic as opposed to circumstantial. I feel that no matter what career path I'd have taken, my love life would have been hard.

Indeed, it's always been hard. Some people seem to just breeze through their marriages, and I'm even talking about some whores. It's never been that way for me. Not before, and not during, and not after, my life as a prostitute. No romance has ever been breezy for me.

Any relationship therapist who reads this will be likely to do a mental review of all the childhood traumas, revealed in both of my books, that have influenced my dire relationship choices. Well, for sure I've got all my baggage. It's been slamming me and tripping me and making me dumb, for all of my adult life. I'll be fighting that stuff until the day I die! And it may even nail me again! But I like to think I've made progress.

The one thing I take a lot of comfort from is that I haven't lost the will to love. And I believe that's the biggest thing that matters. I believe that's the real definition of success.

So okay now, with that said, I'm going to sprawl on my back now. I'm going to expose my underbelly. I'm going to show you a weakness that the sex work-abolitionist feminists may immediately jump onto, in order to try to gut me.

The abolitionist feminists may read through the following chapters, and conclude with a whooping war cry: *AHA!* See? We're right! Prostitution *does* damage women! She's proving it here, right here in this section where she describes her horrendous suffering! See? See how the work violates her! See how it's made her life *HELL!*

Well, before you start skewering me, ladies, allow me to remind you of the truth. The truth is that *YOU*, and *NOT* the work, are exactly what make my life hell. Your part in the oppression, stigmatization, and isolation of whores has been the driving force behind my descent into a bad, abusive relationship that never should have begun. Your part in the oppression, stigmatization, and isolation of whores was the driving force behind my travails in another relationship with another man that's been riddled with the pain of his conditioned incapacity to cope with where I've been. Those treacherous paths that I've slipped on, as a flawed human being in love, might have been completely avoided if *I'D HAD YOUR SUPPORT OF WHO I AM.*

I'll repeat and repeat and repeat this, along with my activist peers, until finally some day you begin to understand: it's not prostitution that causes the damage. It's not prostitution that's wrong. It's *the way the world treats it,* that's wrong. And that's what makes our lives hell.

So with that said, now I'll begin. I'll take you for a ride down the convoluted trail of my love life as a sex worker.

I met Mitch, who became my next husband, sometime after I ran from *that motel.* I've told you how that episode hurt me, how it filled me with sick desolation, that feeling of *got to escape now,* that all-alone fugitive angst.

Right then I should have realized, at the same time I was running, how wounded I was becoming. I should have realized that the pain of the outlaw was going to make me do something stupid.

Something very, very stupid. I should have shut myself down and shut myself off and avoided romance like the plague; I should have known I was becoming too vulnerable, that my loneliness was going to blind me.

But no.

When I got with Mitch, I was staying at a dump. It was the same situation as before—I was visiting the area, perching, because of my son Jesse. But one thing had changed—now I slummed it. I checked into shitty motels now, places I would never get attached to, ugly holes I would never miss, if I had to run again.

I had only done a couple of incalls in that dive, but this time my caution wasn't only because of my fear of getting caught; it was also because I was ashamed of the place. I didn't want the clients to see it.

Most of the time, I only slept there. In the daytime, I always left. When Jesse was busy with his friends, I would journey to outcalls galore. And whenever I wasn't working, I found beautiful paved biking trails. There were miles and miles of them down in the woods, and also out by the sea; I would jump on my bike or strap on my rollerblades, and get myself feeling pretty good. My dog would run alongside of me, veering off to explore or to rest.

I used a local gym, as well.

But I couldn't work out 24-7, so there were times when I had to just deal with the doldrums of staying in that hideous room. The place was getting to me. The skid row décor was making my loneliness more crushing than ever before. To be there for even five minutes depressed me. To even have to pull up at the place, and see the cheap features outside, and feel the rutted parking lot under my tires, was awful. But I had to hang my hat somewhere. I had to wait for calls somewhere.

I didn't always handle it well.

A couple of times, I succumbed to temptations. I bought some yummy goodies to chow on, to buffer myself from the pain. Big mistake. I should have been crying, or therapeutically writing, or something else just as healthy.

I remember the night before I met Mitch. It was one of those times when I ended up food-partying with myself. I was shacked up in that rotten room, and my constant companion, besides my sweet dog, was the specter of desolation.

Some lowlifes were yelling outside. It was summer, and the AC unit rattled; it was just as loud as the drunks.

In retrospect, it's so obvious: I was becoming susceptible. Hindsight is showing me how foolish it was to let my own bravado deceive me. Sometimes my bravado was making me believe I was in better emotional shape than I thought I was. It made me grab food, and recklessly binge, when I ought to have been facing the monsters of hurt, when I ought to have been taking a good hard look at all the Swiss cheese holes inside me, knowing I might do something far, far worse than eat to fill up the black holes, knowing I needed to stay on my guard to never do worse than nosh.

Oh, yeah, I can see it all now. I was so ready for a fall. No, *tumble* would be the right word. With all my good judgment careening. Loneliness? Isolation? Stigma? Watch out for those three ugly sisters. There's no one more lethally hurtful.

And there was another thing. Maybe I was getting a little bit tired of Prince Charming being plural. His practical and agreeable role, in plural form, is something I go on about often; I've shown how Prince Charming, when he's made kaleidoscopic, can color life with money and comfort. But the instinct for monogamy is huge.

It's huge even though it's not practical, even though it's romantic as hell.

Well, *I'm* romantic as hell.

That need to intensely bond with one lover can be really lethal, too. If you have the capacity to fool yourself, that is, and I most certainly do, and I especially did, then. I was starting to stumble from the stabs of the three ugly sisters. I was bleeding so bad that it was blinding. I was getting so blind that I might see a goblin, and think he's magnificent.

Well, Mitch had left me his number at four o'clock in the morning. I usually ignore what comes in before dawn. But business had been a bit slow the day before, and thus far today, at eleven a.m., the pager was still dead.

So I figured I might as well call back a night owl.

When his phone rang, he answered immediately. The hour of four had been eons ago, but he was still game for a tryst; in fact, he'd love to see me, he said, even though he was groggy.

I could tell, as I listened, that he was someone safe to visit, just a horny-guy sleepyhead, harmless. I was all bathed and ready, and this dump looked the worst in the daylight; how grateful I felt to have somewhere to go.

It took forty minutes to get there. I'd never been called to his town before, and as I drove through it, I saw why. By the look of it, few guys who lived there could ever afford my fee. The place wasn't dangerous—it wasn't *that* bad—but it sure wasn't what I was used to. I was used to the upper crust. This vicinity looked very working-class, and it wasn't the least bit pretty.

I arrived at the house he lived in. It was big, and clean white, a not-bad old farmhouse, surviving the prefab industrial buildings that broke out like rashes around it.

His entrance was way in the back.

I found it and walked up a narrow flight of stairs, in a drab little hallway that was dusty and dim. The odor of mildew was strong.

I'd almost never seen dingy places like this one, and whenever I had it was to see the kid clients. The youngest would call me to their slummy apartments, when, once in a blue moon, they had money. They tended to inhabit the grungier parts of otherwise decent buildings; they couldn't afford something better.

This guy had said he was thirty-eight. That was pretty old for this rat hole.

?

Oh well, whatever, who cared. The time of day was sunny and bright; the downstairs family was out in the yard; I didn't feel weird, or unsafe.

When he opened the door, the first thing I thought was, this is a Puerto Rican. He was short and as dark-skinned as a white person can be and still be called a Caucasian. He had very black hair, the kind that curls up so tightly that it doesn't grow very long.

If the date had been post-Nine-Eleven, my heart might have clenched up and whispered, **an Arab?**

He was openly smiling, but he looked a little stupid. Momentarily, I would realize he was stoned.

His apartment was a disaster. Every room looked as though all the detritus of a garage and an attic and an office had been dumped there. Functional things, like a table and chairs, were barely distinguishable.

It was clear he had single-guy-itis up the ying-yang.

And maybe he also had **stoner** up the ying-yang. Or maybe **arrested development**. Or **organizationally challenged**. Or other iffy brain chemistries. But those thoughts receded to the back of my mind when I noticed what he wore around his neck.

He had led me into his tiny living room, to furniture that looked like that cheap chintzy stuff that gets sold under roadside tents. He had shoved aside some mess, and settled himself on the loveseat, and was now grinning up at me. I summarily knelt down before him, so we could be face-to-face.

And that's when I saw the Star of David, on a silver chain, on his neck.

So that was it. He was Jewish! Genetically speaking, he was a very original-Hebrew kind of Jewish. Mideastern ancestry caused his dark features.

Jewish.

That was my father.

A few minutes later, we were in his cluttered bedroom, on the only twin-sized waterbed I'd ever seen in my life. It was small for two people, but we did just fine. I remember he made me come twice.

I wasn't in a relationship then, so I totally let myself go with the clients, when I was in the mood. I was having orgasms whenever I wanted, with anyone who could make me. But when Mitch got me off, it wasn't the usual. It wasn't just a physical, soothing release. With Mitch, it felt kind of special. With Mitch, it felt kind of deep.

Uh-oh.

Now you're probably thinking, how could I feel that? How could this evident loser, this stoned little pony-tailed packrat, living like a kid in low-achieving dishevelment, get to a woman like me? I was older than he was. I was responsible, a parent. Men who got high a lot didn't impress me. As an "escort", I met successful men, men who lived in style and luxury.

So what made *this* guy so special?

Well, for one thing, he acted very Jewish-mother sweet. That got to me right away. He seemed very nurturing and loving, in touch with his feminine side.

Daddy was just like that.

And then there was what he did in bed. The first time he made me come, which was by going down on me, he stayed down there for a few moments after, and gently blew on me. Something about that just floored me. He didn't just lick it and leave it, as most guys would have done; he wanted to care for it, afterwards. He wanted to cool it down.

Priceless!

And then there was his work. It was all about my passion, rock music. He labored as a stagehand at all the local venues. After he informed me about that, even his dope-smoking charmed me. Now it had a purpose. It was integral. The weed was part of his classic-rock lifestyle.

The aroma of it was taking me back…back to the good old days…

We had all lived in lowlife apartments, back then. And we had been happy to be there.

And Mitch was so damned interested in everything that mattered—like my dog. When the hour was up, did he see me out the door? No. He walked me all the way down to my car. The reason was he wanted to meet my best friend.

My back seat was essentially a doghouse, no matter what the season. All of the windows were accordingly rolled all the way down, or up. My buddy hung out there, with his water and food, and Mitch was determined to see him.

And when he spoke to my dog, very lovingly, my dog got over his barking, and quickly.

Ladies, you know how that goes. If our pets take a liking to the guy we've brought over, the softest among us go gooey.

At times like that we should remind ourselves, Hitler had worshipful Dobermans. The same might be true of Osama.

Well, I wasn't in any kind of cautionary mode; I had completely lost my good sense. With Mitch, I had drifted into something so sweet, it was like getting shipwrecked in heaven. I didn't give a damn about anything, right then. All I knew was, I felt happy. As I leaned on my car, reluctant to go, I said he could page me, anytime.

I said that to most of my clients. With them, however, it was business, just a stab at good customer service. It was nice words to punctuate a friendly transaction. My professional feeling was always, *I'm through here*. But with Mitch, it felt very different.

I don't think I told him I'd see him for free—the words hadn't yet reached my mouth. But that truth wafted teasingly between us, like a lovely scent on a breeze.

The next day he paged me, and I eagerly called him back. We chatted like a couple of old friends. When he paged me yet again, on the day after that, the talking felt empty and achy. It felt worse than when I noticed the designs the peels made in the wallpaper at the dump.

I wanted to see him. I didn't want money. I told him so right away.

But Mitch didn't seem to have heard me. He told me his wallet was empty. He said that he'd paid me the first time with a $200 lottery winning. Good fortune like that was the only way he could go for a treat like me; there was no way he'd scrounge up the dough for me again, not any time soon, anyway.

He had paged me just to say hi.

"That's fine," I said. "Can I see you?"

When Mitch finally realized I was serious, that I wanted to visit free of charge, he was absolutely astounded. He came down his stairs to greet me with a smile that could have lit up a midnight. This time, it wasn't the weed. No drug could ever induce such a glow; it was real joy that brightened his features.

Mitch had known several "escorts" during his time here on Earth, and once, he'd helped to manage a strip club. He understood the great magnitude of a sex worker wanting his company, without wanting any money.

He understood he'd been *chosen.* He didn't see how, or why; my favoritism was baffling. But one thing he knew: had he ever gotten lucky!

And then he made *me* feel lucky. The next several days belong in a book about head-over-heels romance. Mitch did five wonderful things. They were amazing things that incited my crush into an avalanche of lover's attachment. The first thing had to do with the dog.

We had cast the working girl time constraint completely to the wind. Suddenly, we were an item. We avidly wedded our schedules, spending hours and hours together. Such changes felt totally natural to us, but for the dog, they were way too abrupt. One night we left him alone in the apartment, while I went with Mitch to his job. Of course, Mitch's place was very new to the dog, and I, in my state of giddy-lover distraction, forgot to leave him a piece of my clothing to make him feel more secure.

Well, my poor four-legged soul mate must have thought I'd abandoned him. I guess he thought I'd gone home without him. He scratched through a screen, and jumped out its open window. He landed on top of a car—we deduced that later on, from a dent—and took off, looking for me.

It was very, very late, it was just about three a.m., when Mitch and I returned. We were stunned by the dogless apartment, and then by the telltale tear in the screen. We set out and searched the whole neighborhood. Our exhaustion from working at a concert all night turned into wrought nerves, desperation. But what got me the most was, Mitch *wept*.

Any guy would have been concerned; any guy would have helped me search; Mitch was taking it further; Mitch was tearful with me.

Well, my dog came wagging on back to me, just about an hour later. And he was completely okay. He didn't even limp, and I can tell you, he should have; he'd leapt through a second-story window.

Mitch wept again, over *that*.

I was intensely relieved to see my dog. But I was also bowled over by Mitch. I drank in his sweet show of caring like a woman who'd been dying of thirst.

Mitch's occupation was menial. It would only impress a groupie. He was poor, got high often, and lived in complete disarray. But his Jewish-mother compassion eclipsed all that stuff, made it minor. Until now, my life had been pure isolation. Until now, my aloneness had been so overwhelming that I'd begun to think painful was normal. And then *poof!* Here was someone who cared. He completely, openly cared. It didn't seem to matter one iota that we were perfect strangers. It didn't matter one iota that we'd been a whore and her client. Mitch just snapped *on,* like a light. It was like we were parents in a beautiful marriage who had just found their lost canine child.

The second and third things that Mitch did, over the course of that week, things that folded me deeper into a beautiful surrendered state, were two incredible things that he said. The first was the best thing any guy could have told me. Talk about "magic words"! He told me my work didn't bother him. He knew it was just a job. And then he proved it to me. He watched me leave to go on calls, and then he cheerfully welcomed me back. He didn't seem to care at all about what I'd just done; instead, he seemed nothing but happy. He was glad I could make such great money without having to work lots of hours.

And then he said, to this been-there-done-that mom, whose tubes had been tied long ago, that he didn't plan to have kids. He didn't want any babies.

So with those two sweeping declarations, it was as though he were telling me, *See? My attitude's perfect. We're on the same page.* In response, I was blissful and thrilled. But that doesn't say it; what I was is ***disintegrated.*** Mitch was a treasure, a precious encounter, the proverbial fits-just-right partner; I was swelling and bursting, I was giving grand birth, to devotion, to pure grateful loving.

The Three Rotten Sisters were slinking away. They were beaten and powerless losers.

Yet Mitch had said something disturbing. At the same time he'd told me he didn't want kids, he'd added a strange little comment. He'd said: "There shouldn't be any little *me's* running around."

I'd filed that away somewhere, thinking, it's nothing. But I'd recall it in the future, and often.

The fourth great thing he did that week was cry with me, over our long-gone dead mothers. He'd buried his mom a few years before; mine, of course, had been gone forever. He wept with me over our permanent grief, just like a soul mate, and maybe like a brother.

I hadn't spoken to my real brother for almost eleven years.

That sealed it. Now I was done for.

The dump motel never saw me again, except when I went there to grab my belongings. I had paid for a week, but spent most of it with Mitch; what a total waste of my money.

But who cared! True love had found me!

Fifthly, and finally, he gave me his spare key.

He was totally letting me in!

Me! The pariah! The fugitive! He loved me!

But there was one very painful problem. Remember, I was *visiting* the area. My current address was a long, long way from Mitch's.

At the time I was living with all of my sons in way-far western upstate New York. But Jesse and I sometimes trekked out here, to southeastern Massachusetts, to visit where he'd lived with his father. His dad had moved to Florida, so for Jesse, it wasn't about seeing him; it was all about being seventeen now, and wanting to catch up with all the friends he'd made here, living here in the past.

For me, it was all about missing the place. Over the years, I'd lived here quite often, and I yearned to move myself back.

I had a feeling that some day I'd return to New England, and not leave, ever again. The last time I'd lived in Massachusetts had been a few years before.

I had left on the advice of my loving Aunt Sarah; she lived in that place in upstate New York. She had suggested that my kids and I move there, and at the time, it had seemed like the right thing to do; she was all the caring family I had, and my two older boys could use a fresh start.

Well, my sons were all doing better out there, but I didn't like it out there. I was accustomed to the lovelier locales of the Greater Boston Area. Ever since I was ten years old, Massachusetts had enchanted me. People would take me out of Manhattan, or dull upstate New York environs, and immerse me into this quaintness, this lush-lovely apple grove greenness, this exquisitely preserved antiquity, this old seafaring charm.

New England had quietly seduced this New Yorker, a long, long time ago.

And now, much later in life I had learned, as an enterprising "escort", about the huge difference in fees I could charge, depending on where I worked. In wealthy eastern Massachusetts, the rate per hour was amazingly more than the comparative pittance the clients forked over in the depressed and downhearted region I'd moved to. I made *twice* the money as a callgirl, when I visited Massachusetts, than what I was making in the Rust Belt— without working any more hours.

And there was something else. That place in western New York was where I'd gotten arrested. The cops were aggressive out there. They went after the women just for placing their ads. Here in Massachusetts, the cops seemed more lenient. Or at least not so gung-ho.

So I was *aching* to move back to this area, and after I fell for Mitch, a native New England son, well, you can just imagine what the ache turned into, then.

By the time I picked up Jesse at his friend's house, to share the long boring drive "home," my separation pain was acute. My current address was almost five hundred miles distant from the dearest love of my life! How was I going to bear that?

I couldn't just pick up and move here. Jesse had his last year of high school to get through, on the furthest western edge of New York. I couldn't just leave my kid there.

All those tortuous thoughts had knifed through me as I spent the last night with Mitch.

Jesse met Mitch as we were leaving, and I could tell that he wasn't impressed. He'd been hearing about this guy all week, and he could see that his mother was stupid-in-love, and he didn't like it at all.

As I introduced my son to Mitch, I said: "I'm going to marry him some day." I knew that when I said that, Mitch wouldn't flinch; during our emotional week together, Mitch had referred to marriage; that was what "nice Jewish boys" often did.

But Jesse looked somewhat revolted. After we left Mitch, and he noticed my despair, he implied that I'd lost my mind.

"Mom. You just met the guy."

Point taken. I couldn't argue. I knew that I looked idiotic. Jesse was peaking at that frustrating age when kids come to realize their parents are flawed. Seeing me like this, all smitten like a schoolgirl, wasn't helping at all. Any lovestruck mom would have known that, and would have allowed her kid his disgust, but I had an additional reason for keeping my yap shut tight: Jesse didn't know for sure what his mother did for a living.

At that point all that I'd admitted to my kids was that I did a little soft-core dominatrix work. That doesn't involve real sex. They pictured me letting guys lick my feet, and me spanking them, and such. Sometimes that was exactly what I did, but certainly not all the time. There was no way I could tell Jesse that the apex, the crowning glory, of my swept-away feelings for Mitch, was his total acceptance of my sex work. There was no way I could divulge to my kid that reason for my passion for that guy, that stoner and stagehand of diminutive stature who personified, to intuitive Jesse, all the bad meanings of *small.*

So I listened to Jesse's lectures, and I accepted his skepticism, and I respected his right to an opinion, and I kept myself prudently quiet.

And four years later, in the storm of my divorce, I would admit that my son had been right as rain, albeit he'd been only seventeen.

The next few months were sheer emotional hell. That is, when I wasn't with Mitch. The most horrible thing was going on calls, all those hundreds of miles from him. I couldn't stand it.

To be missing your man intensely, and to have to be touched by others—I remember the feeling was so cutting and poison that I feared for my sanity. It was as though I was forced to provide tender care for a whole lot of hungry babies, all of them needing my body and mind, while my own baby was lost.

The Rust Belt clients knew something was up. My professionalism was shattered. I got told I looked terribly sad.

I kept at it, though, for my family. At that point only my eldest son, Ayden, was completely on his own. I kept at it to help my son Jeremy in college, and to help with the high costs that Jesse, as a gifted young video-maker, was starting to incur. I also kept at it to pay back some money that I had owed, since my poverty days, to Aunt Sarah. And also to retain the freedom I needed to be able to visit Mitch often.

You can take that emotional torture when you have to. But I wouldn't wish it on anyone, not even the devil himself.

When I visited Mitch, however, and I went to see clients from his place, and then returned to his love, everything felt okay. He was there to tell me not to feel bad, he was there to tell me it was all right, and when I looked deeply into his eyes and saw that he really meant it, the agony totally left me. When I was with Mitch, I felt peaceful. Being with my lover, and seeing that my work didn't hurt him, made everything bearable.

The only limitation Mitch imposed was no incalls. He would never stand for having any clients on appointments with me in his home. *Of course not!* I agreed. His home was our world, the place just for us. The clients were work. Work was elsewhere.

It was getting really crucial to move there. My emotional health was on the line. And then there was the practical reason, the fact that I made much more money there. A nasty irony had developed: Jesse needed my presence, but he also needed my money, and I don't just mean for the basics. He needed more and more video equipment, and he always needed props. He needed time for his craft. A fulltime job, on top of school, was out of the question if he was going to work on his films. To sum it all up, he needed a sponsor, and that, of course, was me.

His father drank away his disposable income in bikini-filled Florida bars.

But the trouble with Mom was, she made her best dough far away. And Mom was much more emotionally serene, and therefore much better able to work, only in that locale.

There was really only one way through it: I had to move in with Mitch.

So Jesse finished his senior year of high school with his mother ensconced at a distance. But it wasn't too bad for him. He lived in Aunt Sarah's big, comfortable house, in his own renovated section. Aunt Sarah was retired, and loved him, and always happy to do for him. And his older brothers were around for him, too, whenever he needed them. And I came back to see him, every two or three weeks.

It was hell on my car, and hell on me, driving, but what was a mother to do?

I always brought plenty of money, aware that when kids are almost grown up, and needful of support for their talents, the green stuff takes precedence. If I had stayed poor, a powerless presence, watching my boys become men, I don't think I could have lived with the pain of not being able to finance the honing of their gifts.

So being away from Jesse, in order to better help him, was an irony I could stand.

Meanwhile, Mitch was letting me down, a little. For the most part, he still acted loving, and he continued to show me that critical acceptance and consistent support for my work. But he was also drawing sharp boundaries between us, and sometimes, it really hurt.

Mitch had never been married. He had never even lived with a woman for long. It was becoming quite apparent that he was something of a loner, and often, he just wanted me to leave him by himself.

But Mitch came from good, strong, stable Jewish stock; he was the youngest of three sons in a solid, conventional family. His two older brothers were both college graduates, with promising jobs and futures. They were the owners of beautiful homes, and they both thrived in good, stable marriages, and both of them had two kids. Accordingly, Mitch's mother and father had enjoyed a good marriage in the years before she died. All of her sons were grown men when she died.

So Mitch had grown up pretty happy, at least on the face of things. But something about him was different. His loner ways weren't like his family. Since the age of fifteen, he'd done a shitload of drugs, something his brothers only dabbled in, only for a while, when in college. For Mitch, weed had never been only a phase; getting high, and also cocaine, I would learn, had been a way of life for him, from adolescence on.

Maybe the drugs were the whole damn thing. Maybe the drugs were the cleaver, the thing that made him black-sheepish, set apart from his responsible family.

Or maybe Mitch had been born different. I'll never know. What I do know is this: he possessed that familial Jewish sweetness, that affection my father had given. That was the Mitch I had fallen for; his people had taught him well.

But...

I was going to find there was much more to Mitch than that lovely ethnic molding, and none of it was good.

He told me that in the mid-eighties, he'd gone on tour as a roadie with the legendary band, *Aerosmith*. He and its lead singer, Steven Tyler, had been friendly. The band had been heavy into coke in those days, and Mitch got lost in it with them.

On one night he ingested so much of the drug that he went into cardiac arrest. Tyler had Mitch rushed to the hospital, and from there he wound up in rehab.

That was the end of the tour for Mitch. It was also the end of his dance with cocaine.

Or so he said.

When Mitch brought me around to his father and brothers, I could see they were a little standoffish. One of his sisters-in-law seemed to despise him. She didn't want her children on outings with Mitch, even when he eagerly offered to take them.

In response, Mitch seethed with resentment. There was tension all around.

Mitch's father told me that Mitch was his "baby." But later on I was going to realize that the man was pretty much saying, that was the *only reason* he could feel much love for that son.

I began to get the impression that Mitch's relatives felt he was a liar. No one ever came right out and said it; Mitch was family, after all. But I heard things, like "I can't believe half the stuff he says."

My secret life, my hidden work, necessarily made *me* a liar. Maybe that's why when I heard them say "bullshit artist", I could just let it go. Mitch lived with *my* lie, didn't he? That made him precious and lovely to me, no matter what liarly leanings he had.

One thing was going on, however, that I couldn't just let go. Mitch's sexual interest was waning. That was hard on me.

I would come back from working and driving for hours, and when it was time for bed, I wanted to make love, or snuggle. As a whore, I very much needed that attention, even more than I would have if I hadn't been in sex work. I needed to come home to loving that was *permanent.* I needed to come home to loving that was *marital.* Every woman needs that, but a sex worker needs it *more.*

It's not that I was oversexed. Twice a week would have been plenty. And just to have Mitch hold me, on most of the other nights, would have been enough. But Mitch didn't want to do that.

I would get in around eleven or midnight, tired and ready to fall into bed, and if he was there, not working a concert, Mitch would look up and greet me with a warm and loving "Hi, honey." But that would be all he'd do. He'd turn back to his online journeys and his burning stick of weed, and he'd stay there into the small hours, apathetic to my needs.

I would lie in bed hopefully waiting, and give up, and sadly doze off.

Mitch was just doing what he'd always done, I guess: entertaining himself, all by himself, with regular help from drugs. He didn't seem to much like the idea of being wrapped up in me.

But Mitch had been raised as a Jew, and part of that upbringing is the fervent belief that a person ought to be mated. On principle, it seemed, he knew that the love I was offering him was something he should endorse.

But he didn't want intimacy.

And when he finally came to bed, he didn't want us to touch. He didn't want us to snuggle. He *did* want us sleeping side by side, and he *did* like the fact that I warmed up his bed, but that was all. He'd get annoyed if I asked to be held.

That was very, very hard on me. I was starving for his affection. Clients often wanted to hold me, and that made my job very sweet, but I wanted Mitch to do it.

And something made it even more frustrating. Mitch was always happy to cuddle up to the dog! He'd hug the dog and pet him and fondle him, but he didn't want to do that to me!

Well, I would just sit there, watching him with the dog, and first I'd feel resentment, but then my optimism took over. I'd remember how loving he'd been with me, back there in the beginning, way before I moved in. If Mitch could remain that way with the dog, then he must have deep-seated affection; maybe some day he'd find the courage to sustain that loving with me.

But instead, things just got worse. After I'd been living there for months, Mitch wanted sex only once in a while. I got very aggrieved over that.

And then I found out he had cyber lovers. I pitched a fit over that.

"But look what *you* do," he said.

"What do you mean?" I said. "I do that because it's my *job!* And it's *only* my job! You know that! You know I want to *make love* with *you!*"

"Okay, you have a point," he said. "But those women online, they're nothing. You shouldn't get upset. They're just *type*."

"No they're not!" I shot back. "They're *real* women, and you're getting *them* off, not *me!!* And you're not doing it for money, like I do! So why *are* you doing it?"

"Don't worry, they don't get me off." Mitch said. "I just like the sense of power. I like knowing I make them crazy."

That may have been true. I'd never seen him with a hard-on when typing that erotic stuff, not even when all the women out there typed back that they were soaking their chairs.

"But why don't you want to make *me* crazy?" I implored.

"I dunno," he said, and I think he really didn't.

Mitch obviously couldn't handle any long-term intimacy, and I was getting distressed. Whatever happened to that adorable lover who blew on me, the first day?

But disappointment wasn't denting my commitment. His total acceptance of my sex work was the glue that kept me there. I realized I could live with almost any way Mitch was, as long as I heard that loving "Hi honey!" when I came through the door.

Being with Mitch taught me something. Knowing that someone accepts your truth is the biggest seduction on Earth. Being accepted makes you soft on that person, so soft that you'll take almost anything.

You also might *offer* almost anything. At one point I started to offer him women. I offered him three-way trysts. I thought that might liven him up. And there was another reason—I figured it was wise to play fair. I wanted to reward him for dealing so well with my profession, my encounters, with men.

We ended up getting with a working girl friend, and paying her for her time. On another occasion, we had a young girl come over, someone Mitch met at a concert, someone who craved a bisexual romp.

Mitch had a lot of fun. Just as it would go with any guy, having two women excited him. As with just about any other guy, he enjoyed being able to touch a strange woman, and have his own woman there, too.

As for myself, I had some mixed feelings, but mostly I liked it a lot. As you know from this book's first chapter, three-ways turn me on. And there was another reason: I was actually proud of Mitch's skills. I loved being witness to what that young girl felt, when he went down on her.

But none of that did anything to improve his desire when we were alone.

I'll never forget the first time that I became aware of his ice. There was definitely ice inside Mitch. There may have been a whole glacier. And I think he'd been careful, up to that point, to keep it hidden from me. I think that he'd learned, some time before me, that people turn away from him when they feel too much of that chill. So he tried to keep on the mask, the one his upbringing provided, that sweet little face of Jewish-mother affection.

Such cold, such a terrible absence of love, spanned like the canyons of the moon, inside Mitch. The first time I felt it we were smoking a joint, on his couch, while we watched TV.

For me, marijuana is an aphrodisiac. I never smoke it often enough for it to become ineffective. When I get high with my lover, I get wet just because he's near. The combination of cannabis and the person who's won my heart makes me instantly lusty and wanting to *merge.*

On this particular evening, my desire for Mitch was further ignited because I'd been away. I'd just returned from two weeks with Jesse. I was extra hungry for love.

My head was on Mitch's chest, and my mouth was near his nipple. Stoned, in love, and in a state of impassioned reunion, it was the most natural thing in the world for me to start gently nuzzling him there.

A few moments passed, and he wasn't responding. It was just as though he were dead. I paused and faced up at him, confused but still smiling. I found myself jolted by a mean pair of eyes.

"Are you done?" he said. His tone was pure ice.

"Yes," I said, and I pulled away, calmly. I sat up, keeping my smile on. But I was stung. No, I was stabbed.

After a few moments, I quietly rose. I left him and went into the bathroom, and softly closed the door, and sank down in the dark, and silently shook with tears.

He should have been feeling a lot more lust for his lover-who'd-been-away, but on the other hand, maybe I'd annoyed him. He was a guy in leave-me-alone mode; he wanted to watch TV. But still, his coldness was horrid; he should have rejected me gently.

I thought: whatever happened to that sweetheart, that guy who'd cried with me?

I should have packed up my stuff that night, and left Mitch behind, forever. I'd just seen a warning, a sign of the truth: Mitch couldn't maintain affection.

But I was in love. And I was alone. And I'd never been one to give up—not so soon.

Oh, Mitch. What a player you were. Or maybe one spark of sincerity blew around inside that glacier; I'll never know for sure.

Believe it or not, not long after that, the Ice Man proposed to me. With only a sixth of a caret, but so what? What got to me, and also my family, was that he asked my sons' permission to marry me, the night before he asked me. I think he asked my aunt, too.

That touched everybody, right to the heart. What a family guy!

And lo and behold, he did something else: he got me to talk to my brother! For the first time in over a decade!

And some time after that, for my birthday he got me a kitten. He knew that I missed a lovable cat that I'd left behind in New York.

So Mitch was physically cold, yet warm and mediating when it came to family and pets. His ironies were dizzying me. But one thing kept me grounded there, just as firmly as a rock: there was no Madonna/Whore complex. Mitch had no problem with wedding a whore, and also with keeping her secret. I felt secure and happy about that, every single day.

And Mitch himself seemed to feel pretty good about becoming a husband. After his proposal, when he talked to my sons, it was stepson this and stepson that; he seemed to genuinely like the idea of becoming a father to three sons by marriage; maybe it made him feel as though he was taking after his dad.

My oldest son Ayden had just made me a grandma, so Mitch would be a step-grandpa. He seemed to like that idea, too.

I guess Mitch figured he was getting it all. He had a woman who made lots of money, and loved to spend it on him; she also let him play with other women. There were stepsons of an age to smoke weed with, and even something biblically juicy, a comfortably righteous role: he could fulfill the part he was raised for; he could feel like a Jewish dad.

Now the roadie rocker, the stoner, would finally be properly married. Now perhaps his family would respect him!

I have to mull over those things, because even though he made it clear that he wanted to marry me, Mitch was ironically chafing against me, and acting more and more annoyed with me, as time went on and on.

I had helped him get his trashy apartment cleaned up and organized. I had hung some beautiful curtains. At first, he sang my praises; he seemed to be truly grateful for my cleaning and homemaking efforts. But later on, when I made it clear that I wanted the apartment to *stay* clean, well, that he appeared to not like.

I got out into the seedy hallway that led to our domicile door, and I cleaned and painted and laid plush stair carpet, all at my own expense. Now we had a nice entranceway, something to be rather proud of. The landlord and neighbors all oohed and ahhed, and so did our visitors.

But Mitch only shrugged, and smoked his joints down, and made a bunch of new messes.

I had started to see a pattern in Mitch, his M.O., if you will. He was wonderful at initiating things. He was bad at following through. And then, when I *expected* him to follow through, he would turn on me, sometimes viciously.

He had started our relationship like some perfect loving prince, but now, he just acted withdrawn. Even though we were engaged, he was almost asexual and somewhat detached, just like a proverbial roommate. And even though he loved the fact that I got the apartment squared away, he couldn't keep it that way. It was getting insanely disheveled again. And I, of course, kept cleaning, again.

Mitch was resisting my wifely affection, and also my neat-and-clean habits, and sometimes getting nasty about it, even though he'd heartily welcomed them, back there in the beginning.

Where was that wonderful lover I'd known, during those first thrilling visits? Where was that guy who had told me I was the best thing since the wheel, because of all my devotion, and my beautification of his home?

Who was this mean little fucker? This increasingly foul-mouthed, miserable gnome, who didn't want me to touch him, and got resentful when I neatened things up?

"Is it my work?" I asked him. "Is my work getting to you?"

"No, it's not that," he said.

The meaner Mitch got, the more I repeated that question, and that's how he answered, every time. He seemed to be telling the truth about that.

In fact, for the entire duration of our relationship, my work was the one thing that *didn't* seem to annoy him. Toward the end of my life with Mitch, even on his darkest, most combative day, when he seemed to need to tear me down until I was paralyzed, he still showed respect for my work.

Mitch didn't even tell whore jokes. He said they were demeaning to me.

But he didn't mind demeaning me in other ways! Much to my dismay, he became hypercritical. He attacked me for all of my flaws, like my low-tech computer shortcomings. That hurt me a lot, because I value relationship-helpers, like positive reinforcement. I took care to not ever put *him* down. I was mindful of the importance of building someone up. I was also very sensitive about his male pride. I was careful not to *ever* rub in that I made much more money than he did.

Well, Mitch was acting so shitty, sometimes, that I had to struggle mightily to not let it rub off.

And then, to my horror, he started to call me a cunt.

Ladies, you know what that word does. And I for one knew that I didn't deserve it. I knew I was far from perfect, I knew I could be annoying, but I also knew that I wasn't a *cunt*. I knew that I wasn't even a *bitch.* I was too good to people to be called that. I was especially too good to my *man* to be called that.

"Why did you say that?" I would ask him, almost nauseated with rage. I'd been with an abuser before—that ex husband who punched me right in the face. But no one, including that husband, had ever called me *that word*, the most dehumanizing word to a woman in the language. And no one, including that wife-beater, had ever been so *constantly mean*.

Mitch would respond that the word meant nothing, but what bullshit, he knew it made me crazy. It seemed that Mitch *wanted* to make me crazy. Bad crazy, hurt crazy, mad crazy.

"Are you *SURE* it isn't my work?"

"Nope. It's just that, you're *here*."

"What do you mean, I'm *here*?"

"Look, I'm not very happy," he said. "I never have been. And it's just that, you're just *here*. I'm just venting on you."

So there it was, out of the shadows: the classic abuser's excuse. And I was the classic enabler, with a sad-little-stigmatized-prostitute twist: I felt lucky, so lucky, to have Mitch to come home to, a man who could live with my work.

What a guy! What a prince! What a marvel!

When Mitch didn't have any dope to smoke, he ferociously smoked cigarettes. I believe it was over a pack a day. His ashtrays brimmed over with bent stubs of filth, and the grey flakes of death's desiccation. The stench of the air he defiled brought me down, and I was quietly disapproving, and I wasn't conflicted about it. Smokers are addicts, they're slaves to a killer, and these days, most of them face it.

After I moved in, Mitch tried hard to quit, and thus began, for the ever-hopeful me, sad episodes of health-nut frustration. Just when I thought he had smoking so beat, just when I thought I'd no longer feel jealous of things in his mouth that weren't me, he'd go right back to sucking his butts. It was very disappointing, a real roller-coaster ride, to watch him quit for two whole months, and then light up again. It happened several times.

At first Mitch would valiantly try to do right, but he just couldn't stick to a thing. Not anything positive, or strong. I saw that in everything he attempted.

Maybe that's why he got so mean. Maybe he hated me for being there, for being a witness to his weakness.

At the rock concert work sites, Mitch was appreciated. He was always on time, and hard working. But he tended to have accidents, because he was stoned. One such mishap disabled him for almost a whole year. He had me to support him, though.

He admitted he'd been fired from other jobs, way before he met me. I inferred that they were the types of employment where he wasn't allowed to get high. It seemed that Mitch had an attitude problem when weed wasn't in his brain. He'd get irritable, and very belligerent, to the point where his bosses would oust him.

He'd been the same way in relationships with women. Mitch had begun to confess to me that even though he adored his mother, he had often been awful to her. And he'd been shitty to the one girl he'd lived with for a short time, years before he lived with me. And his dating relationship with someone else, a very romantic young girl, had ended viciously.

I was starting to see that ugly attitude, daily. Whenever Mitch was stoned, he was stupid, but his treatment of me was okay. But whenever he ran out of weed, which was often, he'd get edgy and mean and offensive.

Oh, boy. I'd sure picked a loser. Sometimes, even Mitch would admit that he knew what a loser he was.

But somehow I loved him, anyway. Mitch accepted my truth, my work. Mitch knew my truth, and lived with it well. That kept him golden to me.

I wasn't alone anymore.

But there was something else that kept me there, the glue that welds any two people together: Mitch and I shared some big dreams. The two of us had some big plans.

For one thing, I had started this book project. Regardless of his meanness in other things, Mitch was supportive toward me as a writer. He pushed me to keep it up. I didn't really need any pushing from him; I had found my own endless drive. But I loved his being squarely behind me.

At first, Mitch proofread my writing. English had been his best subject in school; he was actually rather good. But after he read my work for a while, he began to lose interest in it. It was just like with everything else he got into: Mitch lacked staying power.

We fantasized about how sweet life might become if I were a successful writer. And we had other dreams, too. We wanted to succeed in a business together. We agreed that the money I made as an "escort" could float us through a lot of any start-up costs incurred.

We failed at a dot.com endeavor—a website for nutritional supplements. After that I hit on another idea.

I'd like to describe what that business idea was, but I won't because it's just too revealing. If I talk about that endeavor, anyone who knew us and reads this book will immediately realize this story's about us. What I will say is that it was legitimate, both artistic and sensible, and very realistically feasible, and a service the area needed.

Mitch loved the notion. He was eager to get it going. He was virtually combusting with initiative. That's what Mitch did best.

But whatever got Mitch going was the same thing that made him implode. That was the rotted-out nutshell that I was learning to sum Mitch up in.

He was so afraid of failure that it made him mean as hell. But Mitch was even more afraid of success. On the face of things, he wanted to succeed, just like anyone else. But in truth, Mitch was comfortable being a loser. That was his biggest problem.

The closer we got to starting that business—and with the money I made we were *damn* close—the more abusive Mitch got. The colder, the meaner, the more insulting, Mitch got. He was absolutely determined to get the business going, but at the same time, he needed to smoke more dope, at the same time, he needed to see more stoner friends, at the same time, he called me a cunt more often, apparently because of my dynamism.

I guess to Mitch I was no longer just a sad and lonely little whore. Dealing with that had been easy. Now I was becoming a positive force, the means to make him successful. Now I was making things scary.

I was buying us a place in a beautiful area, a property we'd fallen in love with together. It was a sweet little honeymoon cottage, and there was also a brand new barn. The house would be perfect for our marriage, and the barn would be perfect for our workshop. Mitch had said so, himself.

He loved me for it, yet he hated me for it. He hated me for it *much more*. Mitch never said so, but I could see it.

I'll never forget how things escalated. At the beautiful site where we planned to be married, a site he'd enthused over with me, Mitch dug so deeply into my arm that it was black and blue for weeks. I had no idea what I said or did to make him claw me like that. But one thing I knew for sure: it was a very, very bad omen, getting viciously bruised by my fiancé, at the very locale of our wedding-to-be.

The wedding was three months distant, and I should have cancelled it, right then and there. But of course, this foolish girl didn't. I was planning The Most Beautiful Wedding on Earth.

I was planning a sort of Boomer-priestess event, which I knew would be starry-eyed for everyone gathered. I had two granddaughters at that point, and they would be flower girls. Several other darlings would be flower girls too, the children of close friends. That's right—I had *lots* of little girls to strew the blossoms; the more the merrier, that's what I wanted.

The children were all going to pick their own flowers to throw, from a garden right next to the ceremony, a garden that I'd planted myself; I had purposely picked out a country resort that would allow me to do such a thing.

I also had many bridesmaids, mostly the grown girls of family or friends.

I had three matrons of honor. It was too hard to choose only one.

I didn't buy any dresses for them. I told them to wear what they wanted, as long as there was lavender or purple.

I designed my own gown, and had it made by a seamstress. It mystically glimmered with lavender hues. I labored over numerous garlands from scratch, of silk flowers, laces and ribbons, all for the heads of all the females in the wedding.

I won't tell you what music I was going to walk down the aisle to. It was moving and thrilling, and just the right beat, right out of the annals of great classic rock. To reveal it would blow my cover right off.

The locale was a comfortable antique inn, and the wedding would last a whole weekend. The ceremony was going to be beautifully pagan, and beautifully rock and roll.

The pastor would be Unitarian. He would perform the ceremony, written by us both, under a Jewish arch. There would be a wineglass to stomp on.

So the service would have something for everyone gathered, rockers and Jews, and anyone else, everyone enjoying, together.

Later on, after the dinner, we would drive, as a huge entourage, to a panoramic beach during sunset. There we'd all revel and toast with champagne, all generations in a romp by the sea, until it became pitch dark.

How could I cancel something like that? Something that perfectly summertime-joyful, that perfectly, sublimely romantic, with so many young and beautiful people excited and involved? I was thinking much more like a mother than a bride.

I knew, at that point, that the marriage might not last. Mitch had become so pathologically abusive that I didn't think I could hold on. But I'd have that great gathering anyway! Why not—I could afford it! I saw it as not just a wedding, vows spoken with withering hope, but also as a reunion, a sweet time for everyone there.

That would make it very sweet for me.

Well, the wedding weekend came and went, and it was absolute bliss. Even Mitch acted nice. The only glitch was the absence of Jesse when it came time for the pictures. He'd taken off with a girl.

These days, I know that was prescience.

After the wedding and a short honeymoon, everything slipped and slid back to normal. It was right back to getting called cunt for no reason, and almost never getting touched, and all the time Mitch needing joints and butts.

Actually, it was back to that even on the honeymoon.

A couple of months later, we were out to dinner one night. We'd both had a couple of drinks. Mitch never drank much, so even just a little booze made him kind of sloppy. On this particular occasion, it gave him some very loose lips.

My lips were getting loose, too. I said: "So, why do you hardly ever make love to me, even now that we're married?"

"You have your clients for that."

"*WHAT?*"

Oops. I could see it on his face. He'd let something out that he shouldn't have. The mask had fallen down for a second.

Fucking alcohol.

I gasped, "What do you *mean*, what are you *saying*! What do you mean, the *clients*..."

Mitch tried to fix his blooper, but there was nothing he could do; he had clearly blurted the truth. He wanted to pass making love to his wife right off onto her clients. God help me, the horror was out. It oozed there between us like a big stinking corpse, an exhumed ugly truism, nauseating. How could I process that, or live with that, or look at that for more than a second?

I threw it on the back burner, into the pot full of hell.

Because there were other things to think of. Very compelling things. The bought house. The big move. The new business.

A few weeks after that, when we were getting ready to leave the apartment and move to our adorable cottage, Mitch got so mean and violent that I decided it was time to have a talk with the police. That was also the occasion of my traumatized call to my cross-dresser buddy, Greg—the friend introduced in Chapter Five who I've told you I desperately turned to.

Mitch had kicked in the bathroom door, and ripped it right off its hinges. The violence was so quick and explosive that my dog had forgotten to guard me; he had fled right under a table.

Then my husband glowered at me and told me that the next time, he'd do that to *me.*

I had no clue what I did, or said, to make him go that crazy. I couldn't recall saying anything!

The cops told me I could definitely get a restraining order against Mitch. They said that his violence to things, and his consequent threats to me, thoroughly warranted it.

I decided to wait. I'd pick up that thread if I had to, only after the move.

A few evenings later, we were driving to our new property. We were on one of those boring little back-and-forth trips that occur during hassles of moving. Mitch was driving, and we were avidly talking. I recall it was a discussion about our business plans. We were expressing a bunch of ideas.

All of a sudden, Mitch got enraged. It seemed he was angry because I had ideas. The next thing I knew, he'd hauled off and punched me. He hit me really hard, in the shoulder.

For the next several days, it would hurt to lift that arm.

I slumped against the passenger-side door, with my whole upper arm in pain. My emotional pain was worse. I remember I stayed crouched for a while.

It's not that I was afraid. I didn't think he'd hit me again, not right then, anyway. I knew that for now, his insanity had passed. The reason I remained in that weird, hunched state was that something momentous was happening.

I was just about through.

After several long minutes of silence had passed, I suddenly sat up and told him:

"If you abuse me again, after the move, I'm going to go straight to the police. I'm going to have you arrested."

A whore's lonely gratitude, a whore's compensations, and last-ditch newlywed hope: they had finally all fallen away.

I knew I meant every word.

SHE RISES, SHE STANDS, SHE WALKS

She married Love, then Love abandoned her.

My sons hadn't seen how abusive Mitch got. Whenever Mitch visited them with me, he was careful to behave fairly well. And when they came to see us, he watched himself those times, too. He knew not to get too nasty to me in front of my towering sons.

But the kids knew he was no prize.

They'd been trying to tell me for quite some time that Mitch was full of shit. They'd caught him in all kinds of lies. Jesse, for one, had seen hints of his temper, and something even worse. Jesse was aware of something crazy, something whacko. He'd sworn things to me that I couldn't believe.

He'd insisted, for instance, that Mitch pissed in his shoe. He'd deliberately peed in one of Jesse's shoes, just because Jesse annoyed him.

I couldn't accept that. Jesse had to be wrong. That was just too bizarre.

But now I know it was true.

Shortly after Mitch and I moved into our house, we got a distress call from my eldest son, Ayden. He was having grave problems with Annie, his wife. She was addicted to crack.

Annie was in many ways similar to Mitch. She came from a decent, stable family; in fact, they were pious church-goers. None of them drank or did drugs. Annie was the fuck-up, the black sheep, the one who'd gotten lost.

Annie had had a baby girl when she was just eighteen. Right away, her mother got custody. Then, four years later, Annie got pregnant again. She had another baby girl, and that was Ayden's child.

Ayden was willing, and even excited, to step into the role of a father. He also seemed to take after—God help him—the foolishness of his mother. He thought he could "fix" somebody. He thought he could have babies with a loser, a girl who needed help, and everything would turn out okay.

Oh, boy.

At that point Annie's mother decided that her daughter had done something right; she'd gotten involved with a responsible young man, and seemed to be completely off drugs. In other words, now she seemed worthy of having her firstborn living with her and Ayden.

So Ayden became both a father and a stepfather. He and Annie got married.

Well, he'd chosen a horribly treacherous road. Annie was totally schizoid. Her success as a wife and mother was intermittent at best. With the help of court-ordered rehab, sometimes she seemed to get the better of her demons, but it turned out to never be true. Just at the point when we'd all be agreed that she'd vanquished her addiction, she'd take off again, to do crack.

When Annie was cracked out, she disappeared. She became someone else, in someone else's world. Sometimes she was absent for many, many months.

Ayden was losing his mind.

A strong indication of how bad things had got was her failure to come to my wedding. Her husband, her six year-old, and her toddler had all had a role in the ceremony. Her daughters had been dressed up adorably, and she hadn't cared to see it. Can you imagine? What Mommy in her right mind would miss that?

Ayden told me later on that Annie had apparently used my event as a chance to get free of her family, and run away to her crack.

It was actually Mitch who took Ayden's distress call, a few weeks after our move. Ayden had relocated to Florida, hoping that somewhere new and exciting would straighten Annie out. That plan, of course, had been a mistake. Annie had established a drug contact down there, almost immediately.

Ayden had sunk every dime he had into that fresh new start, and now he was devastated. Now Annie was cracked out in Florida. He was afraid he'd kill her. I was afraid he would, too. This was the son with the violent teen-aged past.

He was calling in sheer desperation, a guy reaching out to his mom, not knowing what else to do.

His step dad didn't hesitate for a second. "Grab the baby and get on the next plane," Mitch directed my son.

The older little girl, my step granddaughter, wasn't in Florida with them. Annie's mother had taken her back, intuiting that Florida would backfire. So Ayden disembarked at Logan Airport, Boston, with his motherless and sisterless two-year old.

I had appointments to go on; with troubled family about to arrive, we needed some extra money. So it was Mitch who drove to the city to fetch them, a round trip of three or so hours.

All that he seemed to want to do was help Ayden all he could, and indignantly rant about Annie. But you know Mitch's M.O. Sublimely perfect at starting things, and dismal at following through.

Poor Ayden. It must have been so comforting, when he was alone and heartbroken in a place so far away, to hear his new stepfather saying, *come home*. And then, right after Ayden arrived, his stepfather's fatherly attitude died.

Because the pressure got to Mitch right away. It wasn't just the stress that anyone would feel, having a guy and his toddler show up, so totally impromptu; I could see his agitation was mostly because he was going to have to behave. Mitch had just lost the freedom to be his miserable self. He couldn't kick back and be a dick to his wife, not with her son in the house. Nope, he'd have to be nice all the time.

It was proving to be too hard.

Mitch would try to keep his mouth shut whenever Ayden was present. But the second my son was out of earshot, he'd be all over me. I can't remember what made him so mad; it was always trivial stuff. But I do remember his hatefulness. It was unforgettable. He'd henpeck me, nag me, and needle me, and drive himself ragged with rage. It was mysterious, unaccountable, but very real rage.

I'd be sitting there with my granddaughter, and Mitch would do hostile things. Once he came at us with a glass paperweight. He held it high over his head. He threatened to bash in my skull with it, even as the baby held onto me, watching.

"Why?" I moaned, incredulous. "What the hell's wrong with you?"

Mitch said the stresses were affecting him: the move, and the unexpected family. But God, I thought, what an overreaction. A little bit of grumpiness would have sufficed. *This* was getting psychotic.

These days, I wonder whether it was cocaine.

A couple of weeks before Ayden's arrival, Mitch had let loose another big blooper. It came out in conversation, just as naturally as you please, that on the day that Mitch met me, he'd had a decision to make. It was whether to pay for an "escort", or to buy a stash of blow.

"Whoa, whoa, wait a minute!" I said. I was taken aback. "I thought you told me that after the *Aerosmith* tour, you never did coke again! That was in '85!"

Oops.

"Yeah, well, uh…no. I've had a couple of relapses."

Oh, the fucking things you can find out, *after* you marry someone. I guess Mitch thought that at that point, I was staying, so he could just tell it all.

When I recall Mitch wielding that paperweight just as though he'd lost his mind, enraged and threatening to clobber me for not even God knows why, in front of a beautiful child, I realize how naïve I can be. I'm not a hard drug user, and never have been, so at times it can take me way too long to connect the obvious dots.

Maybe cocaine was in him, or maybe a terrible itching for cocaine that he didn't know where to find, because we'd moved from his source. Either way, his role as the helper and comforter of two crack victimized children, the stepson and the baby, must have jarred him just like a collision, must have strafed him like daggers of shrapnel inside his drug-jumbled brain.

Because the addict was forced to play rabbi.

What an insane contradiction.

And it was all my fault, of course. *I* got him into this mess.

Whether coke played a role in his craziness or not, I know his insatiable need for weed did. Within days after our move-in, Mitch found a bunch of stoners to smoke with, in a trashy apartment above a little store, about a mile down the road. I never set foot in that place, but I could tell by the way Mitch described it that it must have felt very familiar. It sounded like the dump we'd moved out of.

Mitch was supposed to be working in our barn, turning it into our shop. I was making money for the fix-up; the fix-up itself was his job. Mitch had quit his regular job. We had agreed that he should, so he could focus on the shop. I could financially float us.

Well, Mitch was failing to live up to that agreement in any useful way. He was gone down the road, he was down there *a lot.* He was down there smoking dope all the time, and maybe he also did blow there.

He would putter around in the barn for a while, not getting very much done. I think he felt overwhelmed. My son, who works in construction, was happy to offer his help, but Mitch only wanted to argue with Ayden about things that Ayden knew better. And mostly, he wanted to leave.

I told Mitch, at that point, that I was tired of working. The stresses were getting to me a bit, too. There's nothing easy about taking on a mortgage, struggling through a move, and then having to worry about raising the funds to launch a brand new business. And then there was my heartache for the kids.

I felt as though the pressure was endless. That rhythm thing inside me, as I've described in Chapter Two, was starting to send up strong warnings.

Mitch snapped back, "You've got to keep working! We need the money for the business! You can't slow down now!"

So now my husband was being a pimp. My stoned and lazy, but pushy pimp.

I kept on working. I knew I had to. I didn't need a pimp to tell me.

That lazy-but-bossy bullshit was behavior that Mitch had established, some time before Ayden showed up. So after he arrived, Ayden saw Mitch getting very little done, but his mother kept working at some kind of job, driving many miles daily and nightly, and always coming home tired. And he could see that Mitch was being mean to his mother. Mitch couldn't totally hide it. Ayden knew he was witnessing something really, really fucked up.

After my son had been there for a week or so, one time Mitch got crazy for nothing, just like the time with the paperweight. This time, Ayden *saw*. Mitch became a virtual Tasmanian devil, with Ayden looking on. Mitch knew he couldn't get menacing to me, not with Ayden right there, so he ran out to the driveway and jumped into his truck, and maniacally drove the thing back and forth, spraying driveway gravel everywhere. He dug the tires right down to the dirt.

We watched this insanity from the kitchen. Then Ayden summed things up for himself, and defined my situation. He said:

"He's worse than Annie."

I'll never forget the despair I felt, when Ayden spoke those words. To have my husband referred to as someone whose behavior is even worse than a crackhead who abandons her family...God.

"You made me leave my home!" Mitch whined at me, later on. I could understand his mixed feelings and homesickness. Even when someone moves up in the world, there are always some feelings like that. But Mitch was going too far. He was being dysfunctional and abusive. And he wasn't being fair. I hadn't forced him to do anything; his excitement over our new home and business had been just as intense as mine.

He just couldn't follow through.

Mitch had gone down to the town hall, and had joined a local committee. I think it was "Summer Recreation." But then the town elders never saw him again. He was too busy getting high.

Once Ayden went with him to that stoner apartment. When he returned, he told me that most of the people hanging out there were minors. They were mostly teen-aged kids.

Mitch was forty-one.

Well, about two and a half weeks into his visit, Ayden decided he'd had it. He hadn't seen the worst of his stepfather's behavior, but no matter; what he'd seen was enough. My oldest son has never been one to mince words, or to value restraint and decorum. Not when he's good and fed up. He told Mitch to quit being shitty to his mom, or he was going to kick his ass.

And Mitch immediately called the police, and reported Ayden's threat.

Well, I was fit to be tied. The fucking hypocrisy! My wounds from taking years of his shit were suddenly squirting black venom. The lid blew right off the pot. I was suddenly aware of the energy, I was filled with the ruthless fury, of long-suffering finally giving birth to revenge. It burst into blazes of that legendary scorn, the unforeseen fangs of a woman.

As soon as the officers arrived at the house, and started to take down my husband's complaint that my son had threatened him, I strode right over to them, and explained the whole situation. I made sure that the cops got the picture: Mitch was the real abuser.

And thus began the sick saga of reams of restraining orders. After that first day with the cops, only a warning was issued; we were given a document that said that for now, Mitch could stay on the premises. But one more report of abusiveness would get him arrested and banned.

After the officers left, Mitch tried to make me feel guilty. "Don't even go there," I snapped. "You were warned."

"But I didn't do anything! Ayden made the threats!"

"Yeah, maybe *this time*, he did. But don't you know how *you* are? What am I going to have to do, get it all on tape? What about the times you've bruised me? What's next?"

Mitch responded with a flurry of defensive verbal staccato. I could see that my actions had provoked him into some kind of warrior mode. What got me was that all the things he accused me of—falsely—were the very kinds of things *he* did.

Well, Ayden must have called his brothers, and told them everything, because all of a sudden, a couple of days later, Jesse showed up at the house.

He said he had come to check out the new digs.

Yeah, right. Since when does a twenty-year old drive a whole day, just to see his mother's new place? That was just his excuse.

Jeremy might have come around, too, but he'd moved to San Diego. He was three thousand miles away, and busy with school and work. That was very lucky for Mitch. Jeremy, more likely than any of my sons, would have gone psycho on Mitch. He would probably have strung Mitch up by his ankles, and smacked him until he was begging for mercy, if he'd been there to see what went on.

Ayden packed up himself and the baby; he was headed back to western New York. He liked it in eastern Mass., but felt it was much too expensive. And besides, his mother had married an asshole. And Annie's big family was helpful to him, out there in New York. And most of all, his stepdaughter was there.

I hugged them both good-bye.

Jesse, however, had no plans to leave. He was waiting to hear from some film schools that he'd applied to in Manhattan. Until he heard back, his life was on hold. He was free to hang out, working odd jobs, anywhere he wanted.

But Mitch didn't want Jesse to stay, of course. He had way too much to hide.

Well, Jesse wasn't about to leave, and I wasn't going to make him. There may come a time, in any woman's life, when she ought to side with her husband, even if it means forsaking her son; this, however, just wasn't the time.

Jesse was there *for me.*

Another son wanted to *see.*

Things wound up really fast, after that. I'm omitting some horrible things Mitch did, just to get on with this tale. One thing I do want to mention, however, is that Mitch poured a bottle of grape juice on me. He poured it all over my head. I think he figured he could get away with that. He was careful to do it when Jesse wasn't watching, and he was probably thinking that the cops wouldn't come if I called them over some juice. But what got me about that scene, that rotten little sticky-haired, purpled-skin scene, was that it lent some credence to Jesse's insistence that Mitch once pissed in his shoe. It seemed that Mitch had a strange little penchant for getting offensive with liquids.

And I would be seeing some more of that behavior, before he and I were through. I'll get to that later on.

But for now, I'll cut to the chase.

It was a busy Saturday morning. The main roads were clogged with shoppers. Mitch and I were in his truck, on our way to have a trailer hitch mounted. The hitch was something he'd been hankering for, and I was buying it for him.

We began a discussion about something, I don't remember what; it was something that wasn't of dire importance to either one of us. What I do remember is that all of a sudden, Mitch went into one of his rages. He wanted a yes or no answer, and I hadn't given one yet. I was mulling the subject over, looking at all of the angles, responding a little too slowly. For that, it seemed I deserved to be punished.

He was calling me every name in the book. He was crazily screaming and ranting. I was a cunt, a bitch, a New York brat, whatever hurtful term he could think of. He wasn't going to stop it until I gave him a yes or no.

286

Well, at that point I couldn't remember a thing about the subject at hand. I said "yes" just to shut him up. And then I went into that weird little state, that hunched-over introversion.

And while I was down there, pulled into myself, I realized I wasn't spending one more minute inside this vehicle with him. Here I was, going to buy him something, and he was being like this.

Fuck him.

We weren't going fast down a highway, like on the night when he punched me. This time, I wasn't trapped. We were five or ten miles an hour. The traffic was jammed. He could pull over. I could get out of the truck.

I opened the rider-side door just a tad, just enough to stick out my foot.

"Get off the road. I'm getting out."

"Oh no you're not, bitch. Shut the door."

"I'm not shutting the door. Pull over."

"You're not going anywhere. Shut the door, cunt."

I only opened it further.

He ended up making a right turn onto a less-traveled road. *Good,* I thought. *He's letting me out.* But I was very mistaken.

He speeded up, trying to scare me, to get me to pull in my foot and shut the door.

I didn't. I wouldn't. "Let me out, RIGHT NOW."

He just went even faster.

There comes a point, with a madman, when you know that to challenge him will only make him worse, but you just don't give a damn. You just want out, and you're going, and you don't care how crazy that makes him. I guess that's how some women die.

I would not pull in my foot. I would not shut the door.

And I wouldn't be buying him anything today. I wouldn't be with him anymore today, or maybe even on any day. I'd had it; I was done; stop the truck, end the hell.

I would not pull in my foot. I would not shut the door.

And then he aimed the truck at a phone pole. He aimed *my side of the truck.* If I didn't pull in my foot and shut the door, the door and my leg would be crushed.

NOW.

My self-preservation took over. Mitch got what he wanted, and he swerved away from the pole.

After we got past the phone pole, he finally pulled over and let me out. I guess he was satisfied that he'd shown me who was boss. That seemed to be all that mattered; he could just ditch me now.

We were about two miles from the house. It was a nice sunny day, no problem at all for me to hoof it on home. Actually, there could have been a blizzard, and still, I would have walked home. Anything was preferable to riding with that shit.

For a while he kept circling back to me, repeatedly telling me to get back in. I guess he really wanted that trailer hitch.

I just kept on walking. My head was hanging. My eyes were fixed on the ground.

In a woman, that's a very, very dangerous sign.

Mitch yelled some final expletives, and then, at last, he was gone.

"What happened?" Jesse wanted to know, as soon as I entered the house. "Mitch just packed up some stuff, and left."

"Good," was all I could say.

I knew it was time. It was time to do that thing. It was time to turn in my husband.

But I wasn't completely sure that I should. It was all just so horribly big. I'd be bringing the court, the whole state of Massachusetts, into my miserable marriage.

And I'd be making my husband a recognized wrongdoer.

I sat down with Jesse and told him, in detail, exactly what had just happened.

"Mom. Go to the police station right now, and tell them everything you just told me."

"Okay."

Down at the station an officer read my statement, and then he abruptly stood up. "This isn't only a threat," he declared. "This is *Use of a Motor Vehicle as a Lethal Weapon*. Do you know where he went? We're going to arrest him immediately."

I knew where Mitch was. He was sixty miles away, at a boyhood buddy's house. That's where he always went, when he needed to air all his troubles. He and his chum would smoke dope and butts, and bitch about things, through the haze.

MOURNING THE DREAM, FACING THE MONSTER

I don't wanna be a victim.

Mitch got picked up, and spent Easter weekend in jail. I spent the weekend in tears.

Oh, I knew I'd done something right, I knew I'd taught him a lesson. But what would that do for the marriage? Wreck it forever, was all. Mitch had never understood love, not in any adequate way. And now that I'd got him arrested and charged, now he must totally understand *hate.*

That had never been my goal. My goal had been to just love him. As I sat there clenched up, crying for days, I realized something important. I didn't want to stop being married to Mitch. What I wanted was to stop being married to *abuse.*

Because I still loved Mitch, you see. I loved the Mitch who wasn't abusive. I had never seen enough of that guy, but whenever I did, I felt happy. Even though he was physically cold, and pushed me off on my clients. Even though he epitomized *loser*, I still loved the good things about him. He had always accepted my sex work. He had never said a harsh word about it. And we'd shared the big dream of owning a business. And he'd always supported my work on my book project. And we'd shared a beautiful wedding. And we'd moved into a sweet home.

Besides, I was tired of leaving relationships. In the past, I'd left a husband who beat me. I'd broken up my family to do it. And then I'd split up the family again, to get rid of a stepfather-husband who abused my older two boys. Both times, it didn't take me long to move on.

But I felt different this time. With Mitch, I felt something heart-wrenching. I had a sense of wanting to save something. In spite of all the horrors, in spite of all my awareness of the rot that festered in Mitch, God help me, I still loved him.

We'd only been married for nine months. The hopes and dreams of a newlywed still tore away at my heart.

I realized I wasn't through.

When you know, deep down, that something's totally hopeless, but you still want to give it a chance, I think it's because some grand principle is working its power through you. It wasn't so much that I believed Mitch could change; what I needed to believe was that true love prevails, no matter what sickness erodes it. I needed to show myself that I could love that deeply. I needed to know that when all was said and done, I hadn't just left, as I'd done in the past. I needed to know that I'd done everything, everything I possibly could, to turn things around, to make love the winner.

Because, if we don't have true love, if its precedence isn't invincible, beautifying our hearts, then what do we have in this life we're all cast in, besides darkness and hate and despair?

There was now a no-contact restraining order. Mitch was not to come near me. I could have him arrested just for dialing my number. The state had filed spousal abuse charges, and also a felony charge, on account of his menacing behavior with the truck. The state hadn't hesitated to slap that on Mitch, because he had minor priors.

Of course, he'd gone crying to his father and brothers, and any of his cronies who'd listen. *Poor me, look what she's done to me.* He created an image of the bitch wife, the *cunt*, who'd made up a pack of lies. And then there was the great big mean system, threatening him with a jail term.

I wrote to his father and brothers, explaining myself completely. I described to them, for the first time, Mitch's chronic abuse. I told them I still loved Mitch, but I'd finally taken action with regard to his behavior. I was sorry, so sorry, about everything—I wept as I wrote it all out—but something had to be done, and I'd done it.

And then I wrote to Mitch. I knew where to contact him. After his father got him bailed out, he would only have gone to his buddy's.

In the letter, I told him I loved him, but I would no longer live with his abuse. I included a couple of bridal pictures. I asked him whether he thought we could work things out.

I offered a situation. We'd remain at different addresses, but nonetheless talking and dating, if he would get counseling to stop the abuse. And if the counseling proved to be working, then he could move back in.

"All he's ever done is use you," Jesse insisted, for not the first time. "All you've ever been is his meal ticket. When are you going to face that, Mom?"

I wasn't ready to face that, not even when my common sense nagged me: *If he talks to me, it will only be to get me to not testify against him.*

But I found out that Mitch was doing something that gave me a ray of real hope. He was actually complying with my written request. He was going to anger management classes. He'd signed up for them on his own, before the court even ordered it.

Now, wasn't that a glimmer of the Mitch I'd fallen for? The good Mitch, the caring Mitch, the Mitch who tried to be helpful? The Mitch who searched and cried for my dog in that magic summer predawn?

But it was probably just a smart move on his part, something his lawyer suggested, something to make him look good in court. I, of course, didn't see that. I told myself Mitch sought help for *us.*

His lawyer asked me to downgrade the restraining order, to enable the two of us to legitimately talk. I was more than happy to do so.

I ended up making the assistant D.A. frustrated as hell. I took the "spousal privilege" option and declined to be her witness for the phone pole incident. That pretty much killed her case.

So the felony charge no longer plagued Mitch, because I had helped to quash it. But Mitch wasn't acting grateful. He showed not the slightest remorse. The anger management training was working a little, I guess; I saw some new signs of composure. Yet his bearing toward me was hard as nails, spiky. Mitch was all rigid and armored; he gave a new meaning to ice.

In the past, I had only been his dumping ground. Now, he saw me as *foe*. I possessed a power he hated. It was the power to have him arrested, thrown right behind iron bars, if he made one wrong move.

His odium for me was palpable. It was smoldering, bitter, and evil. But Mitch wasn't through with me, not yet. I had some things he wanted.

He wanted the restraining order, what little of it that remained, to be cancelled, cut down to nothing. Then nothing would hang over his head.

He wanted to be put on the deed to the property. Because of his lousy credit, we hadn't been able to get a mortgage in both of our names. So the mortgage was only in my name, and therefore, so was the deed.

Mitch was very adamant about being put on the deed.

He also wanted Jesse out of the house. He wanted Jesse totally gone.

So many demands from someone who was supposed to be changing *his* ways!

I gave him some compromises. I agreed to reduce the restraining order to what it had been at first: a simple statement of warning, with no restrictions whatsoever on his presence in the house, unless he screwed up again.

I wouldn't agree to oust Jesse. But I granted that whenever Mitch visited, I'd have Jesse go stay with friends.

I wasn't going to put him on the deed.

"Is that so?" he snarled, just barely in control. "Well, I really think you'd better. I could make trouble for you, you know. *Lots and lots* of trouble."

A paranoid "escort", afraid of exposure, doesn't need to hear that threat twice.

Good God, had Mitch ever torn off the mask. Now he stood there before me, stripped down to the pure piece of shit that he was.

He had me, and we both knew it. I put him on the deed.

Our first wedding anniversary rolled around. Mitch rented us the same room at the same inn where the wedding had taken place. For the very first time since I met him, he was the one who paid. That was a nice thing to see, and I'm sure it made him feel manly.

But he never made love to me there. He wanted a blowjob, was all. On a special occasion like that! Mitch could never get things right, not even when he was trying. And he picked a mean argument with me, right over the frozen wedding cake remnant, even as he carefully cut it. He was insisting that I commit to seeing much, much less of my precious granddaughters.

Now, *that* was a new one. And I wouldn't comply. Then he needled me, as usual, to totally get rid of Jesse, and terminate all of the restraining order.

Somehow, not long after, I got Mitch off that track. The thing that helped most of all was that Jesse was moving away. His destiny was calling him to New York.

After the wedding anniversary, the summer of 2001 wound down. It was time for Jesse to go. He was enrolled at a film school in Lower Manhattan, and soon, his classes would start; I helped to secure an apartment for him there.

As he readied himself for the move, I gave him the assurance he needed that I could handle Mitch. Then on Labor Day weekend, I drove him down to the City. I helped him get all moved in. I wished him luck and kissed him goodbye, and contentedly drove back to Massachusetts.

Did you have a child in Lower Manhattan, on the morning of September Eleventh?

As I watched the first tower fall down from the sky, I was certain it was landing on Jesse. I was certain my baby was dead.

He had frantically called me while on his walk to school, when the first plane roared terrifyingly low, and imbedded into the tower. He'd stood there gaping at history unfolding, not a third of a mile away.

He had called me to urge me to turn on my TV. And then he'd abruptly hung up. As soon as I saw what he was yelling about, I knew that my dedicated student of film, my daredevil son with a camera, was running straight into the horror. I knew he was eager to get vital footage.

I hadn't been able to call him since then. No phone was going to reach anyone in New York City that day.

After the tower collapsed, I watched the tail end of Manhattan disappear in ballpark-sized billows of smoke and dust. If he wasn't a cadaver in the rubble, I thought, then Jesse was choking to death.

His friends and relatives kept calling me, distraught. I had become so preverbal that I sputtered and moaned, and hung up.

A couple of hours later, the only call in the universe came. Jesse was okay.

For the next several weeks, you kept hearing on the news that all over the country, hopeless marriages were healing. Divorce trials were cancelled, hatchets were buried, people who hated each other were talking...it seemed the whole country was coming together in one big coast-spanning hug.

Mitch and I were no exception.

At first, Mitch refused to face Nine Eleven. It was just "something that happened in crazy New York." Lots of people seemed to be thinking like that, and I wanted to slap them all, hard. But gradually, a few days after, the reality completely seeped in, and then I saw the empathy, the shatter. The event left a permanent mark on all people. Even my sociopath husband was starting to realize the whole world had changed, that something extremely historic had happened, something extremely monstrous.

Mitch stopped being combative.

Al Qaeda had achieved that.

He stayed that way for a while.

The weather, the early autumn, was ironically, inappropriately gorgeous. Mitch and I got together to paint the outside of the house. He brushed all the cedar shingles. I did all the white trim.

It was truly a lovely joint effort. The world was going to hell in a hand basket, but amazingly, we had found sunshine. Here was some warmth and camaraderie for us, in the midst of our traumatized planet.

Then Mitch, of course, ruined everything.

He was still living with his buddy. He almost never spent the night with me, not even during the painting. He did make love to me once or twice—if you could call it that. He did it in that dominant, impersonal, doggy-style position.

But mostly he'd just come over and paint, and then leave me there. It was weird.

One day, when the painting was almost finished, and Mitch hadn't come over yet, he called me to ask me to help him avoid the repossession of his truck. The dealer was about to seize it.

"But why?" I asked him, astonished. "You're working fulltime, and the rent your buddy charges is nothing. And you haven't spent a dime to help me out—even though I put you on the deed! Where are all your paychecks going?"

"Well, uh...well...I've been spending a little too much money on dope."

My stomach started to clench. Mitch wanted $700 dollars from me, to catch him up on his truck payments, all because of his drugs.

He didn't even seem phased, to be in a fix like that.

Something started to move in me then, something sort of clanking, something hard. I think it was a lot like what happens, somewhere deep underground, whenever an earthquake rumbles, and whole neighborhoods get swallowed.

I couldn't keep revulsion out of my voice. I remember I stayed calm, but disgust curled around all my words.

In the end, I told him to come get the money.

But Mitch knew he'd made me sick. Mitch knew he couldn't take the money from me without feeling somewhat ashamed.

And he wasn't going to take it like a man.

He walked into the house all puffed-up, assuming the air of a tyrant. The money was on the kitchen table. I was taking a bath. He strutted into the bathroom, quite obviously enjoying the fact that I was laid out beneath him, all naked and vulnerable.

I don't remember what words passed between us, but I do recall they were hostile. I was being quietly outraged; he was being hypercritical. He insulted me over some weakness of mine, or some way he felt that I'd wronged him—anything to make *me* the bad guy, anything to take the bright spotlight off him, the pathetic one, the middle-aged druggy, who couldn't even handle his car note.

He picked up my coffee mug from the side of the tub, and poured in all of the coffee. It sullied my bubble bath.

If you recall Chapter Two, then you know about how much I love my baths.

I rose from the tub. I grabbed a towel. "Forget about the money," I seethed.

Fuck you, bitch, his eyes answered. He barred me from leaving the bathroom. He roughly shoved me backward. And then, as I struggled to regain my balance, he ran to the kitchen to pocket the money.

When I got into the kitchen, I just stood there, dripping wet, clutching the towel around me. I didn't want to fight him for the money. It really wasn't all that important. What mattered to me was just making him leave. *Just let the fucker take it, and get rid of him.* But Mitch must have thought I was going for the money, because he grabbed my small freestanding counter, and pushed it into me, hard.

It hurt.

"Get out of my house!" I spat.

Those words seemed to make him insane. Suddenly he dived for the paint cans. I kept them inside when we weren't painting, because the nights were getting cold.

He grabbed one and started to bang it on the floor, to get the damn thing open.

Oh my God! The horror of it hit me. *He's going to throw **exterior** paint all over the **interior**!*

Of course he was. Hadn't he already pissed in a shoe, poured juice on my head, and dumped coffee into my bath?

I ran for the wall phone to dial 911. *Help, oh please help me, he's going to ruin my house!* I'd barely gotten my fingers on the numbers when Mitch ripped the phone from the wall.

That was good. I'd distracted him. Maybe he'd forget about throwing the paint. But Mitch was still in his monster mode, and I still wanted protection. So now I grabbed up my cell phone. He immediately came at me to wrest it from me. He dug into my hand with his fingernails. He was bruising me, cutting me, but I didn't care. I just kept gripping the phone.

Somehow, don't ask me how—I got free of him, and ended up outside. I was naked except for the towel. Mitch grabbed me and raised me and held me aloft, just as though I were his bride on a threshold. Then he threw me down so hard on the ground that he badly bruised my left buttock.

The shock of the impact worked. Mitch got the phone from me.

Then he ran for his truck, and left.

But he wasn't going to get very far. Neither of us knew it, but the cops were responding to my call. In the second before Mitch broke the wall phone, I had managed to dial 911. Thanks to the new laws regarding 911, now the police get dispatched to wherever that number's been keyed from, even if the call gets cut off before the caller can speak.

I stumbled into the house. I managed to pull on some clothes. I was shaking and crying and black and blue and bleeding. That's what the cops saw, when they arrived.

Mitch got arrested again, of course. Six months in anger management class hadn't changed a thing.

And now I possessed a police report that clearly indicated, by an officer of the law, that I had been physically abused.

But you know what? I didn't care.

I didn't care what happened to Mitch. Not any more. I didn't care if he was in jail, or out of jail, or what the State charged and convicted him of, or whether he lost his truck, or what his family was thinking.

I didn't even care about the cell phone I never retrieved.

I just wanted out.

I was through, really through with him, finally. I had done all I could to make the marriage work, and I'd failed but I didn't feel guilty. I didn't feel I was at fault; I'd given it my very best shot. What more could I have done? My conscience was clear. Now all I wanted was my freedom.

I knew I was really free of him, this time, because now I was freed from my own foolish love for him. The terrible need to try to save it was dead. This time, I valued the restraining order, which of course had gotten upgraded, once again, to all-the-way-stay-away status.

How nice that the law was ensuring that that twisted little fucker was gone.

This time, all I wanted was a nice quick cheap divorce.

Well, it wasn't quick, and of course it wasn't nice, but I did make sure it was cheap. I ended up doing the divorce pro se—I represented myself. I couldn't bear to pay thousands to a lawyer, to rid myself of Mitch. I had already spent so much money on him. Over the course of my four years with Mitch, I'd bought him a motorcycle, a computer, eyeglasses, vacations, innumerable nice meals out, and I'd paid uncountable bills for him.

The little bastard wasn't going to cost me any more.

I did pay a lawyer to help me. I gave him a consulting fee. He coached me on courtroom procedure, and how to present and argue my case, which had ended up going to trial.

Mitch and his lawyer had wanted to settle for $15,000.

Yeah right, Mitch. Kiss my ass.

"You're gonna pay for my new bike!" Mitch snickered at me, at the courthouse. That was the one and only location where he could legally get in my face.

I just smiled. I told him, yeah, sure.

In the end, the judge apparently saw Mitch for the gold-digger loser he was. He also considered the short term of the marriage.

Even though Mitch had coerced me to put him on the property deed, the judge gave him nothing he expected. Except for a smelly old secondhand couch that one of his brothers had donated to our happy honeymoon home. Mitch whined about the couch at the trial, and also his dead grandmother's cast iron pan, and a couple of other small things.

Meanwhile, the property, which I'd owned for only a couple of years, had appreciated a hundred thousand dollars. That's the kind of real estate market I live in, and Mitch didn't get a dime. I gave the judge to understand that I paid Mitch $700 for helping me paint the house, and he knew that was all Mitch deserved. He awarded Mitch the old couch. He let him have the pot, to piss in.

Yes, I may be a fool for love, and I may be a drastically lonely "escort" who gets stupid in the grip of isolation. But at least I know how to land on my feet, when it's time to get rid of an asshole.

But to use the term "asshole" might be far too simplistic. Aren't all us victims, of a sort? Somehow, when he was very young, Mitch got himself on drugs. Somehow, his upbringing failed him. Maybe he got too spoiled. Or maybe he got overlooked. Or maybe as a little kid, he ate too much processed food. Or maybe he watched too much TV. Or maybe he got ruined while he was in the womb. Maybe his mother took an iffy pharmaceutical, when she was pregnant with him. Maybe he came out already fucked.

Who knows.

Once, when Jesse looked through Mitch's porn videos, he found one that was gay. Was that it? Mitch was something he couldn't face, and he took it out on me? Who knows, who knows, who knows.

Mitch was like some bright and clear painting, wrought by a steady hand, a creation that somehow got cracked, smeared and broken, and then became toxic with mold.

I found out, many months later, long after Mitch was gone, that while he lived with me in our new home, he'd been getting teens to sell dope for him. And when he thought they were ripping him off, he'd been threatening their lives. The kids themselves came forward about that, to their fellow youth, Jesse, when they met him.

And then Jesse told me.

So that's what Mitch had been doing, in tandem with offering his help at town hall! He'd been a corruptor of minors, a dope peddler, and also a committeeman!

What a complex, well-rounded guy!

Those same kids told Jesse that after the first time I had Mitch thrown out, he'd gone around spreading "crazy lies". He'd said he'd found out that his wife was a hooker, and she was writing a book about it.

Well, whaddya know. At the same time Mitch was demanding my money, in order to keep his truck, he was trying to sabotage me. One thing I'll always give him credit for: he's a whiz at burning his bridges.

Sometimes, though, I think of one thing, and it makes me realize how true it is that we're all in this life together. Even when we've come to despise each other, and we'll never speak to each other again.

When the first tower started falling, I was on the phone with Mitch. He was trying to sleep off a long, long night of working at a big concert. He didn't want his TV on; he was reluctantly hearing the whole thing from me.

And I bet that whenever he remembers that day, the thing that reverberates through his mind is his ex-wife's agonized scream.

And I know that I'll always remember, from now until the moment when I draw my last breath, that it was Mitch, and only Mitch, who heard the sound of my soul wrenching loose.

We're going to share that forever.

THE MASTER, THE RULER,
THE HEART

Some day…my walks won't be alone.

In the aftermath of my life with Mitch, I gained a little sad wisdom. Now I regretfully knew, firsthand, that feelings of fear and isolation in "escorts" are deeply destructive and dangerous. Eventually, they cause deadly cracks to spread through us.

They make our weaknesses stronger.

My weakness was bad men. I had a pattern, a personal history, of entangling myself with losers. After I became an "escort", for a while I got free of that pattern. I enjoyed myself with lovely men, and their lovely gifts of money. I enjoyed an exalted new lifestyle.

But the trouble, of course, was that my lifestyle was banned. It was considered the worst thing a woman can do. So having to hide what I was, and living with nonstop paranoia, began to hammer me down. My own isolation attacked me, like a demolition crew. Slowly but surely, I began to implode.

The boss of that crew was an evil old specter who'd been kicking me since I was little. Alienation is her name, and she'd found a new way to take over. She was ripping away every shelter, and chilling me with desolate feelings, just as she'd done all my life. I became desperate to stop her. I found myself a piece of shit partner, someone who seemed to understand the agony of the outsider, someone who let me right in. I wrapped myself around him, in order to stave off the specter, only to find, to my horror, that he tore me down even worse.

Other women in whoring might have a penchant for drugs. Or maybe their weakness is drinking. Or maybe they get with abusers, as I have. I've said it before and I'll say it again, I can't repeat it enough: when you see self-destruction in whores, the work is never the cause. The cause of our downfall is the punishment we feel, for having **chosen** the work.

Well, after Mitch I made damn sure to take total charge of myself. I wanted to be completely invincible. *To hell with the forces against me*, thought I. *Loneliness, Isolation, and Stigma: I'm not letting those bitches ever hurt me again.*

I had rid myself of my weakness for Mitch. Now I was on the upswing. Now I was all vim-and-vigor. Nothing was going to enfeeble me anymore. Not having to live as an outlaw, and not my own romantic delusions.

I was going to stand strong, all alone. And if I ever found myself falling, again, for some low-achieving, miserable loser, I'd understand why, and I'd back right off. I'd put up with the three ugly sisters, I'd steel myself against their cruel shunning, before I'd ever jump into the world of a jerk like Mitch again.

And my life was smooth sailing, for a while.

I had charge of a very sweet option. I could make the whole world my lover! I could belong to the world! There's no finer way to heal. Every single client I saw was a reaffirmation of my worthiness. Every single client I saw was a comfort, a way to forget. Talk about getting into your work! Sex work can be more self-mending than any other labor on earth.

I could actually live off the praises.

You're so beautiful. You're so sexy. You're so sweet. You're so bright.

You're such a beautiful soul.

I feel so good when I'm with you. You're so worth all the money. I'm so happy to give you so much....

Oh, the power, the beautiful power, of being so highly rewarded! Just for being a woman!

The feminists firmly against prostitution have made the point, with quite negative intent, that frequently women get into the work right after they've been hurt by a man.

Well, *yes!* And don't knock it til you've tried it!

But my freedom was rather short-lived. Was I ever in for a surprise. I was going to find out that there really is a cute little cherub with good aim, and the imp wasn't finished with me. He had another arrow in his quiver for me, and this was the big one, this was the killer, this was the spike that would split me.

Oh, did I ever misjudge my strength. I thought I'd gotten impervious.

Sure.

In all prostitutes, I insist on one quality: a healthy feeling toward men. But you see, there's a problem with being like that. An occupational hazard is built right into that. An unattached, heterosexual, emotionally reciprocal callgirl is going to fall for a client.

Of course she is. It's only a matter of time before she runs into the one with all the right stuff…

I should have been thinking a lot more about that. Once again, my foresight was faulty. How could I have not seen it coming! After dragging myself through the depths of hell with a druggy abuser loser, how could I have failed to foresee my subsequent hunger for a winner!

You know the old saying. It's when you're **not** looking for love—that's when you're going to find it. That's when it's going to get you, and that's how it happened to me. First I fell for a fucked up mess; essentially, he was a pimp. After I got out from under that bullshit, and thought that I'd sworn off love, I fell head over heels for somebody decent. I fell for a real man.

And that's when my troubles *really* began.

I'd been free of Mitch for about half a year. The wheels of my divorce were turning. Mitch had been served the papers, the restraining order kept him away, and all I had to do anymore was wait for our day with the judge.

I was making a lot of money. I had ditched the business idea that Mitch and I had dreamed of; that was an enterprise I'd never dare to try all by myself. So that plan was out the window, and therefore, so was its cost. But I had other obligations. I was supporting two households. There was mine in Massachusetts, and there was Jesse's in New York.

Jesse was working eighteen-hour days, writing screenplays and directing student films. He was laboring so hard on his projects that his jeans were falling down. He'd lost about twenty pounds.

But he was happy. He was where he belonged.

And he never could have been there without me. Before he'd enrolled in the program, the school had warned Jesse to forget about supporting himself with a job. The program was just too intensive to allow for other commitments. If Jesse was going to ever succeed in their demanding one-year course, he'd need the total backing of a sponsor.

So there I was, focused on floating it all. I was making my mortgage payments, and also paying an East Village rent. Jesse had roommates, and the place was a shoebox, but still, his rent share was high; that's how it goes in New York.

And neither was it cheap where I lived.

I had my own credit card payments to handle, and Jesse's living expenses. He was totally dependent on me for it all: his food, phone, subway fares, everything. I even had his student loan payments to make—they weren't deferrable. And I sent him extra money for shooting permits, props, and incidentals, while at my place there were utility bills and maintenance costs hitting me, always.

The families of Jesse's classmates were wealthy. Well, I was required to be wealthy too, for the time that my son, a star student, was there.

But I could handle that. Actually, I *needed* to handle that. To enable Jesse to stay at that school was a ***driving force of my life.*** I was haunted by the memory of a talented nineteen-year old. She had also once lived in New York. She'd been forced, for financial reasons, to drop out of the New York Academy of Dramatic Arts. She had just established herself there, as the most promising kid in her class, when her father informed her that he couldn't come up with the money to keep her there. He was totally financially failing; his credit was suffering, too; he couldn't even cosign a loan for his daughter.

And then the director of the school came at her, and offered her a deal. He had "friends" who would pay her tuition, if she would be willing to "see" them.

Oh my God! she responded, as her jaw dropped in shock. *I'm a nice girl! Don't even go there!*

And she cried in the arms of her favorite instructor, who teared up a little bit, too, and then she was out the door.

Well, later on she had three kids, and one of them was creatively gifted.

That girl was me, and what happened to me *was not going to happen to Jesse*. Not on my watch, not ever again, not ever to one of my children. The "nice girl" had learned to grab the bull by the horns.

But more like, by the balls.

So now every day was a mission. My work was cut out for me, and my life was on track, and I was on top of my game.

Except for whenever I puttered around in my house, my yard, or my barn, and I saw ten million home projects to do that I couldn't handle alone. I did have some help, of course; I've told you all about all those "trades." But sometimes, a hollowness iced me. When I looked at my property, all by myself, I felt more marooned than secure. My pride of ownership was a sweet, strong emotion, but my loneliness ate it like termites.

None of my handymen came to my bed, or even into my house, except to do their work and then leave. Then they waited for me to go "pay" them, in their own homes, several towns over. I had made it clear to all of them that that was how things would be. Only the love of my life would be invited into my bed.

My bed was the inner sanctum.

Because the truth is, I'm meant to be somebody's wife. I could feel that need the way you feel a chronic, growing disease. You go about your everyday business, functioning and even succeeding, and then suddenly, the pain of the affliction overtakes you, and you know that everything you've built will soon be consumed by its power.

Oh, was that truth ever there. My aloneness was almost as abusive as Mitch. To not be mated was to not be whole. To not be mated was to be my poor mother, abandoned and limping and dying. To not be mated was to not be *me*. It's me to belong to somebody.

Just who the hell did I think I was, I chide myself, thinking back. Did I actually think I could stand the pain of being a lonely "escort", and being a lonely divorcé *TOO*?

I met Jordan, the man who would conquer me, in the middle of a typical week. I had lots of appointments, and I needed lots of rest; I had so many places to go. I'd actually been putting Jordan off for a while; I couldn't quite get to him. He was just another fee in the pot, just another encounter, just another screened customer, waiting to be fit in.

Smiled at, listened to, serviced. See yuh, sleep tight, thank you, good night...

He'd told me on the phone he was a lawyer. After I decided he wasn't a cop, *lying* that he was a lawyer, I let the word resonate nicely. So this was a professional. A lot of them are. But "doctor" and "lawyer" sound the finest.

When I finally went to see him, and I was getting out of my car, I could feel how inviting his house was. It was one of those gracious, roomy creations, built in the early nineteen hundreds. It had gaping windows and a doorway and veranda that all had been fashioned to *welcome*.

It was big, and it was *only his summer home*. That's what always got me about the very well off. But this place was more than a trophy. This place was comfortable, homey, and warm. I sensed that, before I even knocked on the door.

When he opened the door and our Hi there's got said, and then I stepped inside, he completed our greeting with a kiss. He kissed me and hugged me as though we were old friends.

Hmmm, I remember thinking. *No one's ever done that. New guys always have jitters.* I could see that Jordan was nervous, yet here he was folding me into this endearing, embracing finesse. He was burying his fear in affection.

That was something I did well, too.

How impressive! He knew to be warm! Then I chopped that sweet thought to bits. He was Everyman and Anyman, just like the rest of them. This was nobody special.

I was always aware that each client is unique, and each deserves special treatment. I knew how to give that treatment, and I did that very well. But at the same time, I lumped them together. Emotionally, I barely distinguished between them. The mastery of that paradox was the primary thing that made me professional.

But Jordan was different. Oh yes, he was. I could feel it...I could already feel it...

NO.

But look—he's a lawyer, not a loser. And listen—he just said he's divorced. See? He's not just somebody's husband. And look at this big cozy house...

I said NO.

On that first night, after our introduction, the first thing we did was go into his living room, and sit down on a big, enveloping couch. It wasn't new or pretty, but it felt good, soft and deep. He had a bottle of Bud for himself, and a glass of wine out for me. He'd taken care to ask me, on the phone, what I might like to drink.

There was something about him...an irony. I'd known him for only ten minutes, but I saw it. He was warm and accommodating and affable, but at the same time, completely closed off. He seemed quite serene, contentedly lounging, yet blocked, like a fish in a fishbowl. I could look, I could enjoy, but I couldn't get close, you don't take a fish from its bowl.

Jordan was friendly, all laidback self-confidence, successful with nothing to prove, and that made him easy to be with. But still, I could tell he was locked down. He was radically focused on only himself. I was aware of an extremely thick wall.

He sat forward on the couch with his hands meshed together, staring straight ahead, like a sentry. It was a pose that said *I'm a fortress. Go ahead and touch, but you'll never get in.* And yet, when he let his hands wander, when he decided that *he'd* get to *me,* that was when he showed me his substance. He seized me in places I love to have touched, like my sensitive legs, and my feet. He deliberately, exquisitely kneaded me there, and my brain began to daze.

We didn't need to talk very much. And it wasn't because of a sense of let's go; he didn't seem to be in a hurry to get me into bed. He seemed to just want us to hang out for a while, like a couple of familiar old pals.

I had felt this sense of being comfortable with someone many times before. Some clients are just very friendly and relaxed, after the jitters are gone, and I tend to be that way, too. And some clients know, just as Jordan knew, how to beautifully knead with their hands.

But Jordan was making me feel a lot *more.* Something about him was making me feel...*right.*

Even though he was distant.

The couch was quite broad, and he leaned so far forward that I saw an opportunity there. I slid myself behind him, and spread open my legs, and totally straddled him. Then I began to rub his back. He grabbed my feet, which were perched in his lap, and rubbed them while I did him.

Is there some kind of two-person meditation, or some kind of Tantric lovers' position, exactly the same as that? Because I felt perfect when we did that. I felt an immaculate balance, a perfect exchange of feel-good, when the two of us sat there and did that.

It's said that your soul is in your feet, and I've never doubted that. Well, Jordan was kneading my soul, while I rubbed his tense lower back; and my pleasure from his hands was the deepest I'd known; no one before him had done it so well.

And I know that's the moment when I became his. I know that's the moment when I fell.

But it would take lots of time to admit it.

He had olive skin, on a smooth, flawless back, not one mole or bump, just a sheath of warm silk. He had dark hair, dark eyes, and a full well-groomed beard; it showed off his age: salt and pepper. His lips were so rounded, so kissably full, that even a dike would take notice. His nose was too big, but no problem; that was a flaw I could love.

He wasn't very tall, but he wasn't short either, and that mattered, because I'm tall. The best thing about him was, he was *solid.* You know the body type I mean. All meaty and comfortable, just a little bit chunky, just right for cuddling up to...

and feel like his little girl.

And oh, was he ever cuddly. He certainly *did* like to snuggle. His eyes remained guarded, the keepers of the fortress—but his body said love me, come love me.

He looked like a fisherman, and he looked like a professor, and that could be a reason for what was happening to me: Jordan possessed something deadly. He had working class toughness and collegiate refinement, the just-right mix in a man.

And of course, he looked something like my father. Of course that trait was there.

He wasn't my junior, and I liked that, too. I was sick of boyfriends younger than I was. I was tired of lovers who'd been riding with training wheels, when I was out saving the world.

All of Jordan, the whole of him, was getting to me, but I didn't see it yet. Love can be like an elixir you've drunk, that works its way through you slowly. My "drink" had been spiked, but I didn't know it. I felt warm and fuzzy, but so what? This was only a *client.*

I took Jordan's money the first four times. I kept him in customer mode. Even though very early on, when he made me come, I cried. And whenever I cried, in the wake of his pierce, I sensed in my joy, my eye-wiping joy, that I was in very big trouble.

But I was invincible! That was the plan! So I pushed the truth far away.

The only good thing about the losers I'd known was that none of them riveted me. None of them could permanently lock me in, and own me. In the end I could spit on them, and walk away, free. To this day, for instance, I feel nothing for Mitch, even though I once loved him fiercely.

On the contrary, a *real* man could win me forever. A *real* man could totally break me. I'd managed to keep every one of them from doing that to me. As an "escort" I enjoyed my appointments with them. I enjoyed their attention, their nice homes and hotels, and I built up my life with their money. I enjoyed being counselor-priestess to them, and also a talented sex worker. But I'd never let any of them into my heart. I'd never let any of them conquer me, because I knew what a real man could do to me.

I'd seen what one did to my mother.

So of course, I fought Jordan off, tooth and nail. I expected the payments, the professional distance, whenever he called me over. Even though I found myself buying new things to wear…things to wear *just for him.*

I told myself that was just a nice little feeling, just a comfortable little affection, just a nice sweet breath of fresh air.

On our second or third appointment, he told me he was *twice-*divorced. He was sitting in his closed-off, walled-up position, staring straight ahead. He said: "It's because I'm a workaholic."

He always told me just enough to give me perfect understanding.

We continued to never have long conversations. Our connection was gloriously physical. He told me he'd never known anything like that, not with his wives, or with anyone. So now I knew that he felt it too—that natural closeness, that effortless passion, that I've-come-home feeling of rightness. We felt it whenever we touched.

Jordan did one thing, all the time, that made me feel perfectly anchored. He grabbed my head and pulled it to his chest, and firmly held it there. It was the simplest of gestures, but it thrilled me. I could feel his strong need for me in that, while my face nestled in his dark chest hair.

My father's chest had been exactly like that.

Sense memory, the shrinks like to call that.

And Jordan kissed me exactly right. His kiss was the proverbial "lip lock." His tongue never darted or dog-licked; it was plump and perfect, just like his lips, and he firmly placed it by my tongue, just like two peas in a pod. His kiss was just like the rest of him: not showy, not fawning, not trying, just completely self-respecting, yet completely present for me.

And then he told me, in the way that men tell it, *not* that his heart had been broken to bits, *not* that it wouldn't mend, ever. He simply confided the event that had done it.

"I caught my first wife, the mother of my children, in bed with a friend of mine."

So now I understood everything. Now I knew I was with a man, a man raised to be faithfully Catholic, nourished profoundly on belief in the good girl, the girl who would honor and never stain the vows they'd made to God. She was the priestess of Holy Matrimony, the mother of his blood, and she would accept him, put up with his ways, and love only him, forever. She would touch only him, and fuck only him, forever and ever til death do them part...and she had made holiness useless. She had made everything sacred a lie.

So nothing was sacred to Jordan, anymore. He had shored himself up, just like a blockade, against that unbearable void.

Our abilities to trust had been locked in the same vault.

"I'm twice-divorced," he repeated, "because I do whatever I want to. I go wherever I want to. If I want to work seven days a week, than that's what I'm going to do."

He was explaining to me how difficult it was for a woman to live with him. He was *admitting* it to me. I liked that. I appreciated the warning. And I knew he'd never change.

And I knew that was okay.

But Jordan was getting addicted to me, just like his addiction to work, and I sensed how it scared him and screwed him up, and it compelled me to acknowledge my own growing love, my growing addiction to him.

Oh yeah, the ground was opening up. Whatever Cupid delivers you to, strafed, that's what was coming for me.

On the fourth and last occasion that I made Jordan pay me, he asked me to have dinner first. He wanted to discuss, over a meal, just exactly "where this is going." That sounded good to me.

"For several years now, I've had this plan," Jordan told me over our drinks. "I'm going to be retiring soon, and my plan's to retire *alone*."

And then he confessed, with the wryest of smiles, "You might screw up that plan."

Yeah! No shit! I thought to myself. ***You** might do that to **me**!*

Then he explained a situation he was in. It was going on in his main house, which was two and a half hours north. Jordan had never invited me there, and I was about to find out that there was a definite reason, and it wasn't just the long distance.

"I let my secretary move in," he said. "About eighteen months ago. She needed to escape an abusive relationship, so I let her come stay at the house."

"After about half a year," he continued, "one night we ended up in bed. It was one of those things that just happens."

Jordan went on to tell me that he wasn't in love with her. "But I think she feels something for me. She's the best secretary I've ever had, and she works for my partners, too. So you see, it's a sticky situation. I've got to let her down easy. Somehow I've got to get her out of my house, without making her want to quit us."

I gleaned that he was saying he wanted just me, but he wasn't exactly free. But he would be, in the near future. Could I deal with those circumstances?

I didn't see why not. As long as he cared just for me.

"Do you still sleep with her?"

"No. Not anymore. We've never even had the same bedroom. She has hers, and I have mine, and I don't want to touch her again. It was a mistake to ever touch her in the first place."

"How long do you think before she'll move out?"

"It's hard to say. Soon, I hope."

"Is she pretty?"

"She's not as good looking as you are."

After our dinner, after we'd made love, and I had an appointment to go on, I asked Jordan to pay me again. I didn't realize it at the time, because Jordan hid it well, that he got extremely upset about that.

He gave me the money, and I told him that next time, I wouldn't want to be paid.

Well, after that I didn't hear from Jordan for a while. It concerned me and made me a little bit sad, but I was so busy making money that I could get my mind off it. It would be some time before Jordan admitted that when I made him pay me, after our dinner and talk, he'd gone right out on a bender that night, and swore that he'd never call me again.

But he did call. And this time, when I went to see him, I asked for no money, he gave me no money, and that was it, now I was done for. The cushion, the safety net, the buffer of whore, was rolled up, stashed, and gone. Now I was falling through space.

I had never used condoms with Jordan. That was a rule I never broke, and that had been the first sign. I had never kept our trysts to an hour; that had been another big sign. And now I gave everything up to him: my address, all my phone numbers, my true chronological age; I gave to Jordan all of my truths, I gave him my whole self.

I let him come into my home. I took him into my bed. Now he had penetrated right to the core.

And when you let someone all the way in, God help you, now starts the pain. Now he's a part of you, and you need him all the time, just like you need your own hands and mouth, just like you need to breathe air.

If there's a brain chemical responsible for that, a glandular excretion that bleeds like a river, deep into thoughts of our beloved, then I must be too well endowed. Jordan had the power to make that stuff flood, and to render me utterly changed. I morphed from being supremely cool, a woman whose life was all business, to being Juliet, Ophelia and Desdemona, impossibly rolled into one. I was reshaped by lovers' anxiety, my days a long train of peaked feelings. I waited each day, with gut clenching, to talk to my lover on the phone.

And Jordan appeared to be just as messed up. One of the ways he conveyed it was a mind-rocking comment he made. He told me he felt just as comfortable with me as he had with the mother of his children. I took that to be a great omen. But then, when I considered what she'd done to him, I realized he had to be coping with some painfully mixed emotions.

You're probably wondering how it felt to be working, in the midst of all that. Well, in the beginning, it wasn't too bad. I do recall some appointments where I felt a heartache so awful that my sanity quivered like jelly. But then I got a handle on it all. Just as it had gone with Mitch, my tolerance for being with other men was gauged by *Jordan's* feelings. Jordan seemed to be okay with it.

That is, he was *at first*. So that made working okay for me too—more or less bearable.

He called me several times a day. Truly, he called me that often. But I didn't get to *see* Jordan often—his workaholism was real. He was one of those lawyers who worked nights and weekends, *besides* the regular hours. At those times he could be in the building alone, and achieve total focus in the quiet.

I had a couple of paralegal friends who told me that on Monday mornings, they found piles of work on their desks. Over the weekend, their bosses created it.

Jordan was that kind of lawyer.

So we saw each other about once a week, and the rest of the time, Jordan called. He called, and he called, and he called.

And I lived for every one of his calls. His calls were my proof that he loved me.

"So, when are you working today?" he'd ask. And if I knew when, I'd tell him. And then he'd usually call me again, just before my appointments, and then after. He actually broke up his meetings to do that. Some of those meetings were *important.*

At first I felt flattered, but after a while, I began to feel apprehensive. That need of his to hone in on my trysts—something about that was troubling.

One night, when we were out to dinner, he confessed that whenever he knew I was working, his heart would start to pound. It wouldn't calm down until he'd spoken to me, after I was through.

Such a physical reaction to what I was doing? That didn't sound good to me.

"Maybe you shouldn't know the exact times of the appointments. It doesn't seem good for you to know."

"Oh no, it's okay," he insisted. Jordan seemed to *have* to know, even though it gave him palpitations.

And there were some things I *had* to know, too. Like the certainty that when he was home, he really did sleep alone.

He did. One of Jordan's routine calls was from his bed at night, just before he fell asleep. It was very reassuring, to hear his groggy voice, and to hear his sheets rustling. It meant he really was in bed, and a man never calls a woman from his bed unless he's in there alone.

Well, I sure wasn't lonely anymore. The void had filled up with worry. I was worried that my work upset Jordan. I was worried that the woman who lived in his house would somehow manage to stay. I was worried, I was worried, I was worried...and it was starting to hurt, all the time.

But I was in love! With a good man! I wasn't being an idiot again, handing my heart to a fuckup! This man was truly worth it! So very, very worth it!

So I kept on working, supporting my son, and I kept on living for Jordan.

Finally, my empty bed had been filled. Finally, a real man slept there. It was only about once a week, but when we were together it was a lovers' paradise, and when we were apart, he called a zillion times, and even though it killed me that I didn't see him enough, I felt as though a steady, committed man was there.

A good man, who wanted me.

"I love you more than life itself," he said as he clasped my head to his chest.

"Do you love anyone besides me?"

"My kids."

Jordan had three kids, just like me. They were about the same ages as mine.

That was just one more reason to love that man absolutely.

The Working Girl
Gets Lost

I fell from my pedestal…

But after a few months, three things were clear, and none of them were good.

First of all, that woman still lived in Jordan's house. She seemed to be in no rush to leave. Though Jordan assured me that she was painfully aware that she certainly had to move on, for one reason or another, the woman wasn't budging.

The second thing that bothered me was that Jordan maintained almost total control over all the times we made contact. He called me several times a day, just like in the beginning. But if *I* wanted to call *him*, that was quite another matter. That was almost impossible.

He didn't want me calling his home phone. Not with his secretary haunting the place, jilted and making him feel bad. So he gave me his private line at work. When I reached him there, however, Jordan didn't seem thrilled; his work was getting disturbed. In response, I rarely dialed that number.

But the worst thing, the thing that irked me the most, was that at night, and also on weekends, Jordan kept his cell phone turned off. He'd given me that number, but what for? He'd turn on the phone just to call me, and then he'd shut it off.

So if I wanted to call him at any of those times—those leisure times when lovers tend to always want to talk—all I could do was leave a message on his voicemail, and wonder when he'd call back.

That one-way access between us was deliberate. I didn't like that at all.

Jordan explained it was a practical habit; shutting off his phone during non-working hours kept the battery charged a lot longer. But I knew that was only a fraction of the truth. I could sense something more. It was clear that Jordan wanted total control of the times when we would talk. My intuition told me there was nothing I could do about it. Those were his terms, period.

Well, Jordan was calling me so often, each day, that really, I decided, one-way's not so bad.

My ears became exquisitely keened for the jingle. My nerves got tightly woven into endless skeins of waiting. It was just as though my life had been turned into a series of smokers' butt breaks. I was fixated. I was addicted. Every morning and afternoon broke up around my grabs for the phone. My needfulness was relieved, like a way too long held breath, only when Jordan called. Nighttimes were even worse. I knew that if he didn't call, I wouldn't be able to sleep. I'd be anguished all night, in the darkness. Every evening morphed into a fretful, restless countdown, which ended, just like a sickness ends, when he finally phoned from his bed.

But I have to say that the secretary's presence, and also my lack of access, were not the worst of my stresses. The third not-good thing, and by far the most painful, was that Jordan was starting to get upset. Jordan was freaking out over my work.

In the beginning he'd seemed rather accepting, but now, his heart ate his head. It was clear he couldn't bear what I was doing.

Yet never, not even on his worst day with me, did Jordan ever even hint that he wanted me to quit. He respected the fact that I made such great money. He was loath to interfere. My work was making him crazy, yet he understood its importance. He knew that I had to support my son, and besides, he was just plain impressed. Six figures a year for a few weekly hours? Who could be expected to quit that!

The conflict was starting to kill him.

At first it had appeared that Jordan could tough it out. And for a while, I had actually thought he could do it. What a strong, self-disciplined man! I could feel the hell he put up with, the visceral horror of knowing I had sex other men. I saw how he stoically fought to transcend it. That made me adore him even more.

But Jordan was losing the battle.

"My stomach doesn't feel right," he told me one day on the phone.

"Why? What's it doing?"

"I don't know. It just hurts."

Whenever we weren't on the phone, however, and we got together for real, it was right, it was always heaven. Whenever we were nestled in bed, I felt secure, my anxiety vanished, and Jordan said his stomach was fine.

Once, while he held me, he said to me: "I think that my feelings are deep enough, and strong enough, so I can get over this thing."

Yet he fretted that we'd run into a client of mine, and the client would talk to me. He said: "If that ever happens...*forget it.*"

But our times with each other never once wavered from the right way it felt at first. In bed, we had beautiful rituals established. Whenever my mouth was on his crotch, his deep-rubbing hands made me happy; they took care of my head, neck and shoulders, much better than anyone's hands ever had. Or his fingers would be on my crotch, tweaking me the way I requested, while I urgently squeezed his manhood. Or else he'd be deep inside me, all the while talking to me, his penis and words overtaking me, until I lost myself completely.

Jordan was a smoker. But somehow he smelled good, anyway. His skin was as sweet as a baby's. I buried my face in the groove of his neck, just so I could inhale him.

And when we went out to dinner, we always got silly-romantic. We only patronized places with booths, so we could sit thigh next to thigh. And we always ordered shrimp cocktail, and fed it to each other. We never fed shrimp to ourselves.

On one perfect May afternoon, under a stunning blue sky, I hung out some laundry in my big, flowered yard. The fabrics were swelling all around me.

"I could watch you do that all day," Jordan murmured, as he contentedly looked on.

Things happened between us that we'd never done before. Our intimacies were so profound that only a breastfeeding mother might exceed them. In bed, I cupped his groin in my hand, even when we were sleeping. And sometimes, after we made love, and we were both drifting off, and Jordan wouldn't be hard again for at least another few hours, I laid my head on his pelvis, and took his soft penis into my mouth, and fell asleep with it in there.

Whenever I did that, we loved it. Jordan began to expect it.

All of the above was wrapping us both into some kind of primal, animal bond that might kill us, if we ever broke it. We needed each other's nectar like a vampire needs to drink blood. We needed to talk to each other in bed, just as anyone else needs to sing.

But for me, such a passion was only half the zeal. I was locked into something even deeper. I was slammed by a double set of forces, the merging of passion with the need to prove loyalty. That need, in me, was almost frantic. A prostitute is desperately driven to show her man that she's faithful. She's aware of many ways to be faithful, even though she beds other men. But she's also aware that her lover might be full of doubts and misgivings. So all the time I was anxious to make Jordan understand that many of the things that we did were *exclusive*. I gave Jordan things that no one else got, and I had to make sure that he knew it.

Sleeping with Jordan's soft cock in my mouth was something I'd never do with a client, and indeed I had never done, ever, with any other man. And of course he was the only man who could fuck me without a condom. To stress that point even better, I was never in a hurry to wash off his come. I kept it inside me for as long as I could. I told him I could still smell it, long after he was gone.

His territory was marked.

And whenever I went down on him, I voraciously ate what he gave me. I sucked it and swallowed each spurt and drop, just as though it were lifesaving medicine.

And of course, I never ate clients'.

Kissing was much the same way. Jordan I kissed with abandon, but the clients I kissed just a little, just enough to make them feel that their money was well spent. Eye contact, or the lack of it, was also exemplary. When Jordan was inside me, I looked deeply into his eyes; but whenever I was with clients, I'd smile for them, but always with my eyes closed.

I had terms of endearment for Jordan that fit every mode of our passion: Baby, Honey, Daddy, even Master. For the clients, there were none.

I was deep inside Jordan's head, and I felt burned by Jordan's torment. He couldn't bear the unavoidable fact that all the time, other men touched me. I prayed that analogies I'd thought of would help him.

I said, "Remember when your kids were little? Remember how you just loved them, no matter what they did?"

"Yup."

"But other people's kids, you just deal with?"

"Mmm. Other people's kids are brats."

"That's how it is with the clients, and you. I wouldn't call clients brats, or bad, but that's something like the difference."

"Oh. That's a good comparison."

"And think about the difference between serving a meal to your loved ones, and serving a meal in a restaurant."

"Can't do that. I've never been a waiter."

"Well, I can explain, because I've cooked for my family, and I've served food in restaurants, too. When I'm serving food to my family, or you, it's a total act of love. I don't want anything for it. It fulfills me just to do it. But whenever I've waited on people in restaurants, of course it's been to make money. I've always been nice to them, and I've always made them happy, and maybe, for a lot of them, I've even made their day. But I wouldn't do that for free. See the difference?"

"Hmm."

Besides all that trying, all that need to reassure him, I took a big interest in Jordan's work. His work, after all, was who he was. I felt that to not get to know his work was to never really get to know *him.*

Jordan seemed surprised by my questions. So I said,

"Didn't your wives want to know what you do?"

"Nope."

"You mean, they never knew what your working day was like? You never discussed it with them?"

"Nope."

That was amazing to me. Jordan sometimes came at me with a million lawyerly questions—he wanted to know everything about *my* life, *my* family, *my* work, all of *my* daily routines; well, I was no lawyer, but I was no different; I wanted to know about *his*. His very own wives hadn't cared to?

All the time I inquired about the details and daily goals of his work. I couldn't remember everything he told me—it's hard for me to keep things in my head when I'm not actually there—but I was determined to try. I needed to show Jordan that *all* of him mattered. Not just his sex. His *all*. His work, his passion for baseball, his family, his health, his *all*.

Oh, how caring that was of me. How devoted. How sincere. And maybe, if it weren't for *my* job, we would have known only bliss. The nice supportive little girlfriend, always wanting to hear about her adored man's work and life—what man on Earth wouldn't love that? But this man's girl was a whore.

There *are* some men who can blithely handle their woman being a whore. I knew about them from whore friends. A couple of them had a boyfriend or husband who didn't mind at all. And those guys weren't sociopaths, they weren't anything like Mitch. According to my friends, they were good men, magnanimous men, who understood the difference between work sex and love sex, just like sex workers do.

One of them was the type of guy—I had a few clients like this—who actually *got off* on the prospect of his wife with other men. If that's not the perfect mate for a whore! Another of them didn't go that far, but just the same, he was okay with what his "escort" girlfriend did. Sometimes he even asked her, with only a show of good will, whether she'd had a good time.

I also knew about men like that from my favorite whores' rights activists. Norma Jean Almodovar had married a man, an actor, who had grown up with a madam. He understood, right down to his core, that a whore's work is *only* work to her, and he wasn't bothered at all. And Dolores French had married her lawyer, and he was okay with it, too. Both women kept working after their weddings, and to the best of my knowledge, their marriages thrived.

But Jordan just wasn't put together like that. And there wasn't a thing I could do about that. And it wasn't like I could just trade him in; that was out of the question.

I fell headlong into his pain.

"You've been with a thousand guys!" he lamented one day, on the phone. "How am I supposed to deal with that?"

I really didn't know how to answer that. What could I say, or do? A guy either accepted that fact, or he didn't.

But both of us diligently tried to get past it. Whenever Jordan was with me, if I got paged he'd tell me I should call the men right back. He wanted me to not lose income, especially because of him, and I also think he wanted to observe those conversations. If I were in his shoes, I would have. It's best to face something squarely.

And I told him that whenever I was working, I imagined him sitting right there at the scene, watching everything. I wanted Jordan to understand that he was always with me. I wanted Jordan to understand that no matter what I was doing, or who I was with, or where, he was the man who stood in my heart, he was the man who commandeered my mind, he was the person I saw in my head, he was the person who mattered.

But in the end, nothing either of us said or did made any difference to Jordan. My work was just plain making him sick.

I'll never forget the first time that Jordan went crazy on me. It was early morning, and he called me while on his way to work. That was what he did every morning. But on this day, something was wrong. On this day, he sounded irate.

Jordan was angry about a voicemail message I'd left him the night before. He had only just heard it, now. He'd just heard, along with my usual lovey-dovey stuff, that I'd gone on a rather late call.

That was nothing unusual. I'd left messages like that before. I guess for Jordan, on that particular morning, it was simply a matter of the proverbial last straw.

And the woman he lived with had contributed to his extremely agitated mood. Just before he'd left for work, he'd seen his new cell phone bill. He'd found a note on it from her. Across the "detail" pages, where my phone number was printed well over a hundred times, in a jagged handwriting she asked him: were the calls to me "business" or "personal"?

Her question was entirely appropriate. Part of her job, as Jordan's assistant, was to track tax-deductible phone calls. But her slash of a scrawl expressed something more. It screamed: *You son of a bitch!*

"I can't stand this anymore," Jordan snapped at me, on the phone.

And he hung up. And of course he shut his phone off.

And just like that, he was gone. The man who called me five times a day. The man whose calls I lived for. He didn't call once that day.

And I couldn't call him back.

I could only leave a message.

I left him about fifteen.

Thus began the excruciating saga of never knowing, from one day to the next, whether Jordan was with me, or not. Oh, I was sure he still loved me, but his feelings for me were a torture, and they complicated his life. Who wouldn't want that to stop?

And there was another problem. It seemed that he didn't trust me to behave like a discreet human being. Jordan was worried I'd turn up at his house. That was because on that first occasion that he didn't call me all day, in one of the heartbroken messages I left him, I told him I knew where he lived.

When I said that, I wasn't being threatening. I was simply conveying that I loved him so much, and I wanted so badly to show him how much, that I'd even travel the many, many miles from my town up to his, and wait for him to walk out of his gym, to tell him to his face that I adored him.

Because a whore in love so desperately needs to prove her dedication. Especially when her man's getting crazy. She needs to show him, any way she can, that he's the only one. But that can be hard to convince him of, because of all the clients. But the clients are only her *job.* Does her beloved really know that? Does he really, deep down believe that? I didn't think Jordan did.

That remark that Jordan took as a threat was only my panicky neediness to show him what I was made of. I needed to make him understand that I'd go the extra mile—I'd go the extra ***hundred*** miles—to show him how much I cared. It wasn't that I was saying I'd go right to his ***house.*** I knew that if I were to go there, and upset his secretary, I'd totally alienate him.

I would never do that.

But Jordan didn't know that. When he finally called me back, on that first day he freaked out, it was very late in the evening. He said that because of all the messages I'd left—especially "I know where you live"—he was afraid that I was "unstable."

So I couldn't tell whether he called me back simply because he missed me, or because he feared I'd show up at his house. That question irked me, and so did plenty else. I didn't know whether I could trust Jordan to continue to be my man. He'd become like a person with a knife stuck inside him. It was slicing crazy patterns all through him. Jordan would dump me for a few days. Then he'd go back to his habit of calling me all day long. Then he'd desert me again.

Then Jordan went in for his annual physical, and learned that his blood pressure had skyrocketed. This was a man whose blood pressure had always been distinctively low. His doctor was very concerned. He wanted Jordan hospitalized.

Well, the workaholic wasn't about to waste time doing that. But he did go for all kinds of tests.

And none of the specialists who tested him could find even one organic reason for his sudden blood pressure change.

The doctor put Jordan on medication to bring the numbers down. Then he ordered him to sever right out of his life whatever disruptive emotional issue was causing the dangerous spike.

So the anguish had gone that far. It was actually choking his veins. Our love was just a blueprint for agony. Our love was just a lethal obsession. It was sadder than *Brokeback Mountain*. "I wish I knew how to quit you" became our helpless refrain, years before it was famous.

On the phone, Jordan told me he'd cried. And: "I never, *ever* cry."

During one of the spells when Jordan wouldn't call me, I drove to the home of my cross-dresser friend, Greg, and wept like a lover bereaved. Greg ended up crying with me. He could see that my attachment to Jordan was just as profound and hopeless as his need to become a woman. He held me just like a sister, never trying to sexually touch me, knowing I belonged to someone else, and I had gone mad with pain. He could see I was there to be comforted, just like a feverish baby.

But Greg also chided me. "You've got to forget him and move on. You've got to find someone who accepts who you are."

I knew Greg was right, but I also knew there was nothing I could do. For the first time in my renegade life, an arrow had completely impaled me.

A few mornings later, Jordan called extra early. He said he was parked by a hospital.

"Why? What's wrong?" I responded, apprehensive. He should have been going to work.

"It's my stomach," he replied, and then I heard him wretch. He said: "I'm throwing up blood."

He vomited again.

"I think I fell in love with the wrong woman," Jordan gasped between his heaves. "I think you're bad for me."

And then he hung up, to go into the hospital, to find out why he puked blood.

What do you do when you love someone, and you know you're destroying him? You want to destroy yourself. I began to understand what the Rolling Stones meant in their classic song, *Paint It Black*. And also that heartbroken Pearl Jam song, *Black*.

The diagnosis: bleeding ulcers.

I had done that to him.

It was right about then that I realized that someone was hovering, close. Someone was watching me. The bigger my pain got, the closer he got. Soon, he was standing just a few feet away. He was waiting to see if I'd greet him.

That guy began to look really good. Through my tears over Jordan, I could see he looked sweet. I found myself gesturing to him.

He didn't hesitate for a second. He sidled right up to me. He draped his weightless arm around my shoulders.

Up close I could see that he was confident, but lonely.

That guy's always with us. He's always with all of us. He claims every single one of us, at the far end of everyone's road. But it's not like we make him feel welcome. Almost nobody's glad to see him coming. How sad it must be for him, every day, knowing that he owns every one of us, but we push him away, we don't want him.

And don't you think he feels like a winner, don't you think he feels like a man, when occasionally one of us lets him come near, completely of her own will?

I was doing that for him.

After some very secretive talks, I began to thoroughly understand that he might become my new lover. I flirted a lot with him. I was fixated on an equation, you see, a fact unbearably true, that made me desperately need him. One glance at that fact made me want to jump to him, just like the people who were burning.

I became a whore because I didn't have Jordan. And now I'm losing Jordan, because I became a whore.

I couldn't see anything else. There was only that one blazing insight. No other concepts had meaning. Not unless they fit perfectly with that perfectly balanced equation.

I did think of something that fit right. I recalled the fact that my firstborn child had been conceived very near Jordan's summer home. That had been the critical act, the moment when I seriously messed up my life. Not that I had conceived; the wrongness was who I conceived *with*. And now I, the survivor, the mother-whore, had brought myself full circle. I had found Jordan, the love of my life, in the same place where I once wrecked it.

And the love of my life smelled the karma. And it was making him sick.

Clearly, it was just about time to get out. That's what full circles were for. You went round and round, and then you spun off. You slammed right into the stars.

Jesse would be finished with the film school course soon. After that, he wouldn't need me. At an overpass near Jordan's summer home, near the place where I'd once conceived Ayden, an outcrop of high cement facing stood out. It was a really good place to exit.

And no one would know what had caused it. No one would know that I meant it. Car-aiming mishaps, accidental collisions— just like getting pregnant, they happened all the time.

My secret companion nodded and smiled, as I shared all those thoughts with him. He would be my loving accomplice. He would be right there with me, steadying my hand on the wheel, and shoving my horrified friend, *Fear*, away.

Only one person had any awareness of where I was thinking of driving. It was David, the anti-terrorism specialist, the man I introduced in Chapter Six. He was stationed in the Mideast. He emailed me sometimes.

You know how truthful you can get, in the disembodied safety of all that cyber talk. (Hadn't Mitch put it perfectly once? Hadn't he said, *it's just type*?) Could someone way far across the world be really affected by *type?* I figured it wasn't so. I figured he wouldn't care. So I disclosed to this person, ensconced so far away, the perfect sense it made to me, for me to be no more.

But David was a good friend. And David understood. You'll recall that David's work was lethally bad for someone he once adored. It had violently gotten her killed. The victim of his work— of a car bomb meant for him—had been his beloved wife.

Oh yes, David knew where I was. And I supposed that I'd known that he knew it, with every desperate tap of my fingers.

And David, being the good soul he was, wanted to help me, as I once helped him. He knew that my deepening romance with darkness wasn't just a passing little fling.

So he applied for a leave, and he got it. He spent twenty-four hours on military planes, switching from one to another. Finally, exhausted, he arrived at my door.

He said: "You can't leave us all, not yet. Not for a very long time. You've got far too much to give."

David saw the outrageousness of allowing love to destroy me. "You're way too strong, way too special, for anything like this. How can you let anything, or anyone, make you forget who you are?"

"An angel is what you are," he continued. "You heal souls."

And David expressed his impressions of Jordan.

"Jordan must hate himself. Only a man who hates himself could fail to see who you are. If he knew who you are, he'd be ecstatic, having you for his love! Jordan can't accept what you do. But none of that's your fault, and nothing that you do, is wrong. Why don't you leave him, and try me? Your work wouldn't bother me."

I considered his offer, and in my despair, I even imagined our union; but really, the option was pointless. I couldn't just fall for David, no matter how wise the switch; he wasn't the one who possessed me. True love is immovable, absolute, and faithful. Dear God, was I ever learning.

I remember letting David sit on my bed, on the place where I made love with Jordan. It was king-sized, and I was sitting there also, and I was helplessly crying. David reclined three feet over. He knew it was futile to move any closer; I was inconsolable. He felt honored to be allowed in the "inner sanctum"—I remember he used that term. But he knew that my heartbreak for Jordan was a moat; he would never be able to cross it.

But David did manage to chase off Death. He did slap me awake. I thought, if someone feels I'm worthwhile enough to cross the world to help me, then maybe I shouldn't be thinking so much about leaving, all the time.

Then David returned to the Mideast, to spy on Death's demented idolaters. I continued to be sadly in love, but no longer in love with unbeing.

Thank you forever, David. You haven't responded to my emails in years. I pray it's not because you've been murdered.

Well I went to the edge, and I stood and looked down.

Those words are from a song by Van Halen. Now I knew what they meant. I knew that I'd come that close. Yet no one could break my commitment to Jordan. No one, not even David, left even the smallest of dents; I was deep in that groove you get into, in love: I was exactly like Kathy in **Wuthering Heights**, who recognized, "I *am* Heathcliffe." The depth or the danger of the pain didn't matter; what mattered was that it was ours. Jordan and I were locked there together, and nothing, and no one, could extricate me—not even Jordan himself.

He could run from me, leave me, make me wish I were dead, but always, I was still his.

Now I'd like to share something about Jordan's childhood. He was born with a "lazy eye." Jordan grew up as a kid somewhat cross-eyed. The operation he needed hadn't yet been devised. His eye straightened out, spontaneously, when he was just about twenty. But up until then, he'd spent his whole life afraid to look people in the eye.

Well, I had been born with my eyes straight and true, but my whole *life* had been crossed.

And now here we were, all star-crossed, two self-made survivors of hell, the baggage between us like recycle dumps, the conflict between us like deadly disease, and yet we could feel the true loving that heals.

.

THE WORKING GIRL
GOES BROKE

Sadly, for her the situation went from bad to worse.

So I didn't kill myself, but I did kill a part. I axed and buried the whore. Just before Jesse was through with his film school, and was through with depending on me, I laid all the plans I could think of for a different kind of career.

I was going to go back to professional childcare. I'd been in that when my kids were little. I could be in that again. I was a homeowner, and I had a big yard; clearly, the whole thing was feasible.

I was sure I could qualify for licensure. I had lots of experience with children. Some of it, even, was current. The time I spent with my grandkids had landed me back in that world. But none of that imminent change of occupation, none of that big about-face, had its basis in what you would call a decision. There was never a time when I pondered, or chose; I was driven, plain and simple, by pain.

The whore had to morph to a nanny. Then all of the pain would end.

One thing, however, would stay the same. I would remain self-employed. That was extremely important. I didn't think I could ever work for anyone other than myself. Not after years of that lifestyle!

I carefully studied the literature that the Office for Children sent me. I knew that my background would be thoroughly checked, and I was a little bit nervous about my arrest in New York. When I looked at the restrictions, however, I saw that in Massachusetts, a known prostitute can be licensed in childcare if her record of conviction is over five years old.

Mine was. And it wasn't even really a conviction. My lawyer had gotten the charge down to only "disorderly conduct."

This was beautiful. I had a solution. Now, at last, I could finally enjoy an intense, enormous relief. I could fix an unbearable problem. I could avoid losing Jordan.

I knew that financially, I was going to hurt. My income was going to drop by *three fourths!* But I figured Jordan would help me out, if things got really bad. He'd told me, once, that if I needed money, all I had to do was ask.

It was going to cost me about a grand to meet the childcare licensing requirements. I had to attend a $75 orientation class. I would have to pay for CPR certification, and also a physical exam, and of course, lots of childcare equipment. Toys, children's books, children's furniture, safety gates, outdoor play apparatus, napping mats, multiple high chairs and boaster chairs—I was finding a lot of it dirt cheap, at yard sales, but still, I could feel the crunch.

Most expensive was the fencing I needed, for the play area outside. The licensing lady had told me that cheap steel garden fencing, four feet high and staked, would be adequate to pass her inspection. But still, it would cost about $400 for a large enough enclosure.

You'd think that none of the expenditures above would distress me, the well-heeled "escort". But the truth is I wasn't so prosperous, anymore. My motivation to go out on calls had faded to almost nothing. I still did what I had to, but I also blew calls off. I was bombed-out from all of the heartache, and I was headed in a whole new direction. In dollars and cents, that diminished me—I found myself scraping the barrel.

So Jordan paid for the fence and the fence stakes. And then he did something even better. He came over and spent an entire day setting the whole thing up.

In the heat of the mid-summer afternoon sun, he drove the stakes deep in the ground. He fastened the fencing to them. With a sledgehammer, he married the stakes to the earth. He fixed metal onto metal with pliers. I stood beside him, assisting, almost fainting from the fierce humid sunshine. Its rays ripped into my eyes. I felt dizzy and tired, but I was so happy, I could care less if I collapsed.

Jordan was being like a husband. And together we were building something strong. We were sweating together, just like in bed, but this had tremendous meaning. This was like a resurrection.

And soon after that, my life turned insane. It changed in a terrible, adorable, way. I gave up the men for small children. For ten hours a day, five days a week, I took care of six toddlers.

I was busy and stressed and a little too self-sacrificing, in that way that you get with kids, but for the most part, I was contented. For the first time in years, I was in lawful employment. I didn't have to hide what I was doing. I didn't have to lie about my work. I got lots of support for the work I was in—I hadn't realized, until then, how deeply I needed that, and missed that.

In the other work, I only got support from the clients. Not from the surrounding community. And always, it was in secret.

Now I had women in and out of my house, every weekday, all the time—mothers and grandmothers, and also overseers, who came from the childcare agency. Everyone seemed to like me a lot. They seemed to admire me. They could see I was good with the children. They could see how devotedly I nurtured. They could see that I helped kids and kept them safe, and gave them lots of good times.

I taught the kids colors, shapes, letters and numbers, way before they turned three. I knew how to make learning playful. I knew how to make playing learnful. I knew how to make a day fun. I didn't mind pot banging, or turds from a bunny, or a tabletop mottled by crayons. I didn't even mind the squished circles of Playdough, burgeoning all over the floor. It was nothing to clean it all up.

I could take the endless cacophony, and the streels of yellow-green snot, and the huge wet sneezes spewed freely. (I had doubled up on my supplements—the kind that bolster immunity.) I endured the appalling sights and sounds of repetitive, signature tantrums. I contended with the daily monstrosities, the beloved, indulged psychopaths, the crazed adolescents of babyhood. These babies could walk, and jump, and run, and worst of all, they ran *away*. They kicked, stomped, mangled, and smeared. They clearly told you in Two-Year Old that you could go fuck yourself. But one thing they hadn't yet learned to do was follow a simple rule. It was my job to teach them, and to manage not to kill them, or otherwise make them feel worthless.

I gave them hugs and kisses whenever they needed them, which was all day long, but so what? Whenever these people were brought to my house, they almost never wailed when they were left there. They knew that I understood them.

I knew that this work was important. Well, so was the other work. But this work was *respected.* The other work should have been also, but it wasn't, and I was a veteran of that war, and I was exhausted from that war, and even though toddlers can be hellish, and disgusting, and ten times more tiring than an overbooked day of clients, and the money is comparatively nothing, I loved the pat on the back I was getting, from the entire world that I lived in, for taking on the ungrown.

And there were additional benefits. For one thing, I liked the way the childcare was impacting my divorce. I figured Mitch was doing everything he could to cause me a lot of problems. Knowing Mitch, I'd be stupid to assume that he *wasn't.* More than likely he'd called the local police, and tattled that I was a callgirl.

Well, if the cops had decided to heed him and watch me, all that they saw was a lady in day care, primly corralling her tots. All that they saw of any "traffic" at my house was the drop-offs and pick-ups of kids. All that they saw, if they followed me around, was a sweat-suited matron, buying groceries.

Heeheeheeheeheehee!!!!!

But of course, the best thing was Jordan. Just as I'd figured, his blood pressure went down. At the same time, his ulcers healed up. And whenever he came over now, he enjoyed building towers of colorful blocks. He bounced laughing children on his knees.

And that was my glory, my reward for the sacrifice. I had dismantled the whore. I had become disempowered. But I'd found an alternative way to exalt, something to replace the whore power, the kind found in loving that heals. I had found it in healing my man. I had found it in healing my heart. I was headed for a wreckage of credit—I'd been way too in debt to strip my income this much—but I didn't give a damn.

Jesse moved in, temporarily. He was there to work and save money to move back to New York on his own. The egomaniacal behaviors of toddlers, and the stench of me wiping up great globs of shit, made him stop and look me over, in horror.

"You were like them yourself once," I informed him.

"You're doing all this for...*that guy*?"

"Yup. And for myself."

"But you're broke. You're sweating your bills. And you're strapped to this place, this kid hell!"

"I'm doing what feels right, right now."

His face didn't change. It harbored great doubt. It was the look of a child who thinks his parent's pathetic. I'd seen that look before, and it saddened me, but this time, I knew I was right.

"I won't be doing this forever, Jesse. Don't forget, I'm also writing."

"Jesus, Mom! You're counting on *that*? That's just as tough as the film business!"

And Jesse walked away, while shaking his head, to escape to his hangout in the barn.

The disgust of my son over toddler snot and shit made me think about something that irked me. Back years ago, when for a while I had worked as both a home health aide and an "escort", I had noticed that a challenge the jobs had in common was my dealings with the body's secretions. One sort of secretion was indescribably harder to cope with than others. The misplaced feces of profoundly sick people were much more offensive, to me, than the semen that spurted from the healthy sort of clients that I saw in my hours of sex work. To be truthful, gushing semen didn't bother me at all. I felt compelled to consider the infuriating issue of sex-negativity. Why were encounters with shit not stigmatized, but my dealings with semen were?

I'll always remember the moment of truth, the hideous scene where it hit me. A dying young woman was constipated, because of the meds she was on. Some laxatives were prescribed. One day she went into a full-body spasm, and crapped all over herself. It was loose and extremely copious muck, and the stench was like murder by the nose. Begloved and gagging, but feeling compassion for this terribly humiliated girl, I cleaned her all up, and rolled up her bed pad, which was heavy with the spillage from her gut. I dunked it in the only toilet she had, a toilet that needed repairs.

When I was through dunking, I pulled out the bed pad. Then I flushed, and the toilet backed up. Rivulets browned by innumerable flecks of shit were streaming all over the floor. I actually had to chase the shit down, to the far corners of the bathroom, in order to rid the place of it. Then I bleached the whole area, and my nose and throat fiercely burned.

And all the while I kept thinking to myself: I can describe this nightmare to the nurse assigned to this case, but never in a million years can I tell her about when I wipe clients' come.

And now it was the same with the childcare situation. I could tell all the parents and agency proctors, and for that matter, most family and friends, about shit, piss, snot, drool, and puke, but never about my past dealings with come.

Come, the secretion of ecstasy, is absolutely taboo, and a woman who professionally handles it is perceived as some kind of slut, creep, or freak.

Hmmm. I can feel a big rant coming on.

I'll refrain.

I'll get back to Jordan.

Well, I'd been doing the childcare for about six months, and I'd gradually, then completely, left prostitution, and just like Jesse said, I was broker than hell, but at Jordan's end, nothing had changed. And I do mean absolutely nothing. The secretary, incredibly, had still not moved out. And Jordan still turned off his phone. And he only showed up at my house once a week, just exactly as before.

I had radically changed my existence. I had sacrificed cartloads of money and time. If I found a few hours to write, I was lucky. And on every single working day, I tolerated the worst of the body's secretions, flagrantly spewed from uncivilized butts.

On the contrary, Jordan's situation was the same. None of the changes I needed in his life had even begun to occur. I'd be sitting there buried in that nerve-wracking kid mayhem, and I'd be thinking to myself, ***SHE'S STILL THERE.***

Yet I knew that it was useless to nag him. He'd painted a picture of his hands rather tied. He'd only repeat, with a helpless little shrug, that we just had to wait.

And Jordan had played things quite shrewdly. He'd never once dictated what I should do. No matter how much he'd suffered, he'd never come out and asked me to quit my former employment. So I figured if I complained, he'd remind me of that fact, he'd insist that he wasn't responsible for anything I'd forgone.

Well, none of that really matters, I thought. I had done something important. I had freed myself from the worst thing, the pain of being pain's cause. That was a sweetness, a true liberation, that couldn't be wrecked by frustration.

But oh, my frustration was growing. It was swelling up, just the same.

"She'll be out by next month," Jordan told me each month, and then, she would still be there.

"She's bought a new condo, but it's not finished yet. There're delays with subcontractors," he explained.

At one point, I ventured a daring request. "You and she haven't slept together for ages. You're not together at all. She knows it's over, she's known a long time—so can I go visit you there?"

"*You can't come to the house*," he retorted, with a vehemence I'd never heard.

And she didn't leave. And didn't leave. And didn't leave. And now I'd been in the childcare for the better part of a year.

Just as I'd predicted to myself, my credit rating had plummeted. For the first time in years, I couldn't make payments on time. The mortgage, utilities, and car note came first; I always made sure they were handled. But everything else went adrift.

It was a shame to watch my admirable credit get shot. It had gone from callgirl-income perfect, to shit. I decided to ask Jordan to help me catch up. I asked him to loan me sixty-five hundred dollars. I offered to do it all legal, with a contract drawn up between us, with my house for collateral.

"I'll help you out," he responded.

But then he didn't do it. He kept saying he would, every time I brought it up. But then he just didn't.

And didn't.

I was hurt, but I decided to let it go. I decided I'd asked for too much, too soon. I knew he had plenty of money, that wasn't the issue at all, but we'd only been seeing each other for a little over a year. It was too soon, I figured, for him to trust me with a loan, or to consider me worthy of a handout that big.

I supposed I could live with that.

But Jordan's untruthfulness had struck me. He'd specifically said "I'll take care of it", and then he never came through.

It had never occurred to me that Jordan could lie.

And then he did something else. He talked about moving in. In response, I was thrilled beyond words. He'd put his main house on the market, he said, and then he'd come live with me. We'd share the expenses, and all would be well.

And the secretary? She could go stay at a motel. She could wait there for her condo to get done. Being a nice guy, Jordan would cover her necessitated lodgings.

Whatever...who cared! Let him pay her way anywhere! We'd finally be really together!

Jordan indicated that his move-in with me was definitely going to happen.

And then it didn't. He never moved out of his house. He never moved into mine. And his reasons were terribly vague.

So now my frustration was also disappointment, with bitterness creeping in. The man just wasn't for real. As I went about my daily routine of trying to keep toddlers from destroying my house, and straining to keep the house paid for, I began to view Jordan, my reason for this struggle, with a mounting sense of doubt.

Something was fishy, and screwy.

My family and friends had been saying that all along. They considered Jordan suspicious. Everyone, from every corner of my life, had been questioning things, a lot.

"Why does he only see you on week days?"

"He's a workaholic," I'd answer. "On weekends he always works."

"Why didn't he give you the loan you asked for?"

"He's twice-divorced. Both wives cleaned him out. So I think he has serious trust issues about women getting his money. I think he needs time to trust me more, before he'll give me a lot."

"Why didn't he move in?"

"More trust issues, I guess."

"Are you sure he doesn't have a wife, hidden away, somewhere?"

"I don't see how he could. He calls me every night from his bed. There's no way there's a wife in his bed. And he seems to always be alone, like when he's in his truck. He also calls me from there, all the time."

"Does he ever want to do anything with you except come over for sex?"

"He always takes me out to dinner. To fine dining restaurants. And he always invites Jesse to join us."

"But dinner, and one night spent over, is all he ever does? Along with all the sex?"

"Hey...don't knock it! I love our sex, too!"

As time went on, I found myself lying, to get them all off my back.

"Can you call him?"

"Sure. Any time I want."

"Has that secretary moved out yet?"

"Oh yes, she's been gone for a long time."

"Have you been to his main house?"

"Oh yes. Many times."

"Have you met his kids?"

"Oh yes."

I knew that my lying to the people who loved me was an indication of rot. Something was rotten, all right. Actually, it was more like, something was *heavy.* It was that woman who lived in his house. She seemed to carry such *clout.* I could sense her bearing down hard, on Jordan, with a force and a power no "secretary" wields.

My very first sense of her power had been way back, at the start. Jordan had indicated something about her that seemed odd, inconsistent, with her status.

I had shoved it to a back burner.

But I'd kept it on steady simmer.

What he'd said was that she was badgering him to paint the outside of his house.

To me, that had seemed pretty ballsy. That had seemed out of line. An employee, an underling, who's only shacking up, demanding to have the place painted?

You never should have mentioned that, baby.

And something else was on simmer. On an evening a few weeks later, Jordan had called me from his summer home. To hear he was there overjoyed me. This was the house that was near where I lived, so I thought I'd be driving to see him.

I couldn't have been more mistaken. I couldn't have been more uninvited.

"Oh no, you can't come over," he'd responded, with an obviously flustered air. "Some friends of mine are here. I can't let them see you. They wouldn't know what to think!"

So I was some kind of secret. And of course it was because of the secretary. Yet these visitors weren't business associates; he had said they were friends of the family.

His secretary had an influence that reached that impressively far?

It's awful, how when a suspicion is growing, you even suspect the blameless. Like, Jordan was currently involved with a neighbor, who was also his very close buddy. The poor guy was dying of cancer. Jordan couldn't stand the way his friend's wife was handling things; he said she behaved just as though her mate were already dead and buried.

So Jordan had taken it upon himself to go beyond the pale for his friend. Every time he was hospitalized, Jordan would go and hang out there.

Well, Jordan ended up canceling two holiday dates with me. He had committed to seeing me on July Fourth, and again, on Labor Day. But then, when each of those special days came, he announced that his friend had been rushed to the hospital, and *sorry*, he was going there, too.

The first time that happened, on the Fourth of July, I felt awfully let down, but accepting. But when Jordan did the exact same thing, two months later, on Labor Day, that's when I fell apart. My ability to believe him went right out the window.

What the hell was going on, here? His friend had wound up in emergency surgery on **two holidays in a row?** What were the odds of that happening?

"He's full of shit!" said a particularly cynical working girl friend I still talked to. "You've really got to check up on him, ****."

She'd urged me to do that before.

I knew that the difficulty of escaping a wife, especially on a holiday weekend, was a reason more plausible than canceling with me—repeatedly—because of a neighbor who's sick.

"You can go online and find out everything about him," my friend instructed me.

I silently responded with an ugly emotion, something like hatred, for her. This woman embodied way too much knowledge of lies and attitudinal filth; she lived by that knowledge, she possessed faith in nothing, and I'd rather be dead than ever end up with a mental outlook like hers.

But I knew it was time to listen.

I got off the phone with her. I bent over my laptop, resigning, like a patient awaiting a shot in the ass. I jumped online, searched the term "background check", and soon I was viewing an impressive selection of websites that sell the truth.

They were vying to ruin my day. They all charged about thirty dollars. I got out my debit card, picked one, and commenced with my clicking to hell.

And after about only a minute, my heart was pounding so hard, my breathing had gotten so rapid, and my hands were shaking so much, that I could have been a great poster girl for the look of emotional trauma.

It was all there in plain horrid English. The truth had been there for the taking, all along.

Jordan's properties, and property addresses, were all neatly columnized. And there was a female co-owner. Her first name was the same as the "secretary's." Her last name was his last name.

They'd co-owned the main house for twenty years. They'd co-owned the summer home for eight.

For the next couple of hours, just being able to keep myself still, or even to keep myself sitting, required my full concentration. Thank God it was a holiday—no toddlers. And Jesse was out with his friends. I was alone, and I needed to be. Shock, shame and heartbreak are things you don't flaunt.

The working girl friend called me later, wanting to know what I'd found; she sounded a little too eager.

I didn't want to talk. I found an excuse to hang up.

Fuck you, fuck you, you rotten, right bitch. Leave me the fuck alone.

But underneath the agony, a balm of hope loomed: I knew things weren't simple. They weren't cut and dried. It was true, of course, that Jordan was a liar, and it was true that Jordan was married…but he was in love with just me. Of that I was pretty certain. I was pretty certain that he didn't fuck his wife. I was pretty certain that his marriage was dead.

But oh, had he ever lied. And lied, and lied, and lied. I recalled the elaborate stories he'd told, on a slew of different occasions, about the illustrious "typist." I recalled the astounding *detail.* Why couldn't he simply have told me the truth? I was still legally married to Mitch, and Jordan knew all about it. Why had *he* chosen to *lie?*

I was in love with a deceiver.

By the time Jordan called me that afternoon, I had made myself deadly calm.

"I have a question," I said to him, serenely. I was exquisitely cool.

"What?" he responded, and I almost felt bad for him. He hadn't a clue what was coming.

"I was just wondering how you manage, every night, to call me from your bed, without your wife overhearing."

"What...? What do you mean?"

"I'm talking about your wife."

"I don't know what you're talking about."

"Yes you do."

We went back and forth for a minute or two, until finally, he admitted it all. Jordan knew that he had to when I said it was the twenty-first century, and that anyone could find out anything about anybody, if they whipped out their plastic and used it online.

And then he got very hostile. He didn't want to talk anymore. It seemed that *I* was the bad guy, for catching him in his lies.

"I still need to talk," I informed him. "There are things I need to know."

"I don't owe you any explanations."

"That's not true. You do."

"Why?"

"Because what I give you is pure."

"Pure? You're pure?"

"*Yes*. My love is. My heart is. My love for you is true, and pure."

"What do you want to know?"

"Why did you lie to me?"

"Because your whole life's been a lie."

THE HAVEN JUST PAST THE TORN HEART

What I mean is, I'm basically optimistic.

Last night I found, for the umpteenth time, that I was getting treated to *Titanic.* On *HBO*, of course. Well this time, just like the first time, in a theatre, I kept myself awake and caught it all.

When it got to where Rose leaves the lifeboat, and climbs back onto the sinking ship so she can be with Jack, I found myself sobbing so loud and hard that I was glad I was alone.

The film has the power to melt you. It leaves viewers helplessly weeping. But last night I would have become an annoyance to anyone watching it with me. A co-viewer would surely have glowered, and shushed me. I was that out of control.

Well, I had my reasons for emoting that much. The scene made me realize I've loved someone that much. And that's an achievement that's all mine; I own that. My cries were a celebration.

Jordan lied, and evaded, and misled me. But yes I still see him, even though he deceived me. Why? Just because I still love him. Even though he seems to have thought that a whore deserves to be lied to. Even though he just couldn't see that the life I was living was sincere. I guess he believed trusted friends, who probably told him a whore is dishonest. I guess he believed all the myths. Why else would he say that my life's been a lie, and use that to justify his lies?

Well, this much I know, and this comforts me: it's not my fault if Jordan can't see the true-loving woman that I am. And it's not my fault if Jordan makes the choice to lie to me.

I've been what anyone would label his fool. Just like water, I've flowed all around him. I've laid myself down like a drunk on a train track. I've let myself waft like a kite in the wind. And Jordan has never once taken me in, and given me anything we could call home. He's been way too lost, himself.

He's been lost in his second failed marriage. He's been buried defensively, deep in his work. He's been this, he's been that; you can say he's been whatever; the point is, he hasn't been all-the-way with me.

But he's taken whatever he's needed. And he's run when he's seen how a whore can destroy him.

And even though he's now seen, for certain, how much I dearly love him and accept him, I'm still afraid he'll run again.

Oh well. I'm still living and breathing. I did almost die, but true love can do that. Nothing's really worth it, I guess, unless it almost kills you. Don't all the famous adventurers say that?

These days, he's supposed to be really and truly getting himself totally divorced. I guess he's not lying, this time. Oh, I could go online, and find out once again, whether he's truthful or not; but somehow, I just don't want to. I guess I just want to see what he does. I guess I just want to watch him lie, or find the courage for truthful. Whatever he does, it's all mine. Whatever he does, it will jump-start my soul, and get all my juices flowing. Jordan makes me feel more alive than anything else in the world.

How can I leave someone, who lies to me or not, when he's the only one who can do that?

And in spite of his lying, I know he's not a monster. He's not a pathological liar. He's not a sociopath. I can see that truth reflected in his children's love for him, and in the people who respect him at work. It's just that it's **ME** who gets the brunt of his wounds. With **ME** he's been afraid to be truthful. I'm the one who he carefully stashes inside a locked vault, in the fortress. He only unlocks the vault, he only goes in there and holds me, at specified, limited times. He's treating me just like a lethal beast that must be approached with great caution. He's still averting his eyes when he holds me. Maybe he's afraid of the power in mine.

Well, a man's fear is no reason to leave him. It's the biggest reason to stay.

And me? I got out of the childcare. I was in it for almost two years, and then I sold my house. I made myself a sweet profit. For a while it helped me out as I wrote. My kids? They're all doing well. Jesse's back in New York for good, and he's hard at work on his first feature-length film. A producer is backing him to write three screenplays, and then to direct them all. Jeremy, who majored in Business Marketing, remains in San Diego, and owns two businesses. He's going to help me market the books. Jeremy's also helped Ayden to market his construction contracting. I'm told that Ayden does beautiful work. He now has a wonderful girlfriend—she's the greatest, a godsend...she's taught me that godsends do happen. My granddaughters call her Mom. His ex-wife, Annie, their "first mom," gets supervised visitation, on Sundays. That's because she's in rehab. When she gets out of there, we figure she'll soon be back on the crack, and then she'll disappear. That's what she's always done in the past.

Lately the proceeds from my house sale are dwindling, and Jordan's been giving me money. He's stepped up to the role of being my sponsor, while I finish the books. I think that's a very good sign. But I worry that it's only a payment for being around as his toy. Sometimes, I'm afraid I'm just a convenience. I'm afraid I'm just someone to visit and fuck. I'm afraid I'm just pussy mileage.

I am so much more than those things. I'm still waiting for him to see. No, never mind; I think he does see; but I'm waiting for him to *do something about it.* I'm still waiting for him to come closer.

How many times did I just type the word *wait*? Remember my quote from the novel **Siddhartha**, "*I can think, I can wait, I can fast?*" Apparently that mantra is the one, true endeavor that really seems to matter.

Well, I don't demand much of Jordan. We still share shrimp and make perfect love—our rituals now bear the lovely gold seal of time—yet I know I can't trust him any farther than throw him, until he gets over his fear.

I'm still waiting for him to discover, quite astonished, that he can heal from the wounds in his soul without having to damage me. He can open the doors to the fortress, and throw open the vault I'm locked up in, and I won't make him sorry he did that.

And I'm still waiting for him to take me home. I'm still waiting for him to see that he doesn't have to lie, anymore. No wife is after his bucks, anymore. No wife is fucking his friend, anymore. And a whore really did stop her life full of money. A whore really loved him, that much.

And lo and behold...she still does.

He doesn't have to grab me, and jerk me around, while a devastating force, like a wife who doesn't care, tries to get everything he's worked for. He doesn't have to say he's moving in with me, when in truth he needs to stay put for now and doggedly guard his assets. Some day he's going to understand that what I all is our love.

Some day he's going to understand that when I take him into my mouth for as long as he wants, just as deep as he wants, whatever the time of day, it's not because I'm a slut or a whore or anyone self-hating or gold-digging. I blow him, whenever he wants me to, simply because I love him.

Because Jordan's the one who got to me. And I don't think there will ever be anyone else who can. You know when you've been cut that deeply. You know when you're all bled out. Other men, nice men, men who wouldn't hurt me, try to take me from Jordan, and I feel like they're impositions. I feel as though they're ugly, from Mars.

Because Jordan's my ongoing project. He's my heart's unfinished business. The jury's still out on this romance, and I can't walk away. Believe me, I've tried to walk away. And then I've found out what a joke it is to try.

Yes I know I'm repeating a pattern. I adore someone I'm not secure with. It makes just a bit too much sense! In every sad stage of my years growing up, everyone I needed was either gone, or half-gone, or else they wanted *me* gone. So of course I turned out as a woman who doesn't know how to love a man who doesn't in some way withhold himself from me.

And that's where I am right now, that's the extent of my self-understanding. That's as far as I've come, in my reflections on the saga of my undying love for Jordan. He and I are both moving and growing, toward something evolved and unbreakable, I hope...and for now, my hope's what I'm sure of.

And I'm sorry, but I have to stop now. I've been told by supporters who've read it that this chapter's inconclusive, and vague. So I apologize, everybody, for being so unclear… this is the best I can do now.

But this I can tell you for sure: in spite of all that I've been through, I still fiercely love life. Even after my heart's been shredded, I still have all of my joy. And I can still share my joy. I can still give where it's needed. And I can still get it back.

That's a very sturdy haven I've built for myself.

Having that, I know I can't lose. I can go without my mother, my father and my brother, and I can survive without Jordan too, if he ever decides (God help me) to leave me. I can lose my heart and feel the black hole and know that I'll just keep on going.

Because one thing I've learned is you can always provide love, and you can always benefit from it, even after everyone you need and love is gone.

****

And now I'll get the second book wrapped up. I've been working on Book Two for a long time. To tell you the truth, I wrote Book Two first. I wrote most of it back when I was sex working hard, and focusing hard on the issues, and I hadn't met Jordan yet.

I want that first book to be the last one you read. This one that you're holding is the right one to read first, because I show you so much of myself here.

Book Two is where I unleash my tiger.

Yeah, there's a tiger inside me. There's much more to me than romantic idealism.

And **YOU** just might be what I pounce on!

Stay tuned.

SOURCES

Chapter One: My Sexiest "Escort" Experience

1   Scarlot Harlot, a.k.a. Carol Leigh, *Uncontrollable Bodies: Testimonies of Identity and Culture* (Bay Press, Seattle, WA 1994). All quotes beneath all chapter titles are from Carol Leigh.

Chapter Nine: Your Husbands Love You...

1   Lawrence Wright, *"Lives of the Saints"* (*The New Yorker*, January 21, 2002).

Chapter Ten: Health Nut, Fitness Buff, Whore

1   *ER* (NBC, aired October 26, 2000).
2   Dr. David G. Williams, *Alternatives* Newsletter (Special Edition, Fall 2004).
3   Nina Hartley, *"In the Flesh"* (*Whores and Other Feminists,* Jill Nagle, editor; New York, New York: Routledge Press, 1997), p. 62.
4   Cosi Fabian, *"The Holy Whore"* (*Whores and Other Feminists*, Jill Nagle), p. 53.
5   Michael Specter, *"Miracle in a Bottle"* (*The New Yorker*, February 2, 2004).
6   Robin Moore, *The Making of the Happy Hooker* (New York, New York: Signet Books, The New American Library, Inc., 1973).
7   Fabian, p. 52.
8   Chellis Glendinning, *"The Healing Powers of Women"* from *The Politics of Women's Spirituality*, edited by Charlene Spretnak (United States: Anchor Press, 1982), p. 282-283.
9   Melissa, *The Harlot's Room* (London, England: Chatto & Windus Ltd, 1987), p. 48.

Chapter Fourteen: Flowers That Bloom in the Trash

1   Dolores French, *Working: My Life as a Prostitute* (New York, New York: E.P. Dutton, 1988), p. 29.

2   Norma Jean Almodovar, *Cop to Callgirl* (New York, New York: Avon Books/Simon & Schuster, 1993), p. 325.
3   Sydney Biddle Barrows with William Novak, *Mayflower Madam* (U.S.A.: Arbor House Publishing Company, 1986), p. 283, 285-6.
4   French, p. 36.
5   Philip Toshudo Sudo, *"The Zen of Lovemaking"* (*New Age* magazine, Body and Soul: Holistic Living Guide special edition, 2001).
6   Caroline Myss, Ph.D., *Anatomy of the Spirit* (New York: Random House, 1996), p. 110-111.
7   Susan Hall, *Ladies of the Night* (New York: Trident Press, 1973).
8   Nellie Arcan, *Whore* (New York, NY: Grove/Atlantic, Inc., 2001).
9   See Chapter One, Source # 1.
10 *Jerry Springer Show* (Universal TV Talk Productions), aired December 31, 1998.
11 Jeannette Angell, *Callgirl* (Sag Harbor, New York: The Permanent Press, 2004), p. 72-73.

Chapter Fifteen: The Priestess Becomes Herself

1   Carol P. Christ, *Laughter of Aphrodite* (San Francisco, California: Harper & Row, 1987), p. 189-191.

Chapter Sixteen: Men, the Goddess, and Me

1   *"Closer"*, by Nine Inch Nails, from *The Downward Spiral* ("Nothing" Label, 1994)
2   Camille Paglia, *Sexual Personae* (New Haven, New Jersey: Yale University Press, 1990), p. 1-3.
3   Tracy Quan, *"The Prostitute, the Comedian, and Me"* (© 1995, Urban Desires).
4   Thomas Moore, *The Soul of Sex* (New York, New York: Harper Collins Publishers, 1998), p. 13.
5   Thomas Moore,143-154.
6   The Doors, *"Hello, I Love You"* (United Kingdom: Elektra Records, 1968).
7   Thomas Moore, p. 9.

8   Gail Pheterson, Editor, *A Vindication of the Rights of Whores* (Seattle, Washington: Seal Press, 1989), p. 158.

Chapter Seventeen: I Love You Jesus, But…But…

1   Seymour M. Hersh, *"Up in the Air"* (*The New Yorker*, December 5, 2005).

2   *Ten Questions for Deeprak Chopra* (*Time* Magazine "Interview" section, January 24, 2005.)

3   *Time* magazine, December 26, 2005.

4   See *Conversations with God, Book One* (New York: G.P. Putnam's Sons, 1996); and *Conversations with God, Books Two and Three* (Charlottesville, VA: Hampton Roads Publishing Company, Inc., 1997) all by Neale Donald Walsch.

5   French, p. 223-224.

6   See *"Mary Magdalene: Saint or Sinner?"* by David Van Biema (*The New Yorker*, August 11, 2003).

7   See *"The Saintly Sinner"* by Joan Acocella, (*The New Yorker*, February 13th and 20th, 2006); see also *"The Authentic Herstory of Prostitution: a Brief Chronicle of Sacred Whoredom"* by Gabriel Loch-Lainn Seabrook, at *www.freedomusa.org/coyotela/history.html*.

8   See *"Stretching for Jesus"* by Lisa Takeuchi Cullen (*Time*, September 5, 2005).

9   See *"Higher Learning"* by Rebecca Winters (*Time*, February 2, 2004).

10   See *"God and Country"* by Hanna Rosin (*The New Yorker*, June 27, 2005).

11   Dan Brown, *The Da Vinci Code* (New York, New York: Doubleday Publishers, 2003), p. 145.

12   David Denby, *"The Current Cinema"* (*The New Yorker*, March 1, 2004).

13   Richard Corliss, *"The Goriest Story Ever Told,"* (*Time* Magazine, March 1, 2004).

14   Bill Maher, from *Real Time with Bill Maher* (Home Box Office, aired August 23, 2003).

15   Merlin Stone, *When God Was a Woman* (San Diego, California: Harcourt Brace Jovanovich, Publishers, 1976), p. 198-223.

16   Stone, p.1.

17 Stephen Jay Gould, *"Nonoverlapping Magisteria,"* (*Natural History* Magazine, August, 1997).

<u>Chapter Eighteen: Outlaw</u>

1   *"For What It's Worth"* by Crosby, Stills and Nash, (Columbia Records, 1970).